THE NEW COLD WAR

How the Kremlin Menaces both Russia and the West

EDWARD LUCAS

BLOOMSBURY

First published in Great Britain 2008

Copyright © 2008 by Edward Lucas

Maps by John Gilkes

The moral right of the author has been asserted

No part of this book may be used or reproduced in any manner whatsoever
without written permission from the Publisher except in the case of brief
quotations embodied in critical articles or reviews

Bloomsbury Publishing Plc
36 Soho Square
London W1D 3QY

www.bloomsbury.com

Bloomsbury Publishing, London, New York and Berlin

A CIP catalogue record for this book is available from the British Library

Hardback ISBN 9780747595670

10 9 8 7 6 5 4 3 2 1

Typeset by Hewer Text UK Ltd, Edinburgh
Printed in Great Britain by Clays Ltd, St Ives plc

The paper this book is printed on is certified by the © 1996 Forest Stewardship
Council A.C. (FSC). It is ancient-forest friendly. The printer holds
FSC chain of custody SGS-COC-2061

FSC
Mixed Sources
Product group from well-managed
forests and other controlled sources
Cert no. SGS-COC-2061
www.fsc.org
© 1996 Forest Stewardship Council

To Cristina

CONTENTS

Maps   viii

Introduction   I

1. Putin's Rise to Power:
   How the KGB Seized Power in Russia   25

2. Putin in Power: The Winners
   and Losers of the New Regime   47

3. Sinister Pretence: The Kremlin's
   Use of State Power Against Dissent   73

4. Why Money Is Russia's Greatest Strength
   and Our Greatest Weakness   113

5. The 'New Tsarism':
   What Makes Russia's Leaders Tick   133

6. How Eastern Europe Sits on
   the Front Line of the New Cold War   169

7. Pipeline Politics:
   The Threat and the Reality   211

8. Sabre-rattling, or Selling Sabres?
   Russia's Foreign Policy Unpicked   245

9. How to Win the New Cold War:
   Why the West Must Believe in Itself   269

   Notes   281

   Acknowledgements   321

   Index   325

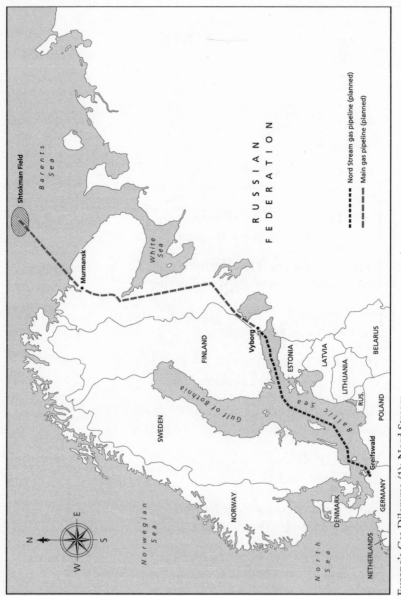

Europe's Gas Dilemma (1): Nord Stream

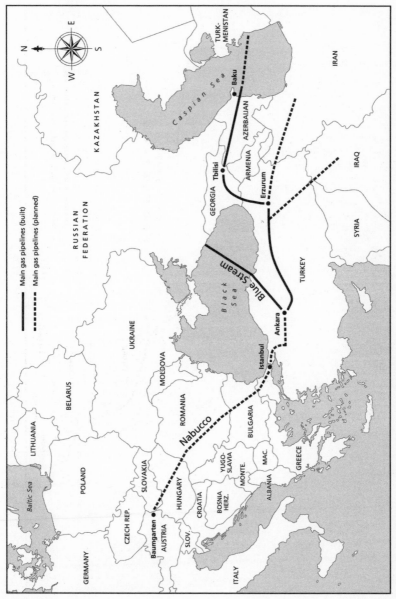

Europe's Gas Dilemma (2): Nabucco and Blue Stream

Introduction

It is chilling to see a friend's name on a death list.

It was 7 October 2006. I had been meaning to phone Yevgenia Albats, a gutsy Russian journalist colleague, since I had seen her name on an extremist website[1] a few days earlier. A page (now defunct) on the site, www.russianwill.org, denounced as 'enemies of the nation' some of the country's finest activists, lawyers and journalists – all of them vehement critics of Vladimir Putin's Kremlin.[2] It gave their home addresses and telephone numbers, and their dates of birth – plus ominous question marks for the dates of death: in effect, a brazen incitement to murder.

But it was Yevgenia who called me first, to say that our mutual friend Anna Politkovskaya had just been gunned down in the entrance to her home. Politkovskaya[3] was not just Russia's bravest reporter. She was the foremost critic[4] of the Kremlin's savagery in crushing the rebels in breakaway Chechnya, scathingly depicting the authoritarian, cruel and wasteful turn that her country had taken under Mr Putin's leadership. The murder took place as the president turned fifty-four; many of her friends assumed it was a macabre birthday present. Regardless of the timing, Yevgenia was scared. Politkovskaya, like her, was on extremists' blacklists. Who would be next? The offical reaction was even more chilling than the murder. Politkovskaya's murder should have been a national tragedy. But no senior Kremlin figure attended her funeral, and Mr Putin took three days to comment on her death; though he condemned it, he dismissed her as a person of 'marginal significance'.[5]

That highlighted the threats faced by those who criticise the authorities inside Russia and the decline of press freedom there. But only weeks later came a wake-up call to the West,[6] delivered in the heart of London. On 1 November Aleksander Litvinenko, a former officer of Russia's internal security force, the FSB,[7] who had fallen out with the authorities and fled to London, was poisoned with a rare radioactive isotope, polonium-210. After three weeks of agonising suffering in a central London hospital, his last words directly blamed Mr Putin for his murder.[8] Certainly it was no ordinary assassination. Almost all the world's polonium is produced in Russia; there, as in every country, it is subject to strict legal controls in large quantities.[9] It decays quickly. Ordinary criminals would have no chance of buying a lethal dose of polonium on the black market. British officials became convinced that the FSB itself – the renamed version of the internal arm of the old KGB – had a hand in the murder. But Russia scoffed at requests for help, contemptuously blocked the British authorities' investigation and then rejected the request to extradite the alleged killer, another former FSB man called Andrei Lugovoi.[10] He had met London-based Russian officials both before and after the assassination, and had left a trail of polonium on his travels from Russia to Britain and back.[11] Mr Lugovoi denies all wrongdoing, but regardless of the rights and wrongs of his involvement, the affair amounted to nuclear terrorism in the heart of London, resulting in the death of a British citizen and putting countless scores of others in danger.

The two murders, and the Kremlin's reaction to them, are symptomatic of the subject of this book: the direct menace that

Russia now poses, not only to its own citizens, but also to outsiders. Twenty years after Mikhail Gorbachev started dismantling communism, Russia is reverting to Soviet behaviour at home and abroad, and in its contemptuous disregard for Western norms. Yet the outside world has been inattentive and complacent, partly thanks to greed and wishful thinking, and partly because of serious distractions elsewhere. Western public opinion and policymakers alike find it hard to focus on more than one or two problems at a time. That proved a costly mistake in the 1930s,[12] when, ignoring the links between Stalin and Hitler, the West regarded the Soviet Union as a useful bulwark, and ultimately a key ally, against fascism.

The 'war on terror' is leading to a similar mistake now. After the attacks on America on 11 September 2001, Mr Putin hurried to offer cooperation which the West gratefully accepted, with little regard for the cost: a free ride for the Kremlin as it tightened the screw at home and bullied its neighbours abroad. Russia gained in another way, too: the 'war on terror' weakened the Atlantic alliance. European countries were so preoccupied with their distaste for President George W. Bush that they all but ignored the direction in which Mr Putin was taking Russia. Even those that were prepared to stand by America's side, to join the 'coalition of the willing' in Iraq and to allow 'extraordinary rendition' of suspected terrorists, soon wished they had stood back. The bungled and blood-soaked aftermath of the invasion of Iraq, the legal black hole of Guantánamo Bay, the mistreatment of prisoners at Abu Ghraib and their systematic torture elsewhere, were not just unpopular among the public in the West and elsewhere. These abuses and blunders became the Kremlin's most potent propaganda weapons against America and its allies. During the 1990s, such a Russian stance would have been inconceivable: in the aftermath of victory in the Cold War, the West's moral stock was high, while the Soviet Union's anti-Westernism seemed a laughable historical relic. But as that period has passed, Russia's public rhetoric has become increasingly caustic. In February 2007 Mr Putin denounced America as a 'pernicious' force in world politics. At the Victory Day parade in Moscow on 9 May he even compared American foreign policy, obliquely, to that of Hitler's Third Reich.

My shorthand term for the new era of uneasy confrontation between the West and the Kremlin is the New Cold War. Despite all the bad news from Russia since Mr Putin took power, this description is fiercely contested by those who find it exaggerated, senselessly provocative or historically illiterate. Indeed, many who claim to be experts on Russia dismiss it as outright nonsense. In their own terms, they are right. For anyone who remembers the first decades of the old Cold War, and the years of stony détente that followed them, even the stormiest spats with the Putin Kremlin seem like minor squabbles. That, after all, was a time of global confrontation, when a surprise conventional attack in Europe by the Warsaw Pact could have reached the Rhine within three days, forcing the West to choose between conceding surrender and starting a nuclear war. Half the continent was under the ice cap of communism,[13] with even the most fleeting human contacts constrained by the climate of fear. Inside the Soviet Union, the Communist Party and the KGB controlled almost every facet of daily life, from housing to the workplace, from holiday plans to schooling, from every published word to the most banal public organisation or association. Practising religious belief was risky, homosexuality illegal. Private enterprise was outlawed; every job depended on the state. Foreign travel was a rare and coveted privilege, not a right. For those outside the nomenklatura,[14] the communist state's charmed circle, finding out what was going on meant painstakingly parsing the leaden prose of misnamed propaganda sheets like *Pravda* (Truth) and *Izvestia* (News).

For all the intimidation and manipulation I outline in the book,

Russia is no longer a closed society. Those determined to tangle with the authorities risk trouble, but people can largely say what they like and read what they like.[15] If they don't like life inside Russia, they can (almost always) easily go abroad. Such safety valves would have seemed inconceivable freedoms for most of the twentieth century. Paradoxically, now they exist, they are not greatly needed. Unlike the Soviet Union, Russia is not riven by economic discontent and failure. On the contrary, investment is pouring in and living standards are rising. Most Russians have never had it so good, and Mr Putin's approval rating is consistently over 80 per cent.[16] If he chooses to change the constitution to stay in power in the presidential election due in March 2008, or maintains behind-the-scenes influence afterwards, Russians will be delighted.

Nor is Russia a global adversary, despite its increasingly assertive presence on the international stage. Indeed, it often looks like a partner. Russia is a member of the G8 club of big rich Western countries and of the Council of Europe, a talking shop that also guards the continent's human rights conventions. It is part of the quartet that tries to broker peace in the Middle East; it says it is an ally in trying to check Iran's nuclear ambitions; it tries to bring sense to the megalomaniac leadership in North Korea. It takes part in peacekeeping in ex-Yugoslavia. Russia has allowed nearly a dozen of its former satellites to join not only the European Union (EU) but also NATO. Kremlin complaints about NATO's eastwards enlargement strike many as understandable geopolitics, not a neo-imperialist revanche. How would America like it if history had gone differently, if the Soviet Union had won the Cold War, and persuaded the states of New England to declare independence and join the Warsaw Pact? That is, they argue,[17] pretty much what happened to Russia, which was reduced from superpower to a state of shrunken weakness in the space of three years.

Even under the newly assertive regime in the Kremlin, Russia has not become a military menace to the West. It cannot manage even to subdue fully the remaining separatist fighters in Chechnya, a province of barely 600,000 people with the land area of Cornwall. In its decrepit, drunken, demoralised military, bullying (hazing) is endemic. On average twelve Russian soldiers commit suicide every month. Russia's newest warplanes are formidably manoeuvrable, its submarines super-silent, its torpedoes terrifyingly fast; but it has not – yet – been able to produce these brilliantly designed weapons in any quantities. Those in service are under-deployed. Only the strategic nuclear arsenal gives Russia the right to call itself a military superpower. But two-thirds of its missiles are obsolete. The Kremlin's ability to launch a disabling nuclear first strike on NATO has disappeared into the history books. So has its capacity to project military power around the globe, or even to launch a crippling conventional attack on Europe. In so far as a nuclear threat still exists, it is that paranoia and incompetence might lead to an accidental conflagration.

The old ideological conflict is over, too. Radio Moscow no longer pumps out lectures on Marxism-Leninism: far from wanting to overthrow capitalism, Russia embraces it. The Kremlin's own ragbag philosophy of 'Sovereign Democracy' (see Chapter Five) has replaced the jargon and dogma of communist ideology. The main aim is not world revolution, but self-justification: chiefly to explain why the Kremlin's overweening political and economic power is part of the natural order, not an aberration from the European mainstream. That may have more to do with psychology, in the form of an ingrained inferiority complex about the West, than with political philosophy. At any rate, the new ideology's main ingredients are unexceptional: an edgy sense of national destiny, a preference for stability over freedom and a strong dislike of Western hypocrisy and shallowness. Similar views are held in many countries outside Russia; it is the combination and intensity that are unusual.

All that is true, and only a fantasist would claim that nothing has changed since 1991. The old Cold War is indeed over: I remember it when it was alive and I was there at its funeral. I grew up in an Oxford academic household deeply committed to fostering freedom of thought behind the Iron Curtain. My father smuggled Plato's *Republic* and the Greek New Testament into communist-ruled Czechoslovakia for fellow philosophers who had been banished to jobs as stokers and window-cleaners. In the early 1980s I campaigned for Poland's Solidarity trade union. I studied German in divided Berlin, Polish in communist Poland. I covered the death throes of the so-called 'GDR' (in truth, the Soviet-occupied zone of Germany) for the BBC. In 1989 I was the only Western newspaperman living in communist Czechoslovakia, and watched as the Velvet Revolution swept away that dreary grey regime. As the Baltic states struggled to regain their independence, I was deported from the Soviet Union by the KGB, having entered Lithuania 'illegally' with the first visa issued by the reborn but unrecognised authorities in Vilnius.[18] As Mikhail Gorbachev's *perestroika* (restructuring) and *glasnost* (openness) flared and faded in the Soviet Union, I saw that wretched country crash into pieces. The week of the evil empire's collapse was one of the happiest of my life. It is closely followed by the day when the last remains of the Red Army occupation forces finally left the Baltic states that they had crushed five decades earlier.

So the old Cold War will not return, and analogies with it are anachronistic and outdated. But so too are the rosy sentiments that succeeded it. The most catastrophic mistake the outside world has made since 1991 is to assume that Russia is steadily becoming a 'normal' country. From this Panglossian point of view, any problems that arise are mere bumps in the road that will be left behind in the inexorable progress towards Western-style freedom and legality. That idea always seemed optimistic, but now it looks downright fanciful; those who still advocate it are deluding themselves and those who listen to them.

The gloomy signs started under Boris Yeltsin, Russia's first democratically elected leader and in some ways of greater stature than Mr Gorbachev, who had dismantled Soviet terror at home and abroad. For a few brief months after the failed coup of 1991, the power of the KGB indeed seemed to be broken, and Russia showed glimmerings of wanting integration into the civilised world without ifs and buts. Though the Communist Party never returned to power, the damage it had inflicted in the past seventy years proved too deep, the forces of darkness in Russia too strong, and the task facing Mr Yeltsin and his allies too great. For all their brains, charm and bravery, the 'reformers' proved incompetent, weak and ultimately venal; as they failed, Russia fell into the hands of those driven by a selfish desire for money and power, not an idealistic desire to make their country prosperous and free. These swashbuckling tycoons called themselves 'oligarchs'.[19] In a largely lawless environment, financial and political corruption became endemic, and colossal fortunes could be made within months. The intelligence and security services came creeping back from the shadows, bringing their own Soviet-era values and habits: authoritarianism and xenophobia. The means Yeltsin and his advisers used to stay in power were lethal to Russia's attempts to establish the hoped-for system based on legality and freedom. In 1993 he used artillery to dislodge Soviet-era hardliners holed up in the Russian parliament. That was followed by a rigged referendum on a new constitution,[20] matched in 1996 by a presidential election in which a gravely ill Yeltsin trounced his communist challenger thanks only to flagrant manipulation of both the media and the count. The greed and influence-peddling of the clique around Yeltsin discredited pro-Western policies, the multi-party system and the market economy.

Given what came next, the Yeltsin years now look less bad. Though the state sorely lacked credibility, at least it was not feared. The 1990s had distributed wealth and power with chaotic unfairness, but nobody had full control of either. Russia's rulers were imperfect, but at least they were under constant, even debilitating challenge. Every point of view was represented on television: even when his advisers urged him to crack down on the media, Yeltsin demurred. Only a return to totalitarian rule was out of bounds. In the regions and republics of Russia, local rulers did as they wished, for better or for worse. But after the calamitous financial crash of August 1998, when Russia defaulted on a large chunk of its debts and devalued the rouble, the sense of failure surrounding the Yeltsin clique and its tycoon-friendly rule was absolute. The banking system collapsed overnight, wiping out the savings of the new middle class. Russia was ridiculed as the sick man of Europe, seemingly destined to survive on transfusions of Western credits and expertise. Words such as *Afrikanisatsiya* (Africanisation) became fashionable.[21] As the lower house of parliament, the Duma, in those days still a rumbustious and powerful body, tightened its grip, the members of the presidential 'family' started looking for an exit.

Their preferred candidate was a little-known bureaucrat: quiet, efficient and above all loyal. He seemed the ideal guarantee for their continued wealth and safety. Mr Putin has indeed honoured that part of the bargain. But when Yeltsin named him unexpectedly as prime minister in the summer of 1999, few imagined that he would soon be dispatching Russia's political freedoms to the cemetery. The means were simple: he matched the public's disgust at the chaos and greed of the Yeltsin years with fear of the immediate present. Within weeks, mysterious bombings of apartment blocks in Moscow and elsewhere stoked a panicky public appetite for more security and less freedom. War restarted in Chechnya. Mr Putin's ratings rocketed, turning him from back-stage zero to national hero in four months. At the time, the bombings seemed to most people to be genuine terrorist outrages, the clear consequence of Russia's past weakness in dealing with separatists and militants. In retrospect, they look like a cynical plot to panic the public into supporting the country's new rulers: the ex-KGB.

When on New Year's Eve 1999 Yeltsin stepped down, Mr Putin automatically took over as acting president. Russians liked his clipped, businesslike manner, his sobriety and physical fitness, his aptitude for hard work and the glamorous aura surrounding a veteran of the Soviet Union's elite foreign intelligence service. But 'who is Mr Putin?' was a pressing and unanswered question. As Chapter Two shows, Russians and outsiders alike were soon to know him a lot better, as a political squeeze began within months on the presumptuous tycoons, lawless regional barons and out-of-control bureaucrats who had flourished during the later Yeltsin era. Some sort of clean-up was certainly overdue, but Mr Putin also betrayed the positive legacy of the Yeltsin years: a Russia com-mitted to friendship with the West, to pluralism in politics and the media and to keeping the old KGB corralled, away from the heights of power. Though the swaggering cronies of the Yeltsin era left office unmourned, they gave way to a new ruling class: quiet, grey KGB veterans, mostly from St Petersburg. An unwieldy new word appeared in the political lexicon: *efesbefikatsiya* (FSB-fication). The FSB, the successor to the KGB's domestic wing, was back in business.[22] Under Yeltsin it had been just one government agency among many, using its powers to bug and blackmail chiefly for self-enrichment. Now that its former chief, Mr Putin, was in the Kremlin, the FSB was, in effect, running the country.

The trend was unpromising. Yet Mr Putin has been highly popular in Russia, and, at least initially, abroad. From the start, Russians have been pleased that after the shocking muddle and moral emptiness of the Yeltsin years, someone was finally bringing order to their country. As with Benito Mussolini's Fascist rule in Italy, people were pleased about the superficial appearance of stability, and did not look too closely at the arbitrary exercise of power that lay behind it. Yet the Kremlin, and the mighty state bureaucracy below it, use the law in their own interests but are not bound by it. As I show in the book, Russia has first tacitly and then explicitly abandoned the aim of becoming 'normal' – an advanced industrialised country marked by political liberty and the rule of law, whose people could stand on equal terms with their counterparts in Western Europe and America. In the view of Russia's rulers now, Western values were tried during the Yeltsin era and found wanting. At best they were simply unsuited to local conditions. At worst they were part of a dastardly plot to weaken Russia and promote Western hegemony. Now, for better or for worse, Russia is seeking its own way, based on a controlled political system, a strong presidency and a tough stance towards the outside world. The result is a menace both to Russia, which now stands little chance of avoiding long-term decline, and to the West, which is struggling to cope with the Kremlin's bombast, bullying and bribery.

In the 1990s, any such attempt to find a home-grown future would have been doomed by Russia's economic weakness: it was dependent on billions of dollars in outside loans and grants to pay for imports and plug the government's deficit. When sky-high interest rates tempted a flood of hot money into the government bond market in the late 1990s, it merely highlighted the economy's humiliating vulnerability to any outside loss of confidence. That red ink has now turned black. Russia's economy is booming.

The biggest reason is high prices for oil, gas and other raw materials – the best possible environment for a country rich in natural resources. That has sent tax revenues and exports soaring. The second reason is political stability. Investors, foreign and local, may find Russia's rules for business tough. But unlike in the Yeltsin era, they stay fairly constant. In most of the economy, conditions do not change overnight. The result of this economic bonanza is that the Kremlin can afford to do what it likes. It no longer fears its foreign creditors: it has paid them off. It no longer fears the capital markets: investors have been queuing up to buy shares, lend money and start businesses. Greed has overtaken fear. Optimists hoped that financial security would give Mr Putin the confidence to liberalise. They could hardly have been more wrong. Not only have the limited economic reforms of his early years come to a halt, the Kremlin has adopted a tougher stance both at home and abroad. Russia wastes much of its windfall because of the lack of reform (as I show in Chapter Four), while using money freely to stifle criticism abroad.

The biggest victims have been the freedoms of speech and association. The independent media have shrivelled, with television in particular coming almost completely under the authorities' control. A forced change of ownership is the main tactic, a new law on extremism intimidates the rest. Critics of the Kremlin are not just muffled in the media, but shackled at the polls. New electoral rules mean that independent candidates and small parties are in effect completely excluded from parliamentary elections. But the true test of political freedom is not elections, but what happens in between them. Here the verdict is depressing. Almost every possible channel for complaint and dissent is blocked. Enough individual activists have experienced judicial and bureaucratic harassment, as well as physical threats, to deter all but the bravest from speaking out or getting involved. My friends are increasingly unwilling even to talk on the phone. Foreigners with a record of criticising the Kremlin have been finding it hard to get visas. Even small opposition demonstrations have to surmount exhausting bureaucratic obstacles. Rallies that go ahead anyway are violently dispersed by the police and security forces. Mr Putin and others publicly denounce not-for-profit organisations as cover for foreign espionage. The judiciary's brief flirtation with independence has ended. The message to outside critics is simple: Mr Putin is popular. Russia is doing well. Mind your own business.

Repression at home is matched by aggression abroad. Russia has started suspending arms control agreements and started sending its warplanes to probe the airspace of NATO countries: both nearby ones such as Estonia, and even those farther away such as Britain. It has announced ambitious rearmament plans, including a return to a naval presence in the Mediterranean. It has restored the Soviet-era practice of keeping a fleet of strategic bombers (which can launch nuclear missiles) permanently airborne. It has threatened to target its nuclear missiles at European countries – a practice dropped in the Gorbachev years. Such military manoeuvring may recall the confrontation of the old Cold War. But the real threat is a different one. When it comes to military might, Russia is still too poor and too weak to do more than posture: the nuclear arsenal and conventional forces are more a background psychological factor than a physical one. Instead of menacing the other side with high explosives, hardened steel and enriched uranium, the New Cold War is fought with cash, natural resources, diplomacy and propaganda.

Cash is the key. For those prepared to take the risks, pay the bribes, and ignore the dirt, Russia is a tempting business environment. At least at first, Westerners there feel that they are in a bigger, brasher, brighter version of their own countries. The profits are colossal and the people seem to be glamorous go-getters with a

whiff of intoxicating Slavic charm. It is easy to ignore the blithe
contempt with which the new Russian friends treat external
constraints. It is hard for foreigners to make a fuss about human
rights questions when such issues do not seem to bother the locals.
Russian patriotism may be prickly and irrational, but the wise
outsider does not let such considerations get in the way of profit.
That is shortsighted, for Russia is no ordinary trading partner. The
New Cold War is in part a struggle for market share. Russia is
building up its clout as an energy supplier, while diversifying its
customer base. In the coming years, Europe, and even North
America, will experience growing dependence on scanty and
expensive Russian gas, but with little chance of alternative supplies.
Russia wields the energy weapon to bully its enemies and bribe its
allies, and uses its financial clout to buy friends and influence. The
big strategic worry used to be the Soviet navy's capacity to
blockade Europe's sea lanes. Now it is Gazprom's ability to
blockade its gas pipelines. Once it was the Kremlin's tanks thundering into Afghanistan that signalled the West's weakness; now it
is Kremlin banks thundering through the City of London.

Behind the scenes Russia's behaviour is even more confrontational. The Kremlin's representatives throw habitual tantrums in
international organisations such as the European Bank for Reconstruction and Development (EBRD), the Organisation for Security
and Co-operation in Europe (OSCE) and the United Nations
Development Programme. They block programmes in countries
they don't like, and demand hefty pay-offs and concessions in
return for their consent. Russian spying exceeds even the heights of
the old Cold War.

The battle lines of the New Cold War are increasingly clear:
America, Britain and some European countries, mostly ex-
communist ones, are trying to stand up against the Kremlin. In
the middle are countries such as Germany that want close business

ties with Russia but hope, probably in vain, to keep their political distance. The Kremlin's close friends are a rogue's gallery: Syria, Venezuela and Iran, plus a handful of ill-governed ex-Soviet republics such as Belarus and Tajikistan. Increasingly, it shares positions with China, with which it is linked in a security organisation of growing importance called the Shanghai Cooperation Organisation. Albeit at a price, this, if it develops further, will provide Russia with a global weight not seen since the 1950s.

Even seasoned Russia-watchers who flinch at the geographical and historical connotations of the 'New Cold War' still agree that something pretty bad is going on: a favoured phrase is a 'sharp strategic conflict'. Like the old Cold War, it is being fought chiefly in Europe, though this time the battleground has shifted east, to the once-captive nations that lie between Russia and the rich half of the continent. Russia makes no secret of its desire for a *droit de regard* in its former empire: it wants to know everything that happens and to have the power to stop what it does not like. That means a tussle in Central Europe, the Balkans and the Caucasus, and particularly in the Baltic states of Estonia, Latvia and Lithuania. They are the Soviet satellites whose loss the Kremlin resents most sharply. Their thriving economies and lively, open societies are a constant and glaring contrast to the authoritarian crony capitalism across the border. Russia is putting the Baltic states under an energy squeeze, cutting off oil supplies to Latvia and Lithuania.[23] It has incited riots in Tallinn, the Estonian capital.[24] It has abandoned Yeltsin's policy of historical reconciliation. The Kremlin's line now is that the occupation of the Baltic states in 1940 – part of the Hitler–Stalin pact – was legal. That should come as no surprise: Mr Putin, who says the collapse of the Soviet Union was the 'greatest geopolitical catastrophe' of the twentieth century, believes the history books written in the Yeltsin years paint the past in too bleak a light; Though the Balts are small in population terms,[25] they are

members – and loyal and active ones at that – of NATO and the EU.
The West has, so far, defended them loyally. When Estonia came
under attack in May 2007, Mr Bush promptly invited its president
for a high-profile visit to the White House. Rather like West Berlin
in the days of the old Cold War, the Baltic states are militarily
indefensible but symbolically vital: if they succumb to Russian
pressure, who will be next? That has not deterred the Kremlin,
which is determined both to divide them, and to isolate them. As it
strikes bilateral deals with other European countries one by one, it
hints hard that the arrogant, troublesome Balts are standing in the
way of mutually beneficial (and still more lucrative) ties.

The less resistance Russia meets, the more assertive it becomes.
Language and behaviour that would have once seemed unimaginable crop up, first as something that can be dismissed as for internal
consumption only. Then it is seen as a regrettable exception.
Shortly after that the world gets used to it. The limits of the
tolerable are constantly changing, and in one direction only. The
uncomfortable but unavoidable question is where this will end. If
Russia gets what it wants in the Caucasus or the Baltics, the Balkans
and Central Europe will be next. And what then? The Arctic?
Western Europe? Slice by slice, the Kremlin is adding to its sphere
of influence.

Russian tactics can also be more subtle. The Kremlin wants to
build up its influence not only *on* the West, but also *in* the West.
The growing business lobby tied to Russia represents a powerful
fifth column of a kind unseen during the last Cold War. Once it
was communist trade unions that undermined the West at the
Kremlin's behest. Now it is pro-Kremlin bankers and politicians
who betray their countries for thirty silver roubles. Western
investment in Russia has already created a lobby for good relations
with the Kremlin in the City of London, in German big business
and in the energy industry across Europe. That is reinforced by the

billions of dollars of Russian investment pouring into Western
Europe and North America. When Russian tycoons – who these
days run their businesses at the Kremlin's bidding – own big stakes
in the West's biggest companies, they are no longer outsiders, but
insiders. Russia is becoming a giant, nuclear-armed version of Saudi
Arabia: a country so rich and powerful that even its direct support
for terrorism does not bring Western disfavour.

The ideological clash behind this has changed, but it has not
disappeared. Instead of an explicit argument between Marxist-
Leninists and the supporters of welfare capitalism, both sides seem
to endorse the same capitalist model. But it would be a mistake to
think that the Kremlin is just aping the West. That was the mistake
Russia made in the 1990s, when it tried to adopt standard templates
for the market economy and political freedom wholesale, with
what now seem like, at least from a Russian viewpoint, disastrous
results. Far from copying the rules of the Western game, it has
rewritten them. The first and simplest rule is: the Kremlin is always
right. At home, any challenge, any resistance, will be crushed by
brute force of money and the levers of state power. No court, no
law, no appeal to good manners or ethical principles will help: just
as a backwoodsman knows not to get between a bear and his lunch,
anyone dealing with Russia knows not to get between the Kremlin
and its profits. Russian oligarchs have learned that bitter lesson. So
have even the mightiest Western investors, including oil giants such
as BP and Shell.

The difference between Russian and Western models of capitalism can be deceptive, for respect for the law is so central to the
Western approach to life that many of those who benefit from the
security and predictability that it brings hardly think about it. But in
the background, the idea that contracts are to be respected; that
judges cannot be bribed; that court rulings must be upheld, is part
of daily life. That is not the way it looks in Russia. The law is a tool

for the powerful against the weak. Appeals to legal norms are dismissed as just disguised political pressure. The separation of powers, ethics codes, human rights treaties and multilateral obligations are nothing more than convenient fictions, easily brushed aside when real considerations are at stake. If the West cites them in argument, it sounds hypocritical and insincere to Russian ears. Don't Western countries break the law in pursuit of their national interests? Don't their politicians take bribes? Don't their officials help their business chums?

Indeed they do, deplorably. Nevertheless such behaviour is not the founding principle of the Western system, but a blemish on it. Multilateralism is frayed by self-interest and exceptionalism, but it is still the governing principle of the world legal order. The EU in particular (to the mystification of many Russians) does truly work as a sophisticated multilateral institution in which common rules and interests trump national ones. So, to a more limited extent, does the World Trade Organization in its rule-based approach to international commerce and investment. (Russia has yet to join this body.) Similarly, when corruption is exposed – in most Western countries at least – it is penalised and punished. In Russia, by contrast, it is little exaggeration to say that bribery and corruption are not part of the system; they *are* the system. The fortunes of senior politicians are measured in billions of dollars. Kremlin officials run state-owned companies as sidelines. Nobody complains, or asks about conflicts of interest. The most telling indicator of corruption is not Russia's low standing in the corruption rankings published by outfits such as Transparency International (see Chapter Three), but the lack of a public fuss about official crookedness. No senior official ends up in court unless he has first fallen foul of his political masters. The ideological conflict of the New Cold War is between lawless Russian nationalism and law-governed Western multilateralism.

The strangest feature of all this is the West's unwillingness to admit what is happening. This is only partly because of a pro-Russian business lobby that has beguiled the foreign-policy establishment in countries such as Germany. It is also because of an unwillingness to confront the uncomfortable consequences of Russia's new direction. Officials and politicians ask haplessly: 'If Russia is a political menace again, what on earth are we supposed to do about it?' The old Cold War imposed a demanding regime of mental and moral toughness on the countries of Western Europe: they knew that if they did not hang together they would hang separately. Now the Kremlin's central tactic, of 'divide and rule', has an almost free run. Western security rests on multilateral agreements: the idea that pooled sovereignty, shared security and joint decision-making are the best way to defend free societies. But memories of that vital principle have faded and loyalty to it has frayed. Greece and Cyprus dependably lobby on Russia's behalf. Silvio Berlusconi, the former Italian prime minister, once went so far as to describe himself as Russia's 'advocate' in the EU.

During the old Cold War, no NATO member would have considered doing private deals with the Kremlin: any overtures from the Soviet Union encountered hard-headed scrutiny, while few in Western officialdom made a career out of being nice to the Soviet bloc. Anyone in the business world who made a profit out of dealings with communist countries was an instant target of suspicion, and risked ostracism. In the New Cold War, such deals are commonplace: Austria (which is not in NATO but is in the EU) plus Bulgaria, Cyprus, France, Greece, Germany, Hungary, Italy, Latvia, the Netherlands, Portugal, Turkey and Slovakia, to name but some countries, have all succumbed in recent years, in differing degrees, to the temptation to be a 'special friend' of the Kremlin. Sometimes it stems from effective flattery, peddling the line that other countries's reservations are based on a short-sighted and biased view of the real Russia. Sometimes the private commercial interests of senior politicians and officials play a role. Typically, the first stage is accepting dependence on gas supplies delivered along Russian-controlled pipelines. Next comes allowing Russian energy giants to buy assets such as refineries and distribution companies. That soon creates a powerful local lobby for good relations with Russia, and unwillingness to defend those being bullied or brow-beaten elsewhere. Germany, for example, has been notably un-willing to stick up for Georgia or the Baltic states. The effect of such policies on their allies elsewhere – and in the long term on their own security – has barely been considered.

Fear of the Soviet Union cemented not only mutual solidarity in Western Europe, but also the Atlantic alliance with the United States. However much some West Europeans distrusted Richard Nixon, despised Jimmy Carter or flinched at Ronald Reagan's cowboy rhetoric, the bottom line was clear: it was the American nuclear guarantee that kept Europeans of all kinds safe and free. Keeping those psychological muscles toned once the old Cold War ended has proved too demanding for many. Complacency is much more comfortable than vigilance. Trust is nicer than suspicion. And remembering the grim grey days of the past is hard. Memories of Russia now are shaped by the optimism that surrounded the end of the Cold War, not the realism of the previous four decades.

Those old reflexes would be useful now. Mr Putin is heir (see Chapter One) to a frightening and barely remembered figure from the Soviet past: Yuri Andropov, a former KGB chief who took power briefly when the geriatric Leonid Brezhnev finally died in 1982. Like Andropov, Mr Putin believes that ruthless discipline is the key to economic recovery. Like him, he places great weight on the use of the secret police, both to collect information and to intimidate opponents and backsliders. Like him, he believes that the West is both weak and hypocritical and can be easily faced down with a mixture of threats and selective arm-twisting. The Andropov era was doomed to failure: it was trying to revive a country that was crippled by the Communist Party's desire for total control, which calcified every part of life and restricted innovation. When Andropov took over, the Soviet Union was already groaning under the cost of maintaining its status as a military superpower, made all the harder by the preposterous economic system bequeathed by Lenin and Stalin. Central planning consumed colossal amounts of raw materials and provided a pitifully low standard of living for the population. A country in which condoms were so crude that they were called *galoshy* (galoshes), in which contraceptive pills, blue jeans and sanitary towels were coveted luxury items, in which foreign travel was an unimaginable privilege, was a beacon only to the most masochistic socialist. The Soviet way of life was a combination of economic backwardness, plus repression at home and abroad. That was a hard sell.

Now the Kremlin has stopped wasting time, money and people in trying to make a flawed economic system work, and in pursuing an unworkably utopian political idea. Instead it has adopted the trappings of a Western system – laws, elections and private property, to conceal a lawless, brutal and greedy reality. That is not only a problem for Russians. Though the country is still too weak militarily and economically, and too dependent on the outside world, to use brute force against the West, it has plenty of other tactics that are just as effective. Chiefly, it can menace and subvert the weaker and smaller countries in the ex-Soviet neighbourhood. For them, Russia is like an aggressive man on crutches – no threat to the able-bodied, but still a menacing bully for someone in a wheelchair. It uses the Soviet Union's most powerful legacy, the monopoly hold on gas and oil pipelines running from east to west, to blackmail and bribe its former satellite countries. In response, the West not only fails to support its allies, but is also

succumbing to pressure itself. The Kremlin uses its limited economic and diplomatic weight to paralyse its opponents' decision-
making, playing 'divide and rule' with extraordinary success.
Against irresolute opponents, clever manoeuvring and posturing
has proved remarkably successful. As in Soviet days, the Kremlin
uses *dezinformatsiya* (disinformation) to camouflage its policies and
discredit its opponents. Yet above all, money remains the West's
greatest weakness. Having cast off the dead weight of ideology, the
ex-KGB men in the Kremlin are presiding over a Russian Klon-
dike, a source of irresistible temptation for greedy outsiders. When
all else fails, Russia uses the methods of terrorists and gangsters, in
the murder of foreign citizens and in the cybercrime attack
unleashed on Estonia in May 2007.

In short: the West is losing the New Cold War, while having barely
noticed that it has started. Mr Putin and his Kremlin allies have
seized power in Russia, cast a dark shadow over the eastern half of
the continent, and established formidable bridgeheads in the main
Western countries. And the willingness to resist looks alarmingly
feeble. It is that which has prompted me, after more than twenty
years of covering the region, to write this book.

I start by showing how Mr Putin and his ex-KGB colleagues
captured a country exhausted by economic upheaval, disgusted by
corruption and yearning for strong and competent leadership.
What it got was a cynical putsch, which used what looks like
mass murder to create the public panic necessary to seize power.
Chapter Two shows how, after a hesitant start, Mr Putin consolidated his control of Russia. It explains how he built a political
base among the winners and losers of the past fifteen years, and
attacked the most unpopular people in the country: the oligarchs.
Chapter Three depicts the result: a sinister sham in which dissent is

punished by arrest, forcible psychiatric medication and bureaucratic harassment, in which elections are rigged, politicians tamed, the media muzzled and the institutions of state hollowed out. Chapter Four examines the Russian economy – superficially strong but weak underneath. Chapter Five deals with outsiders' most common misunderstanding of modern Russia: that there is no ideology. It explains how 'sovereign democracy' includes powerful criticisms of Western shortcomings, but is used to justify the xenophobic and authoritarian style of government in Russia. Chapter Six introduces the main battleground so far of the New Cold War: the ex-communist countries of Eastern Europe. Weak and badly governed, they offer easy pickings for the Kremlin's mixture of bribes and bullying. Chapter Seven explains the Kremlin's most potent weapon: energy. It shows how the Soviet-era monopoly on east–west oil and gas pipelines allows Russia to dictate terms to customers and penalise those who resist. Chapter Eight deals with the military and security dimension to the New Cold War. It shows the hollowness of the Kremlin's aims to become a military superpower, but shows how much more damaging and threatening are its activities in arms sales and in building strategic ties with China. Finally, Chapter Nine explains how the West can win the New Cold War: first by resurrecting collective security to deal with Russia's 'divide and rule' tactics, and secondly by restoring the moral self-confidence that fuelled our victory in 1989.

Putin's Rise to Power:
How the KGB Seized Power in Russia

Vladimir Putin hardly seemed worth a footnote to Russian political history when an ailing President Yeltsin made him prime minister on 9 August 1999. The fifth prime minister in less than a year,[1] he looked like a run-of-the-mill Russian bureaucrat: dull, unappealing, and all too likely to end up as another casualty of the country's unmanageable economic troubles and chaotic politics. Initially, little was known about him, personally or professionally. He liked judo and spoke German.[2] After working as a KGB officer in the former East Germany, he had returned to his home city of St Petersburg[3] and quietly worked his way up the bureaucratic ladder. From the university's foreign relations department, he moved to a job dealing with foreign investors[4] and then to the Kremlin, where he worked in the presidential property department, a huge business empire based on the assets of the former Communist Party. After a brief stint overseeing the ties with Russia's regions, he became head of the FSB.[5]

But even then, a closer look suggested his appointment was more important than it seemed. A KGB career was a red-hot sign of distinction in the Soviet Union. Apart from the Communist Party leadership itself, the KGB had been the country's most knowledgeable, efficient and privileged organisation. It not only attracted the brightest people; it gave them a formidable training and an unbeatable network of contacts. They harboured a sense of great superiority over the shabby, humdrum and ill-informed lives of the ordinary citizen. For many, that sense was stoked by special training in psychological tricks: how to manipulate strangers, to gain their trust or break their resistance. The result was more like a cult than a government bureaucracy: omniscient, omnipresent and omnipotent. In a perverse sense, KGB officers felt themselves to be almost a lay priesthood. Being uniquely well placed to see its shortcomings, many harboured private doubts about the work-ability of communism. But they compensated both with a passio-nate patriotism, and an unbending loyalty to their fellow officers.

The presence of any KGB veteran at the head of government would have been significant, but Mr Putin was not just a run-of-the-mill KGB officer. He had served abroad. The First Directorate of the KGB, which handled external espionage, was an elite within an elite. Its members were specially selected and trained to with-stand the temptations they would be exposed to during foreign travel – something that was an almost unimaginable luxury in the closed society of the Soviet Union. It is still unclear what exactly Mr Putin did while he was in Dresden. The files of the East German secret police, the *Stasi*, are curiously sketchy on his career there. Some believe that he was a lowly counter-intelligence officer, whose job was checking up on more glamorous frontline operatives. Others think he was given, but botched, an important job in managing the survival of Soviet intelligence networks as communism crumbled in East Germany. Both versions may be true. At any rate, Mr Putin was handpicked for his loyalty, brains – and toughness.

An early sign of how his background might influence his behaviour in political office came during his brief stint as prime minister, when Mr Putin spoke to his former colleagues: 'A group of FSB operatives, dispatched, under cover, to work in the government of the Russian Federation, is successfully fulfilling its task.'[7] At the time, many thought that was a tasteless joke. In retrospect, it seems pretty close to a statement of fact. Since 2000, veterans of the Soviet intelligence and security services have taken control not only of the Kremlin and government, but also the media and the commanding heights of the economy. Olga Kryshtanovskaya, a sociologist at the Russian Academy of Sciences, estimates[8] that three-quarters of the top posts in Russia are held by *siloviki*, an untranslatable term for current and former intelligence and security officers, derived from the Russian word *sila* (power).[9]

The rise to power of Mr Putin and his friends is the culmination, accidental or deliberate, of a process that started in the early 1980s, when the KGB became frustrated by the gerontocracy surrounding the increasingly senile Leonid Brezhnev and the Communist Party leadership. Under communism, even the KGB was not all-powerful. It was not allowed to spy on the Soviet military intelligence service, the GRU, or on the Communist Party, which regarded its 'sword and shield' with a mixture of awe and contempt. Like its terror-inducing secret-police predecessors – the NKVD, OGPU, the *Cheka*, and before them the Tsarist-era *Okhrana* and even the black-cowled monks of Ivan the Terrible's *Oprichniki* – the KGB could terrorise the powerless but only advise the powerful: it had no political authority of its own.

That came close to changing in November 1982 when Brezhnev died and the KGB chief Andropov was elected General Secretary in his place. For fifteen months, the KGB was at the summit of power. The austere, intimidating Andropov tried to restore the Soviet system in both economics and politics. He had little success, partly because the Soviet Union was inherently unsalvageable, and also because his diseased kidneys gave out within months of his taking

over; when he died, stagnation returned under his successor, a
doddery Communist Party hack called Konstantin Chernenko
who lasted only eighteen months. Resigned to the inevitability
of change, the KGB then became a strong supporter of Mr
Gorbachev's reforms – at least until they seemed to be leading
to the country's disintegration.

That may seem a paradox. Certainly the main aim of many
liberals and reformers in the Soviet Union's provinces in the
Gorbachev era was to outwit the central institutions of power:
the Kremlin, the armed forces, the bureaucrats who ran (or mis-
ran) the planned economy, and most of all the cold grey men of the
KGB. The two main levers of Soviet power, economic planning
and the one-party police state, seemed one and the same thing.
What nobody realised was that collapse of state planning would
soon give the savviest people in the former Soviet Union – the ex-
spooks – a chance to beat the West at its own game: capitalism.
Political freedom and human rights, which seemed to be at the
heart of public life, were just optional extras. They were dispensed
– and then dispensed with.

It is Andropov, not Mr Gorbachev, who is Mr Putin's role
model. In July 1999, while still head of the FSB, Mr Putin laid a
wreath on his grave. Later, he had a wall plaque restored on the
wall of the old KGB headquarters, the Lubyanka, and praised
Andropov as an 'outstanding political figure'. Since Mr Putin's rise
to power, the FSB has achieved something that the KGB never
quite managed: its members, current and former, are running the
country. The difference between the two types is largely cosmetic.
Shortly after becoming prime minister in 1999, Mr Putin told
Russian television 'there is no such thing as an ex-Chekist'.[10]
Viktor Cherkesov, a close Putin ally who, as the KGB chief in St
Petersburg in 1988, ordered the last political repression in the
Soviet Union and now runs Russia's drug control agency, wrote in

2004: 'We [*siloviki*] must understand that we are one whole. History ruled that the weight of supporting the Russian state fell on our shoulders. I believe in our ability, when we feel danger, to put aside everything petty, and remain faithful to our oath.'[11]

In the book on judo that he co-authored, published in 2004,[12] Mr Putin repeatedly makes the point that success is achieved with 'minimum effort, maximum effect'. That is a salient feature of both his foreign and domestic policy. Trying to control everything, as his communist predecessors in the Kremlin did, makes the grip on power rigid and brittle. Much more effective, then, to concentrate not on crushing opponents crudely, but keeping them unbalanced – and therefore vulnerable to a deft throw and armlock. Although the FSB has in effect mounted a successful putsch, recreating a semi-authoritarian political system, it shuns total control. Instead, it has retained the outward appearance of political pluralism, in a way that still fools outsiders and wishful thinkers.

At first sight, the story seems simple. Russia was already in a terrible mess when Mr Putin became prime minister. Then a spate of deadly and mysterious terrorist attacks, costing some three hundred lives, put the country in a state of national panic. Mr Putin's response, of tough talk and still tougher deeds, made him the nation's most popular politician within weeks. He was therefore the logical and popular choice to succeed Yeltsin as president. Since then he has reversed the abuses of the Yeltsin years and made Russia strong and prosperous. For many Russians and outsiders, that is still the essence of the past seven years. Later chapters will deal with the abuse of power. But the means used in Mr Putin's ascent to the presidency should dispel any illusions about the real nature of his regime once in office.

The story started with an obscure news item, barely covered outside Russia. Fighters from the breakaway province of Chechnya raided villages in neighbouring Dagestan in August 1999.[13] A few

days later, on 31 August, a seemingly unrelated bomb exploded in
Moscow, in an underground shopping mall – a glorified term for a
warren of kiosks around the entrance to a subway station. One
person was killed and forty injured. Many blamed a mafia feud,
though a previously unknown anarchist group left a note claiming
responsibility. On a much bigger scale was the outrage on 4
September, when a car bomb outside a military apartment block
in Buinaksk, a town in Dagestan, killed sixty-four people and
wounded dozens. Russia blamed separatists from Chechnya. Mr
Putin authorised attacks on what he called 'illegal military units'
there. It was not until four days later, when a large bomb planted in
the basement blew up a nine-storey apartment building in south-
east Moscow, killing ninety-four people and wounding 150, that
Russians began to think that they were under a sustained attack by
terrorists. That impression was confirmed by two more mass
murders. On 13 September, the day of mourning for those victims,
another bomb blew up an eight-storey building, also in southern
Moscow, killing 118 and wounding 200. Three days after that, a
truck bomb in Volgodonsk, in southern Russia, killed a further
seventeen people.

The atmosphere created by this sustained assault was frantic. At
night, vigilante groups patrolled the back streets of Moscow. The
Chechens had long been Russia's least popular ethnic minority and
the attacks demonised them further. Mr Putin immediately
authorised a military operation against the 'terrorist' republic.
Russia would 'wipe out' the culprits, even 'in the shit-house'
he said. That was a shocking piece of gangster slang that no
previous Russian leader would have dreamed of using in public.[14]
Some educated Russians winced; but it caught the national mood.
The time for being nice was over. But puzzling questions remained. The Chechens had no record of attacking such targets, or
using such means. The bombs had been expertly planted in

buildings whose construction made them most vulnerable to attack. Military specialists have that sort of expertise (and ready access to high explosive). But the Chechens had previously shown no sign of having the organisational clout needed to get hold of big quantities of explosive, or the knowledge of how to use them so professionally.[15] The bombings had been well planned, probably months in advance, yet the fighting in Dagestan was quite recent. Chechen terrorist tactics in the past involved taking hostages and making practical demands: for the release of prisoners, or for negotiations with the Kremlin. This time, the supposed perpetrators had no motive. The inevitable result of the attacks was a war in which their already ruined republic would be obliterated.

The real beneficiaries were in Moscow. Rumours had been swirling around the Russian capital for a year that senior figures in the Yeltsin Kremlin were planning to use violence to head off what seemed like their impending downfall. The country's most powerful tycoon-politician, Boris Berezovsky, was under investigation for diverting foreign cash revenues from the national airline, Aeroflot. Another controversy surrounded Pavel Borodin, the head of the presidential property department. He had commissioned a controversial Swiss firm, Mabetex, to carry out richly priced renovations[16] on the Kremlin's historic buildings. In September 1999, the Yeltsin family came under renewed scrutiny when Swiss investigators claimed to have found documents confirming that Mabetex had paid $15 million in bribes, including by providing credit cards for the president and his two daughters. The Yeltsin family has consistently maintained its innocence.[17]

In response, the Kremlin played dirty. The prosecutor-general, Yuri Skuratov, had to resign after a video of a man bearing a strong resemblance to him cavorting with two prostitutes was shown on prime-time television. Only blatant bribery of deputies postponed an attempt in the Duma to press ahead with Yeltsin's impeachment. Another seemed certain to succeed sooner or later. Yuri Luzhkov, the powerful mayor of Moscow, had thrown his political and financial weight behind Mr Primakov's presidential candidacy. Elections were due in 2000, but they could happen even earlier were Yeltsin to be impeached. Appointing Mr Putin prime minister and giving power to the 'Chekists' was, in effect, the Yeltsinites' last desperate throw of the dice. The bombing campaign and fighting in Chechnya gave the move all the more impact: attention shifted from the shenanigans about official corruption to the authorities' commendably tough response to a terrorist onslaught on Russia. Few wanted to make the accusation outright, but the bombing campaign was certainly a remarkably convenient coincidence.

Such theories would have remained at the fringes of discussion, but for the 'bomb' that didn't go off. On the night of 22 September, Aleksei Kartofelnikov saw a white car parked outside his twelve-storey apartment block at 14/16 Novosyolov[18] Street in Ryazan, 200 kilometres from Moscow. An unusually observant man, he noticed that the licence plate had been doctored to look like a local registration. He looked more closely, and saw three people carrying sacks into the building's basement. He called the police. Experts investigated what appeared to be a bomb and removed the sacks, a detonator and a timer that had been set for 0530. Hundreds of people living close by were evacuated; eventually a nearby cinema was opened to take them in. A local police explosives expert, Yuri Tkachenko, used a gas analyser to examine the sacks' contents: yellowish granules, resembling pasta. The machine identified them as hexogen, a powerful explosive. The detonators were real and correctly wired. The police immediately put checkpoints on main roads.

The car spotted by Mr Kartofelnikov was found; it turned out to have been stolen.

On the evening of 23 September the head of the FSB's public relations division, Aleksander Zdanovich, appeared on a top talk show, *Geroi Dnya* (Hero of the Day). Though happy to take the credit for the foiled bombing, he seemed oddly confused about what had happened; perhaps because he was ill-briefed, or perhaps for some other reason.[19] The interior minister, Vladimir Rushailo, speaking at a conference the next day, nearly forty-eight hours after the 'bomb' was discovered, criticised the law-enforcement agencies for lack of vigilance, and praised the public for theirs. The next day, 24 September, Mr Putin praised the air strikes on the separatist capital, Grozny. On Ryazan, he said:

> If the sacks which proved to contain explosive were noticed, that means there is a positive side to it, if only in the fact that the public is reacting correctly to the events taking place in our country today. I'd like . . . to thank the public . . . This is absolutely the correct response. No panic, no sympathy for the bandits. This is the mood for fighting them to the very end. Until we win. And we shall win.[20]

Neither he nor any other official source made any suggestion at this stage that the discovery had been of anything but another terrorist plot. Then the head of the FSB, Nikolai Patrushev, stunned Russia by saying that the whole thing had been merely an exercise. He congratulated the residents of Ryazan for their 'vigilance'. The sacks had merely contained sugar and had been planted as part of a series of practice drills.

The Ryazan FSB reacted with fury to the news that the bomb was a hoax. They issued a statement saying:

> It has become known that the planting on 22.09.99 of a dummy explosive device was part of an ongoing interregional exercise. This

announcement came as a surprise to us and appeared at a moment
when the . . . FSB had identified the places of residence in Ryazan
of those involved in planting the explosive device and was preparing to detain them.[21]

One reason for the Ryazan FSB's anger was that on the night that
the 'bomb' was planted, Nadezhda Yukhanova, a telephone
operator in Ryazan, reported overhearing a suspicious fragment
of a trunk call to Moscow that she had connected: one caller said
that his group had been noticed and needed to leave town quickly.
The other replied: 'Split up and each of you make your own way
out.' When the local FSB traced the number dialled, it was
registered at the FSB headquarters in Moscow. Mr Patrushev
claimed that his men 'were among the residents who left the
building in which an explosive device was supposedly planted.
They took part in the process of producing their own photofit
pictures, and held conversations with employees of the agencies of
law enforcement.' That was not the case. In fact the Ryazan
authorities had arrested two suspects who then produced FSB
identity cards. A high-ranking officer from the agency's Moscow
headquarters came and collected them.[22]

Even by the Russian bureaucracy's bumbling standards, the
initial explanation seemed unconvincing. The newspaper *Novye
Izvestiya* (New News) caustically challenged Mr Patrushev's account, wondering if he also confused colours, or failed to recognise
his relatives. Others wondered if the bombing campaign might be
the work not of Russia's terrorist enemies, but of the authorities,
cynically trying to manipulate public opinion. It seemed unlikely
that the Ryazan experts had mistaken hexogen for sugar. And if the
sacks contained only sugar, why had they been swiftly removed for
'expert analysis' in Moscow? Was it perhaps to get the incriminat-
ing evidence away from Ryazan? The FSB added to the confusion

by saying that the sacks' contents had been 'tested' at an artillery range and found to be inert. Why would anyone bother to do that with sugar planted in an official training exercise? Why had the exercise used a stolen car – against all regulations – in a dummy drill when one of the agency's own vehicles would have done just as well?

The FSB appeared to be scrambling to produce evidence that Ryazan was indeed one of a series of planned exercises. Dozens of other 'tests' took place, mostly so amateurish that they would have shamed Inspector Clouseau. (In Moscow, FSB officers left a dummy package marked 'bomb' in a police station office where it was discovered two days later.) None showed the sophistication and extent of what seemingly had been mounted in Ryazan.[23] At a meeting with the apartment block's inhabitants, FSB chiefs struggled to explain what exactly was being practised in the 'exercise'; why no local authority had been informed; why no preparations had been made to look after the evacuated residents. Other details were even more puzzling. The building was an odd choice to test alertness, as it included an all-night supermarket; deliveries there would not arouse much suspicion. However, the flimsily constructed brick structure would have been an ideal choice for a terrorist attack: of similar construction to the one bombed in Moscow the previous week, it would have not only collapsed instantly, but the debris would have slid downhill and quite likely damaged a neighbouring building, too.

In March 2000 an FSB officer told a television interviewer that he and other officers had found by chance an unlocked basement in Ryazan, had bought sacks of sugar at a local market, and a gun cartridge at a firearms shop, and had then ostentatiously planted the mock bomb to test local residents' awareness. A senior retired FSB officer, Gennady Zaitsev, said that the instrument used for testing the 'explosive' had given a faulty reading because it was dirty – for which its operators had now been punished. That was meant to clear things up, but the result was yet more baffling. He may have been genuinely mistaken in his assertion, but staging innocent-seeming activities such as the purchase of sugar at a market, and of a cartridge at a gun shop, could be seen as odd ways to test public vigilance. Why come all the way from Moscow in a stolen car to leave three sacks of sugar in an unguarded basement? On the contrary, no disciplinary proceedings had been launched against Mr Tkachenko: he and a colleague had been officially rewarded for their courage, as had Ms Yukhanova, the telephone operator, for her alertness. If anybody deserved punishment, it would have been those responsible for such an extraordinarily inconsiderate, badly planned and pointless exercise.[24]

The authorities reacted with outrage to any suggestion of official complicity. Mr Putin said it was 'immoral' even to raise the question. It would indeed be unwise to rely only on the Russian media: it makes mistakes, just as reporters do everywhere. Mr Putin's enemies could have planted rumours and red herrings. All the Russian officials involved vehemently deny any wrongdoing, and insist that the conspiracy theory has been cooked up by their political opponents. Proponents of the theory that the bombing had official backing can produce considerable circumstantial evidence, but nothing that directly implicates Mr Putin, senior officials or his political allies. But the Kremlin could have easily cleared up the story. Instead of doing this, it sealed all material relating to Ryazan for seventy-five years and repeatedly blocked investigations by independent-minded Duma deputies.[25] Two Duma deputies who pursued the issue, Sergei Yushenkov and Yuri Shchekochi-khin, have since died in suspicious circumstances.[26] A journalist associated with their investigation, Otto Lacis,[27] was badly beaten. He later died in a car crash. The commission's lawyer, Mikhail Trepashkin, is in jail on charges of breaching official secrecy;

Amnesty International campaigns for his release, saying that the charges are bogus.

The Kremlin's strongest arguments, if they cared to make them, would be that Russian officialdom simply excelled itself in its usual capacity for bungling and secrecy. Perhaps planning for the 'exercise' was merely irregular, callous and incompetent. Maybe the right paperwork was never issued, or went unread. Instead of admitting that, the Kremlin denies that serious questions are raised by the events, and concentrates hard on depicting those who persist in asking questions as the creatures of Mr Berezovsky, an able propagandist with a vested interest in making Mr Putin's Kremlin look bad. But the alternative version is supported not only by Mr Putin's sworn foes, but also by the statements and actions of dozens of independent witnesses and participants who have no reason to portray their government as homicidal maniacs, and who in some cases run a considerable risk in sticking to their story. The official version does not properly account for any of the strange details: the people, the 'bomb', the car, the evacuation or the initial official explanation. The handful of 'culprits' who were eventually caught, tried and sentenced for the bombings had no convincing links to the crimes.

The biggest reason for disbelieving the conspiracy theory about Ryazan is that it is so energetically pushed by Mr Berezovsky, who – at least by his own account – is Mr Putin's arch enemy. Given his controversial record (see page 61) while at the heart of power in Russia during the 1990s, Mr Berezovsky's favourite causes certainly deserve careful and cautious scrutiny. His analysis of Russian politics is interesting but self-interested. It should never be taken at face value. But a theory may have dubious backers and still be true. And Mr Berezovsky is clever enough not to promote a version of evidence that could easily be rebutted as fictitious. The weight of evidence so far supports the grimmest interpretation: that the attacks were a ruthlessly planned stunt to create a climate of

panic and fear in which Mr Putin would quickly become the
country's undisputed leader, as indeed he did. It is a measure of
how far opinion has shifted that the conspiracy theory has gone
from being an outlandish hypothesis to something believed by
serious opposition politicians such as Grigory Yavlinsky,[28] leader of
the main liberal party, Yabloko. It is as if mainstream contenders for
the Democratic nomination in America's presidential election
publicly supported the contention that the terrorist attacks of 11
September 2001 were an inside job organised by Vice-President
Dick Cheney. Perhaps even more terrible than the murder plot
itself is the thought that Russian public opinion may be so
accustomed to official brutality and abuse of power, and so relieved
to have a strong man in charge, that it prefers not to worry about
what really happened.

At the time, most of the Russian public set aside any theories
about official complicity in the bombings. Mr Putin's popularity
was soaring against the other contenders for the presidential
election due the next year, in 2000. He was a straight-talking
tough guy, visibly sober and well organised; the best-educated and
best-travelled Russian leader since Lenin. He was young, compared
to one rival, the decrepit-seeming former foreign minister, Yevgeny Primakov. He was not burdened with the Soviet political
baggage of another: the Communist leader Gennady Zyuganov.
Unlike a third contender, the mayor of Moscow Yuri Luzhkov, he
was not linked publicly to any controversial business dealings.
Perhaps most importantly, he was hitting Russia's enemies hard.

Mr Putin's taciturn competence looked all the better compared
with his lame-duck predecessor. In the final years of his presidency,
Yeltsin was the most unpopular politician in Russia, seen as an
embarrassing drunk whose scheming family and tycoon friends had
cynically looted the country. It was his toxic touch that helped
make Russian politics seem so unmanageable. Yet in the Soviet

Union fifteen years earlier, Yeltsin had been hugely popular. A bear-like Communist Party boss from Sverdlovsk, a big city in the Urals region (which has now regained its pre-communist name, Yekaterinburg), he was originally a strong supporter of Mr Gorbachev's reforms. He moved to become the party chief in Moscow, but then clashed with the Soviet leader in 1988 and then shed his communist ideology, becoming an earthy populist politician. Elected the leader of Russia – in those days not a real state, but just one of the country's fifteen republics[29] – he was Mr Gorbachev's chief critic and rival. Russians admired his honesty and outspokenness, though the outside world worried that he was too nationalist, too unpredictable and (some whispered) too drunk. The waffly and indecisive Mr Gorbachev might have his faults, foreign diplomats and politicians conceded, but undermining him by backing an unknown rival would be crazy.[30]

Such doubts evaporated, at least for a while, in a few hours in August 1991, as the world woke up to find that Yeltsin was leading resistance to a hardliners' putsch that had toppled Mr Gorbachev and was trying to restore Soviet-style dictatorship. As Yeltsin defied the danger of snipers to stand on a captured tank outside his office building, Moscow's 'White House', he embodied Russian and foreign hopes for a future free of fear. Within a few months, he had dissolved the Soviet Union and the Communist Party, put the KGB under civilian control, declared Russia to be a multi-party democracy and appointed a team of radical economic reformers to run the government. The intentions were admirable: he sincerely wanted to make Russia good as well as great, ditching both the ruinous doctrines of economic planning, and the murderous ways of the secret-police state. But the difficulties were even greater than the hopes. The human, physical and economic legacy of the evil empire remained and poisoned what grew among its ruins everywhere, especially in Russia. Communism was more deeply ingrained than in the captive nations of Central Europe and the Baltics, where the rule of law, capitalism and, in some countries, even political freedom were living memories. If any elderly Russians alive in 1991 had childhood memories of Aleksandr Kerensky's brief provisional government of 1917, they were in no position to act on what they remembered.

Under Mr Putin, and among foreign critics of the Yeltsin era, the 1990s are now dismissed as a period of unalloyed failure. Yet it is hard to imagine a Russian leader who could have succeeded. Even the best policies in the world, implemented in the ideal sequence with unlimited outside support could not have made up for the nightmarish problems that Russia's rulers faced. But Yeltsin certainly blundered. Woefully ignorant of economics, ignorant of the world outside Russia, and in the habit of promoting thugs and crooks, he aggravated the effect of three highly unpopular but inevitable developments: vanishing savings, jarring economic dislocation and a growing gap between rich and poor.

The loss of savings, contrary to popular belief, predated Yeltsin's presidency. In the collapsing months of the Soviet Union, the central bank had run the printing presses red hot, destroying the value of the rouble, which slipped from a nominal parity with sterling to first 30 on the black market (in early 1990) and then 300 (by mid-1991). As inflation soared and the exchange rate plummeted, money began to lose its function. At the ridiculously low prices fixed by economic planners, goods simply stayed out of the shops: for lucky foreigners, that meant that you might for a wad of roubles worth pennies pick up a pair of clunky cross-country skis or a noisy but effective coffee grinder. If you were an ordinary family needing the necessities of daily life such as sausage or soap (and towards the end even bread) you would be staring at empty shelves, queuing for hours, swapping favours to get what you needed, or paying what seemed like sky-high prices on the black market. Wise Soviet citizens started saving in cash in hard currencies, and, if they could, exchanged their roubles, too – though this was hampered by crude stunts such as the cancellation under Mr Gorbachev of the highest-value rouble banknotes. Many people's savings existed only as numbers on a bank statement, in banks that had no real assets to back their liabilities. Most people believed that the 'shortages' were only temporary: once prices returned to 'normal' they would then be able to spend their savings. That created what economists call a 'monetary overhang' – a mountain of unspendable money. When Yeltsin's government rightly, and belatedly, freed prices in early 1992, goods reappeared on sale, first hawked on the pavement or at informal markets, then in makeshift kiosks and eventually in the shops. The rouble became money again. But the goods were on sale at prices far higher, sometimes hundreds of times so, than those of the Soviet days. For millions of households, the worthlessness of their savings was suddenly and pitifully visible. Many Russians have never forgiven Yeltsin and his team of young economic reformers for that, though their anger should in truth be directed at Mr Gorbachev and his long-forgotten colleagues for printing too much money in the first place. After a few years of growing but still precarious stability, the currency devaluation of August 1998 added insult to injury. Under Mr Putin, by contrast, the rouble's value has remained rock-solid against Western currencies in nominal terms, and appreciated sharply in real terms. The banking system has recovered. Russian households regard the rouble as real money. For all his virtues, that is something that Yeltsin never managed.

The economic dislocation of the 1990s was unavoidable, too. In the Soviet system giant factories produced huge orders on the instructions of bureaucrats in Moscow. Waste was colossal, quality abysmal, attention to customers' wishes unknown. Outside a planned economy, much of the production was worse than useless: worth less than the raw materials used to produce it. As Jan Winiecki, a Polish economist, put it: 'The Soviet cow drank more milk than she produced.'[31] Management disciplines such as product development, sales or marketing were unknown. Most enterprises had enormous social obligations. Slowly and painfully, the penalties and incentives of the market began to bite. Russia's economy began to modernise, initially by shedding labour and ending production of useless goods. But the price was years of hardship and uncertainty for many. Again, that seemed to be Yeltsin's fault: it was on his watch that the economy was contracting and unemployment was soaring. Few thought of the real culprits: Lenin, Stalin and Brezhnev. Under Mr Putin, the economy (see Chapter Four) has grown month by month for more than seven years. Russians appreciate that; few ask how Mr Putin would have fared had he taken over the ruined Soviet economy and low oil prices, or how much better Yeltsin would have looked had he taken charge of Russia ten years later.

Most Russians were ill placed to judge Yeltsin's policies. The market economy was a mystery, and one they had to unravel almost overnight. Nothing in their past lives had prepared the population for rapid economic change. Soviet-era survival skills consisted chiefly of stoicism, made endurable by alcohol and tobacco. Suddenly, drive, initiative and adaptability were what counted. Many of the ordinary Russians who went into business found life tough: selling pathetic assortments of second-hand goods at seedy markets provided pocket money at best, but not a living. Many didn't even want to try. They retained a lingering Marxist belief that one man's profit was necessarily another man's loss. For many in middle age or older, it was too late to learn new tricks. Worse, those who knew the new rules were poor ambassadors for capitalism: speculators, spivs and outright gangsters, whose profits were dependent more on unscrupulous quickwittedness than talent, effort or ingenuity. For those suffering years of hardship and uncertainty it was little consolation that others were grasping the opportunities – literally – of a lifetime. Brisk commercial relationships and cutthroat competition seemed as disgusting as the string-pulling and hypocrisy of the earlier regime. 'Everything they told us about communism was false – but everything they told us about capitalism was true' was a common complaint. For those on public sector salaries, living standards plunged.

Manual workers fared particularly badly. Under communism their jobs had been arduous and even dangerous. But they had been secure, relatively well paid, and often with privileges such as cheap holidays on the Black Sea – sometimes even a coveted jaunt to Bulgaria. Laziness and incompetence were unpenalised, just as talent and hard work were unrewarded. The informal motto of the Soviet workplace was 'we pretend to work and they pretend to pay us'. Now life had gone from predictable to precarious, almost overnight. State-owned enterprises provided not just employment, but also housing, heating, education and healthcare. When the parent business collapsed, so did everything else. As unemployment rocketed, many middle-aged manual workers wondered if they would ever find employment again. New jobs meant harsh bosses and arbitrary discipline. Social benefits were pathetically small, and often paid late.

Chaotic economics was matched by chaotic politics. Though Yeltsin wished Russia to become a modern, prosperous, indus-trialised country, he had only the haziest idea of what this entailed in practice. His three immovable principles were free speech, friendship with the West and to keep Communists out of power. These were fine things, but not enough to run a country properly. Viktor Gerashchenko, for example, a Soviet-era holdover who ran the central bank until 1994, simply did not believe that printing money caused inflation. Jeffrey Sachs, a Harvard economist, said: '[He] may be the worst central-bank governor of any major country in history.' The state was all but powerless: it could liberalise, but not regulate. The laws and institutions needed for a market economy, such as tax administration, a land register, banking supervision and courts, existed either not at all, or only in distorted and inadequate Soviet versions. Reforms were also haphazard and incomplete because Yeltsin never had a reliable parliamentary majority: indeed, for most of the 1990s legislative power lay in the hands of people who were determined to thwart change, not support it. The easy way round that was bribing legislators. This got things done – but at the price of entrenching the idea that political power was a commodity to be bought and sold, rather than a reflection of the will of the people. The Yeltsin-era Kremlin became an increasingly pungent illustration of a well-worn proverb, that fish start rotting at the head. Not a notably greedy man himself,[32] Yeltsin proved quite unable to rein in the clique of family and friends that surrounded him. Their greed and ostentatiousness became a byword for the failure of his rule.

By the time of the 1998 financial crisis, the multi-party system and the market economy, along with Yeltsin's personal reputation, were deeply discredited (see opposite). Russians talked of *dermok-ratsiya* (shitocracy) and *prikhvatisatsiya* (piratisation) instead of *de-mokratiya* (democracy) and *privatisatsiya* (privatisation). Poor people wanted pensions and salaries paid on time; business people wanted stability. Patriots wanted their country to be respected. Almost everyone wanted the oligarchs to be cut down to size. It was the perfect setting for a quiet putsch by the heirs of the KGB.[33] At first hypothetically, then tentatively, and soon with confident enthu-siasm, Mr Putin was discussed as a future president. Then and thereafter, his leitmotif has been that he represents a clear break with the past. His style of rule was well choreographed and disciplined, quite unlike his predecessor. His policies are sharply different. Yet it remains the fact that he first rose to high office in the period he now decries, starting as an unemployed ex-spy and ending up running the country's most powerful government agency. However much his supporters dislike the notion, Mr Putin is a product of the Yeltsin years, and the handpicked choice of the Yeltsin 'family' and their tycoon friends.[34]

Gloomy Russians

Who more effectively and quicker than anyone else can bring order to Russia now?	%
Putin	41
The Communists under Zyuganov	14
Armed forces	9
Fatherland–All Russia	8
Yeltsin	1

How would you describe politics in Russia today?	
Rise of anarchy	63
Democracy building	9
Old system, new names	8
Approach of dictatorship	6

What phrase best describes the political situation in Russia today?	
Tense	60
Critical, explosive	29
Quiet	3
Good	0

What economic system would you prefer?	
State planning and distribution	48
Private property and the market	35

It would have been better if the country had stayed as it was before 1985?	
Yes	58
No	27

Source: VTsIOM, October 1999 © The Economist Newspaper Ltd

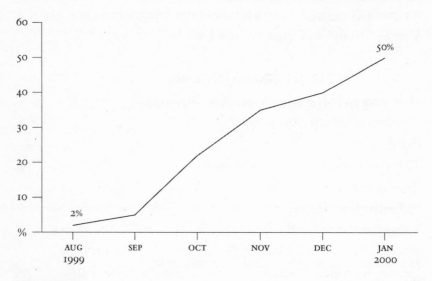

Zero to Hero
Mr Putin's popularity ratings in his first months in public life

As Mr Putin moved smoothly into the acting presidency and
then won a presidential election in March 2000, the big question
became not whether he would exercise power, but what kind and
over whom. Three possibilities were open. Mr Putin might stay a
mouse, timorously observing but not effectively influencing the
workings of money and real power in Russian politics. He might
be the longed-for magician, who would get reform back on track,
modernise Russia, and help it finally step over its post-imperial
shadow. Or he might be a monster: an autocratic leader who would
rule by fear, and who would return Russia to its xenophobic and
authoritarian past.

Putin in Power: The Winners and Losers of the New Regime

It was hard to tell at the beginning of Mr Putin's rule who would suffer and who would benefit. As the creation and creature of the Yeltsin Kremlin, it seemed unlikely that he would be able to change the system that had taken root in the 1990s. How could he tame the oligarchs, whose private security services and bulging coffers made them more powerful than most institutions of state? And how would the centre bring to heel the mighty tribal chieftains, bandit kings, mafia dons, strongmen and warlords who ruled many of Russia's regions? At first it was hard to see how Mr Putin could make a difference: a mere mouse seemed to be running round the Kremlin's endless corridors. The new president's inner circle was an uneasy mixture of the 'family' – the Yeltsin cronies who had brought him to power – and two St Petersburg clans, the *siloviki*, and the economic reformers. The president shifted indecisively between all three, seemingly agreeing with whoever had advised him last. 'Putin jokes' were common, most of which had obscene punchlines.[1] Carefully staged photo-ops aside, the Russian leader cut an unimpressive figure in public: tetchy, foul-mouthed and unsympathetic. If trouble brewed, he disappeared. When the *Kursk*, one of the most advanced vessels in Russia's nuclear submarine fleet, sank after a botched torpedo launch, Mr Putin stayed on holiday for a week. When he was finally asked by an American television interviewer what had actually happened (Russian naval officials had blamed everybody and everything but their own incompetence), Mr Putin seemed to find it impossible to show sympathy, distress or contrition. He grimaced and said simply 'it sank'.[2] Progress in the Chechen war was slow, the casualties appalling. His popularity looked set to ebb as fast as it had flowed.

But the mouse had a taste for magic. Mr Putin came out strongly for economic reform, saying that he wanted Russia to reach Portuguese standards of prosperity in a decade. His government pushed through a 13 per cent flat tax in 2001; as in other countries where this has been tried,[3] the results were impressive. His ministers talked of setting up a 'one-stop-shop' for registering small businesses, replacing the baffling and expensive trek between different state institutions that faced Russia's hardy would-be entrepreneurs. Then, as the months went by, the Putin-mouse's squeaks turned to roars. Stumblingly at first, and then moving more systematically, he began squeezing independent sources of political and economic power. For those who thought that the winners and losers of the 1990s were set in stone, it was time to think again.

The landscape of Russian society now is marked by three phases in recent history: the Soviet era, when political loyalty was at a premium; the Gorbachev/Yeltsin era, which prized talent and adaptability; and now the Putin era, which punishes only dissent. Each period has had its losers and its winners. The foundation of Mr Putin's success is that so few have lost, and so many have gained. They include both those who have felt hard done by in the past and those who have done well through all three eras. Under Soviet rule, the biggest winners by far were the nomenklatura. Through a mixture of family connections, brains and opportunism, they acquired, usually rather late in life, the best that the Soviet Union could offer: princely country houses, access to special shops where Western goods were sold at knock-down prices, chauffeur-driven cars, healthcare and prostitutes. Only contact with foreigners was restricted: distrust was so ingrained in the Soviet system that even the elite could not be allowed to mix freely with the enemy and his temptations.

The collapse of the one-party state and the planned economy suddenly made ideological purity and party connections matter less, while talent and flexibility were at a premium. The able members of the old power structures moved on, dumping their communist allegiances along with the grey plastic shoes and nylon suits of the Soviet wardrobe. Some moved into the private sector, setting up well-connected banks or import–export businesses. Others stayed in government service, such as the young Mr Putin, handling municipal foreign relations in St Petersburg, a city that some hoped might even eclipse Moscow in importance as Russia rediscovered its European roots. Many of the KGB moved to the 'active reserve', working in the private sector but keeping their alumnus contacts alive, just in case.

For these able apparatchiks, as the members of the communist establishment, or *apparat*, were known, Mr Putin's rise to power was the best news possible. Their Soviet past gave them contacts and credibility, the new conditions offered them the chance to turn them into money. The best examples come from the top of the Kremlin: Sergei Ivanov, a career KGB spy who is now first deputy prime minister, has become chairman of the board at the new state-controlled aircraft manufacturing company, UABC. Igor Sechin, a deputy chief of staff in the Kremlin (whose Soviet-era job as a 'military translator' in Africa strongly suggests a background in the Soviet Union's military intelligence service, the GRU) worked alongside Mr Putin in St Petersburg and is now chairman of Rosneft. Thanks to the bargain price at which it has acquired

assets, Rosneft is now Russia's largest oil company. Sergei Naryshkin, a fast-rising deputy prime minister,[4] who is a former
colleague of Mr Putin both from St Petersburg days and before
that the KGB, is his deputy there and chairman of the main
shipbuilding company. Viktor Ivanov, a KGB veteran and a senior
Kremlin figure, chairs the boards of Aeroflot and the air-defence
systems giant Almaz-Antei. Similar types also run, or are in powerful positions at, the ministries of economy, transport, natural
resources, telecommunications and culture. At least a quarter of
Gazprom's management is made up of ex-KGB veterans. Aleksei
Gromov, the Kremlin spokesman, whose Soviet-era postings
abroad strongly suggest a past career in the KGB, sits on the board
of the main television channel. The railway monopoly, Russia's
second largest company after Gazprom, is headed by Vladimir
Yakunin, a former diplomat and ex-KGB officer.[5] Soviet apparatchiks unable to make the transition, by contrast, disappeared like
dinosaurs. Their last hurrah had been the failed putsch against Mr
Gorbachev. They could barely conceive a world without the
institutions of Soviet power, much less operate in it. In a country
where the male life expectancy had plunged below the age of sixty,
many followed communist ideology to the grave. Few mourned
them. Russia's new rulers regard with contempt the way that the
old guard misruled the Soviet Union, turning it from superpower
to basket case.

For different reasons, the old Soviet ruling caste is also despised
by the chief losers during the communist era: the phantom middle
class of principled and well-educated people who were deprived of
the life they would have enjoyed in capitalist countries. Advance-
ment in any line of work was limited for those not prepared to
swallow what Czesaw Miosz, the Polish Nobel Laureate, called the
'Pill of Murti-Bing'.[6] Some became scientists and engineers,
professions largely uncontaminated by communist ideology. But

many of the middle-class occupations that make up the bulk of employment in an advanced capitalist economy did not exist. The phantom middle class could not run small businesses because none existed. Professions such as medicine and teaching were of far lower status than in Western countries. The life of the mind was imprisoned by a system that prevented travel abroad, and severely restricted access to the cultures and ideas of the outside world. Speaking out – which was almost unthinkable – risked severe punishment: the thought of being forced to move to a communal apartment, sharing a kitchen and bathroom with noisy alcoholics, was usually deterrent enough. The result was internal emigration. People retreated into drink, despair and the intense friendships of their private lives, where in a narrow circle of trusted friends they could – they hoped – at least speak freely.

The Yeltsin years were good for many of this phantom middle class, at least initially. The professions opened up. Russian business needed commercial lawyers; Russian women wanted cosmetic surgery and decent gynaecology and obstetrics; everyone wanted to learn English. Journalism went from being a closely guarded branch of Soviet propaganda to a profession open to anyone with a quick pen and a sharp mind. Professions mushroomed that had been unknown in the Soviet Union: travel agent, estate agent, salesman and tax accountant. Obscure hobbies turned into specialist businesses. Good things came in return; foreign travel went from unimaginable luxury to part of normal life in a few years. People who once knew London only from the pages of Dickens and Conan Doyle could see the real thing for the price of a coach ticket. Visa lines at Western consulates lengthened, first shamefully and then outrageously. Squalid and tatty Soviet apartments have had a *Yevroremont* (Euro-makeover) and become gleaming and some-times gaudy. Diet transformed: vodka sales dropped; wine and beer consumption soared. Russians bought cars, to the point that big

cities have become unmanageably congested. Some started edu-
cating their children privately.

The Yeltsin years were also good for a second group of losers
from the Soviet system: the commercially talented. The planned
economy offered few openings for the ambitious, quickwitted, and
sometimes less principled people who would have been the back-
bone of a capitalist system. A few got jobs running Soviet foreign
trade, usually in close collaboration with the KGB. For the others,
the only place for their talents was the black market. Denounced as
'speculators', and subject to severe punishment if caught, they
skulked on the margins of society, sometimes enjoying rich rewards
if the KGB allowed them a little licence in return for information
about their clients.[7]

While offering both groups unparalleled opportunity, capitalism also created some jarring juxtapositions. In the chaotic
1990s, even the most fastidious members of the country's
intellectual and cultural elite found themselves rubbing shoulders
with people they would have previously regarded with horrified
distaste. Mr Berezovsky, a respectable Soviet-era mathematician,
spotted an opening in the car business and became one of the
richest men in Russia. Vladimir Gusinsky, a theatre director, used
$1,000, his entire savings, to open a store selling women's
clothing and copper bracelets. Ten years later he had the largest
media business in Russia. Aleksander Smolensky, after years
tussling with the Soviet authorities over his semi-legal business
activities, set up one of the first cooperatives in the construction
industry, and shortly thereafter a bank. Within five years he was
one of the richest men in Russia. Others took a more direct
route to riches. Hardened criminals were a natural basis for the
newly emergent Russian mafia, whose ruthlessness and mutual
loyalty outstripped a police force that had always relied on now-
vanished political and KGB back-up. Their businesses ranged

from looting state property, establishing monopolies and cartels, to simple extortion.

For the dodgy and distinguished alike, the quickest gains came from goods that were portable and readily saleable, such as valuable raw materials.[8] Anyone crossing the former Soviet border into Poland would see roadsides dotted with signs offering to buy non-ferrous metals. Wily middlemen began buying the most sought-after products of state factories and smelters, paying a nominal price to the nominal owner, plus a stiff 'enabling payment' to the manager, and then selling the products on the open market. In the rudimentary post-Soviet legal system, it was not clear if any of this was illegal. The profits were even more fantastic for those who could run not only businesses, but also whole chunks of government. The most successful tycoons became the oligarchs, making multi-billion dollar fortunes by snapping up state assets at what seemed like knockdown prices, at a time when most Russians were struggling to keep their families fed and clothed. Those sell-offs were perhaps less bad than they looked then; in the mid-1990s, with the Communist Party seemingly on the verge of regaining power, few others wanted to buy these companies at all. But the auctions were strangely rigged, and, once in charge, the new owners proved better at stripping assets and diddling the other shareholders than building real businesses. The richer ones sent their offspring to the grandest English schools such as Eton and Winchester and bought boltholes in London's most upmarket districts. Russian good-time girls started shunning the foreign clients they had once chased so assiduously; the rewards for bagging a rich compatriot were so much better.

The tycoons set up institutions that they called 'banks', but which would have been better described as a mixture of personal piggy banks, pyramid schemes and *bureaux de change*. The boring business of making sensible loans to dependable borrowers, or competing for savers' cash by offering convenience and good service, featured only for cosmetic reasons. In the 1998 financial crash, these 'banks' mostly disappeared, along with their deposits. The nascent Russian middle class had lost their savings yet again: in 1991 it was to inflation, this time to fraud and incompetence.

Mr Putin's single biggest achievement is that this crisis – against many expectations at the time – proved only a temporary setback. For all his attacks on other freedoms, Mr Putin has preserved the ones that the 'new Russians' most care about. More than ever before Russians can plan their lives: they can save, educate themselves, travel and bring up their children as they like; they can buy anything they can afford; own property at home or abroad; worship (mostly) as they wish; read almost anything they like; live according to their sexual preference (if not always publicly). Though they lack the freedom to choose their elected representatives, to organise publicly to influence their government, or to change their political systems, never in Russian history have so many Russians lived so well and so freely. That is a proud boast, and one that even those who dislike Russia's current path must honestly acknowledge.

The most significant changes are in the core middle-class preoccupations of travel, education and entertainment. Private cars used to be a luxury in the Soviet Union. In 1993 there were fifty-nine per thousand people. That figure has risen fivefold. Around 15 per cent of all Russians have been abroad at least once – something unimaginable in Soviet times. Indeed, Russians have become the ninth biggest spenders in the world on tourism. Hundreds of thousands come to Europe to shop, study and relax. Russians took 1.47m trips to Turkey in 2006, 900,000 went to Egypt (in both countries visas are available to Russians on arrival). Russians feel linked to the outside world in a way that their Soviet predecessors never were. Whereas once the international departure lounge of Moscow's Sheremetyevo airport was a sanctum for the elite, now dozens of airports all over Russia offer cheap and frequent travel abroad for any customer who can afford it.

For all but the very brightest in the Soviet Union, access to good education depended on parents' connections. Despite the communist system's egalitarian rhetoric, higher education in particular was highly elitist – well under a third of the eighteen-plus age group went to university. Now the figure for post-eighteen study is nearly 80 per cent. At the good universities corruption is endemic both to get in and to get a good grade. Political connections (such as a job in a pro-Kremlin youth movement) may mean that you get higher education free of charge, or get in more easily. For those without such connections, costs at the best universities are soaring. In some institutions, studying law or business can cost an American-style $40,000. Elsewhere, the quality of the teaching is often far lower than in Soviet days. The qualifications on offer may be Mickey Mouse affairs such as diplomas in 'marketing and international PR' involving often only part-time study. But the doors are not barred to anyone.

The life of the mind is still limited by politics, but only partially. Mr Putin has not blocked off the emergent middle class from outside intellectual life. It is true that the Kremlin's internal propaganda machine swamps most outside influences – but that reflects also Russians' own preferences. The internet remains largely uncensored[9] for any Russian with the time to browse it (7 per cent of Russian adults use it daily, 17 per cent once a week and 22 per cent at least once a month; in the last two years the number of Russian citizens with access to a computer at home has risen from 14 to 25 per cent). Those who want to listen to foreign radio stations can still do so, at least on crackly, cumbersome shortwave receivers,[10] or online. If bookshops do not stock politically controversial material, it can be ordered from ozon,

Russia's equivalent of amazon. Small-circulation newspapers and magazines still write largely what they want; Ekho Moskvy (Echo of Moscow), the sole remaining independent domestic radio station, remains a symbolic trophy of media freedom.

The bourgeoisie that enjoys this lifestyle is small by the standards of advanced industrialised countries, where a majority of the population typically describes itself as 'middle class', but it is certainly growing. The Kremlin reckons that what it calls the 'middle class' (those earning a monthly salary of $900–$1,100) will make up 35 per cent of Russia's population by 2010. That is up from 20 per cent in 2006, and from only 16.5 per cent who identified themselves in this category in 2003. The consolidation of the middle class is creating a social force, albeit so far a politically passive one, that Russia has never had in its history, and its future political behaviour is the biggest question facing the country. A big middle class may not be a sufficient condition for political freedom and pluralism, but it seems to be a necessary one. So far, Russia's new bourgeoisie strongly supports the status quo, but when (or if) it begins to chafe at lawlessness, corruption and other ills, it may demand more freedom and tolerance. The evidence so far, though, is that prosperity correlates with what might be called 'soft nationalism': the number of people who want 'Russia for the ethnic Russians' is highest in the most advanced and prosperous cities: Moscow and St Petersburg. 'The more well-off Russians become, the more they need something beside money to gain respect – and they seem to be looking for this respect in ethnic status,' says Dmitri Polikanov, a pollster.

While the middle class gets richer, the workers are not doing badly either. Not only has real disposable income doubled; unemployment, the great curse of Russia in the first fifteen years of transition, is down to a largely fictitious 7 per cent. Employers complain of labour shortages. It is no exaggeration to say that any

Russian who is not a drunkard (and some who are) can find work. That appeals to the 'old Russians': the losers of the 1990s, those senior in years, poorer in incomes and more backward in outlook. Their wages and pensions are paid punctually. Employers have to offer better terms than ever before. A bloated public sector offers a safe, undemanding and increasingly well-paid life for those prepared to stomach the necessary political compromises. For such Russians life has turned full circle from the Soviet era, for which they are thankful.

Russian capitalism is not Western capitalism: connections matter more, and laws matter less. Improvements have been infuriatingly slow and patchy. Many of the promises of Mr Putin's first term have not been fulfilled. Public services are still dreadful, especially in rural areas. More out of fear than generosity, the governments have only trimmed the country's sprawling and inefficient network of social benefits, such as subsidised housing. Small businesses are still waiting for their 'one-stop-shop'. Interaction with the legal system threatens normal life, rather than safeguarding it. Despite cosmetic changes and paper reforms, bureaucracy remains a huge burden for households and businesses.[11] State ownership is growing not shrinking. But for such failings disgruntled Russians tend not to blame Mr Putin. Polls show most Russians think that the government is doing a bad job, while giving high approval ratings to the president.

For all that, modern Russia is a country in which it is possible for a private citizen to dream about personal fulfilment through brains and hard work. The promise of a prosperous and civilised life began in the Gorbachev and Yeltsin eras, but for many Russians it has only become a reality under Mr Putin. As a result, even the most self-consciously modern 'New Russians' are proud of their country and mostly regard criticism with a mixture of irritation and bewilderment. Surely, they ask, this is just Western ignorance and hypocrisy? Why are we not being praised for our progress, rather than nagged about our shortcomings. Despite all the West's blunders, Russia has constantly extended the hand of friendship. It has cooperated with NATO on terrorism and closed down Russia's Cold War bases in Vietnam and Cuba. Not only are relations with many European countries (such as Germany) excellent, but Russia is respected and admired in much of the rest of the world for its ability to carve its own foreign-policy course. The criticism says more about the critics than Russian reality. If relations with America are frosty, the blame for that lies mainly in Washington, DC, not in Moscow. It is the Americans' fault if they incite their puppet states such as Estonia, Georgia and Poland to get on Russia's nerves. And it is Britain's fault if it harbours traitors, terrorists and fraudsters. Modern-minded Russians regret the occasional chilly episodes in their foreign policy, but they do not take them too seriously. After all, they reason, what the West really cares about is business, and on that score Russia can't be ignored for long.

So much for the winners of the Putin years. But what of the losers? One clear category is the mafia. It was already retreating towards the end of the Yeltsin era. Now it has been squeezed out of the extortion business by a newly confident state. Amateur gang-sters are no match for those who have the might of officialdom behind them. Small businesses still need to pay protection money to their *krysha* (roof) but this is far more likely to be to a powerful local politician or official than a swaggering thug in a shiny tracksuit and leather jacket. Clever gangsters have become respectable businessmen or public officials. The stupid ones have retreated back to the fringes of the economy. That change makes life more predictable, but not necessarily more comfortable, for legitimate enterprise. Instead of a rake-off from the profits, the new state-run mafia may demand a share in the business. If the owner refuses, he can lose everything overnight. For those with big businesses, the

Putin Kremlin has brought more risk than reward. Prosperity means a larger cake – but only if you are entitled to a slice. The price of failure is now jail, exile or assassination, while only total obedience to the Kremlin guarantees survival. The wise tycoon now portrays himself as a well-remunerated steward of the nation's wealth, rather than its proprietor. The prime example of this is Oleg Deripaska, who interrupted his physics studies in 1990 to go into business, became a billionaire in Russia's terrifyingly competitive aluminium industry and married Yeltsin's granddaughter. 'If the state says we need to give it up, we'll give it up,' he said in mid-2007. 'I don't separate myself from the state. I have no other interests.'

The first victim of the Kremlin's squeeze was Vladimir Gusinsky, Russia's biggest media tycoon. His empire produced most of Russia's best-quality broadcast journalism, albeit under questionable editorial control from the top. Having strongly opposed the first Chechen war, Mr Gusinsky's news coverage then swung unflinchingly behind Yeltsin in the 1996 election. This was the time when the newly free Russian media sold its soul: believing that it was vitally important to keep the old communist guard out of power, the first generation of independent journalists in Russia's history produced – without much central direction – a public-relations blitz worthy of the most ardent Soviet propagandist. Though gravely ill, Yeltsin rose from seemingly hopeless unpopularity to beat his communist challenger, Mr Zyuganov. The cause was perhaps noble. The means were anything but. Two years later, Mr Gusinsky's main outlet, the television channel NTV, switched sides again, excoriating the Yeltsin Kremlin for weakness and corruption and supporting Mr Luzhkov, who had his sights set on the presidency. (The Moscow mayor's energetic and hands-on approach to municipal capitalism made some term him an unlikely champion of clean government.) NTV's punchy Sunday night

political programme, *Itogi* (Summary of Events), could strike outsiders used to Western political broadcasting as outrageously biased
and sententious, although it was still an unmissable part of the week
for anyone interested in politics. NTV's business coverage seemed
to sway according to who was paying (or who was refusing to pay).
Though it would have been too kind to call the station independent in the full sense of the word, it was at least independent of the
Kremlin. For those optimistic about Russia's future, NTV looked
the most likely candidate to evolve eventually into a respectable
channel where professional journalists would broadcast dispassio-
nate news.

Though the Gusinsky media empire had disliked Mr Putin from
the start, few thought it would experience serious problems. Its
satirical puppet show, *Kukly*, ridiculed him[12] – but every other
politician in Russia, including Yeltsin, got similar treatment. Its
commentators lambasted him over the authorities' response to the
sinking of the *Kursk*, and its journalists investigated the Ryazan
bombing. But in a country where the state had enforced a monopoly
on all information for seven decades, the freedom of even an
imperfect media was treasured. That had been one of the few
consistently commendable features of the Yeltsin era. Surely under
Mr Putin, the authorities would continue to be cautious in dealing
with the country's top independent television station? Not a bit of it.
Not only did the Kremlin order *Kukly* to stop making fun of the
head of state, but in the spring and summer of 2000 Mr Gusinsky's
offices were repeatedly raided by different law enforcement agencies, on allegations that seemed either selective or invented. On 13
June he was arrested and spent several days in one of Moscow's most
notorious prisons. A month later, he struck a deal with the government under which he would sell his media company to Gazprom.
He then moved to Israel, eventually setting up a satellite channel,
NTV+, that – for those able to watch it – is now Russia's only

independent national broadcaster. Some of NTV's best journalists left; others were fired; a few switched sides. Some refugees from NTV moved to two small independent channels, TV-S and TV-6; both were shut down in the course of the next two years. Many of them now work at REN-TV, a channel with limited reach that has retained some independence. NTV now pumps out much the same mixture of apolitical entertainment and Kremlin propaganda as its supposed competitors.

Mr Berezovsky, the manic manipulator of Russian politics, was the second target. To many Russians he symbolised the looting and influence-peddling that had characterised the Yeltsin era. Starting seemingly from nothing, he had acquired an oil company, a television channel and control of the foreign currency revenues of Russia's national airline, Aeroflot. He was so powerful in the late 1990s that for some time he had an office adjoining that of Mr Chernomyrdin, the then prime minister. A close associate of the Yeltsin family, he played a crucial (and still unclear) role in brokering Mr Putin's rise to power. In the summer of 2000, Mr Putin unleashed the prosecutor's office on him too. Mr Berezovsky responded toughly, claiming that dictatorship was looming. Few wanted to listen. Within a few months, he had lost his most important assets. His television channel, ORT, was back in government control. Prosecutors and accountants were poring over the books at Aeroflot. His control over his oil company, Sibneft, had shrivelled. Mr Berezovsky moved to London, where he gained political asylum. Some wondered why the British government allowed such a controversial figure to take up residence in the capital; that question was posed more sharply when the Russian authorities began demanding his extradition. The most likely answer is that it was a quid pro quo for Berezovsky's efforts in 1998 to bring about the release of two British citizens who had been kidnapped in Chechnya.

It was hard to sympathise greatly with Mr Berezovsky. From a journalistic point of view, he was an excellent source, often willing to chat in his rapid, sibilant Russian, or his confident but eccentric English, at his ludicrously luxurious private club in downtown Moscow. But the fact remained that at every company he touched, the other shareholders, employees and customers tended to curse his name. He said he had fallen foul of a monster that fused political ambition and business greed, using the dirty tricks of the intelli-gence-service world. If so, it could equally be argued that it was one that he had himself created and which he epitomised. Once based overseas, Mr Berezovsky's mystique evaporated. His public pronouncements were increasingly shrill. He became politically toxic: an association with him might mean some extra cash – but it spelled doom for anyone wanting a political future in Russia.

The other oligarchs dived for cover, offering fulsome political compliments to Mr Putin and pledging to shun all involvement in political opposition. Only Mikhail Khodorkovsky, the founder and main shareholder of the Yukos oil company, was prepared to stand up to the Kremlin. His company was the best run of all the Russian business empires. It had a controversial and even (some said) bloody start. Outside shareholders who had bought minority stakes in its production subsidiaries complained furiously that they had been cheated. Shareholders' meetings were shifted to remote locations at short notice, where the agenda and votes were rigged to produce decisions of outrageous unfairness. Some talked of more brutal means: a mayor and an oil refinery manager who had obstructed the company's rise had both met early deaths (Mr Khodorkovsky vehemently denied involvement in either case). But the most interesting thing about Yukos was not its history – unexceptional by Russian standards – but the direction in which it was going. After the 1998 crash it had started cleaning up its accounts, brought in foreign managers and independent board directors, and replaced clunky and wasteful Soviet-era habits and technology with the most modern foreign expertise and equipment. At its peak, Yukos alone was producing 2 per cent of global oil output. Compared to other Russian businesses, it was a model corporate citizen. Yukos paid $1.9 billion in taxes in 2000 – more than the entire firm was worth at the time of privatisation five years earlier. Mr Khodorkovsky donated heavily to charities in both Russia and abroad, from Omsk to Oxford. For those who believed that Russia's robber barons were going to go from banditry to respectability in a generation, Mr Khodorkovsky, the richest man in Russia and the sixteenth richest in the world, was a shining example.[13]

His strength was undermined by overconfidence. Mr Khodorkovsky was not only publicly at odds with the Kremlin on issues such as the Iraq war (which he backed) and friendly relations with America (ditto). His beneficence, official and unofficial, had begun to create menacing political clout. Hundreds of members of both houses of the parliament, plus senior officials and government ministers, were all heavily influenced in their decision-making by the attentive generosity of the Khodorkovsky empire. By the standards of past years, that was nothing special. Every rich Russian had a payroll, and the bigger the coffers the more impressive the help it bought. But this was a new era: Mr Putin was not willing to tolerate any competitor for power, and particularly not one with grand plans in energy, foreign policy and domestic politics. Mr Khodorkovsky's preparations to build an independent export pipeline threatened the vital Kremlin monopoly on oil exports. The trigger may have been Mr Khodorkovsky's plan to merge with Sibneft, another Russia oil giant, and then bring in an American energy company as a big strategic investor in the new firm. That would gain not only expertise and commercial clout, but also heavyweight political insurance from America. If it went ahead, he would be close to invulnerable. The Kremlin started firing warning shots, arresting a close colleague of Mr Khodorkovsky's, and giving unmistakable signs of its discontent. Mr Khodorkovsky countered with a well-publicised tour to meet regional leaders in eastern Russia. The Kremlin took that as a declaration of war. It was a fight Mr Khodorkovsky could only lose.

On 25 October 2003, Mr Khodorkovsky's private jet landed for refuelling at Novosibirsk airport in Siberia. Masked FSB agents stormed the plane, confiscated his bodyguards' weapons and arrested him. He was taken to a prison in Moscow and charged with fraud and tax evasion. For Yukos's shareholders, including many Westerners, the bonanza of the past years turned to disaster. The company's share price tumbled as it was looted by its state-backed rivals, with its key assets sold off in order to pay gigantic tax bills. However fast Yukos tried to raise the money, the authorities increased the amount, while setting impossible deadlines. On 14 April 2004, for example, the authorities insisted that Yukos pay $3.5 billion in unpaid taxes by the end of the day.[14] Bailiffs then froze Yukos's shares in Yuganskneftegaz, its main production unit. Yukos's assets were sold at knockdown prices to companies close to the Kremlin. On 19 December, for example, the Russian authorities auctioned a 76.79 per cent share in Yuganskneftegaz, in order to recover what was now an alleged $28 billion in unpaid taxes. Western companies boycotted that auction, as Yukos had filed for bankruptcy in America and said it would sue anyone who took part in grabbing its assets. Only two companies took part, a Gazprom subsidiary and a previously unknown company, Baikal-finansgrup. The latter won, with a bid worth nearly $9.4 billion, barely half the $17 billion at which Yuganskneftegaz had been valued earlier in the year. Baikalfinansgrup had been registered only two weeks previously with a share capital of 10,000 roubles ($358) in a small office building in a provincial city. Despite this, it was able to borrow $1.7 billion from Sberbank, a state-owned financial institution, in order to pay the deposit needed to take part in the auction. Four days later, it was acquired by Rosneft.

In May 2005 Mr Khodorkovsky was sentenced to a nine-year jail term[15] for fraud and other offences, which he is serving at one of the country's most remote prisons near the Chinese border in eastern Russia, an eight-hour drive from the nearest airport.[16] The fire sale of Yukos's assets has continued. Sometimes this involves the collusion of international energy companies who turn up to take part, but not to win, or who win the asset only to sell it on to Gazprom. For smaller assets, the rigging is even more blatant. In July 2007, for example, Rosneft bought Yukos's transport subsidiaries, which chiefly owned leasing contracts on railway oil tankers, plus pumping stations and pipelines. The only other company at the auction, an unknown company called Benefit, pulled out of the auction after Rosneft's first bid. The next month, a similarly unknown firm called Promneftestroi snapped up Yukos's overseas assets for $306 million in an auction in which only one other company, equally obscure, took part. Rosneft said before the auction that it was connected with Promneftestroi; afterwards it said it had been misinformed and had no link with the company. If those participating in these events were worried that the auctions might be seen as shams, they made little effort to dispel such misapprehensions.

Any company that buys Yukos assets without Kremlin permission, by contrast, is asking for trouble. A salutary example of that came from the crushing of Russneft (confusingly named, but no relation to Rosneft), an oil producer controlled by Mikhail Gutseriyev, a pioneer of Russian business in the early 1990s with strong ties to Chechnya. After Russneft acquired, indirectly, some Yukos assets, a court froze all shares in the company; Mr Gutseriyev became the subject of criminal proceedings but he vehemently maintains his innocence. His company, worth up to $9 billion, is set

to be acquired for around $4.5 billion by Mr Deripaska, the
Kremlin's favourite oligarch, who will presumably pass it on to
Rosneft. In a revealing moment, Mr Gutseriyev denounced his
'unprecedented hounding' by the Russian authorities, which included regulatory harassment of the company, a tax probe and
criminal charges. 'They made me an offer to leave the oil business,
to leave "on good terms". I refused. Then, they tightened the
screws,' he complained. But within hours he had recanted, removing from the company's website the page bearing his protest
and insisting that he was selling his company entirely voluntarily.
After his son died in an unexplained car accident, Mr Gutseriyev
fled abroad.

At the time, it seemed as though this assault on property rights
would discredit Mr Putin's style of Russian capitalism in the eyes of
outsiders. But it proved just a blip. In the tussle between greed and
fear, greed won. As the Russian stock market resumed its jet-
propelled ascent, foreign investment, both direct and indirect, continued to pour in. Yukos was an 'exception', world-weary Russia-
watchers explained. This was what happened to a business when its
boss made a direct political challenge to the Kremlin; nobody would
be so foolish as to do that in future. The oligarchs were certainly a
deserving target, and Mr Khodorkovsky's past was packed with
unanswered questions. But the attack on Yukos was outrageously
selective. Its tax-avoidance schemes, based on the use of tax holidays
awarded by regions trying to attract investment, were certainly
ingenious. Any government would have been justified in scrutinising
them carefully, and probably closing them promptly. But other
companies had used similar schemes, without attracting official
displeasure. And the calculations of unpaid taxes were exorbitant.
The amount claimed for 2003 was, according to Yukos, 111 per cent
of the company's entire revenue. Companies that the Kremlin
favours seem to get away with paying far lower taxes: Gazprom,

for example, had revenues of $28 billion in 2003 and paid a tax bill of a mere $4 billion. Secondly, the Russian state had other means of ensuring that citizens regained what they had lost in the looting and chaos of the 1990s. It could have renationalised the oligarchs' empires and paid compensation, or levied a stiff windfall tax when the oil price started rising. Investors would have whined, but they would not have squealed murder. Instead, the Kremlin used the legal system to get what it wanted, sending a double message: these are our enemies, and these are the means we will use to attack them.

So by 2004 Mr Putin had the media and business under his thumb. But other strands of power remained outside the Kremlin's grip. The elected chiefs of Russia's regions and republics[17] could still cite their own electoral mandate in disputes with the 'centre'. Their clout dated from the 1990s, when Yeltsin had once promised Russia's provinces 'as much sovereignty as you can swallow'. That experiment in ultra-federalism had been a disaster: in a strong Western country such as Canada or Germany, powerful regions such as Quebec or Bavaria may reasonably run their own affairs. But Russian officialdom's desire for extra revenues, private and official, multiplied with each layer of government. The single market became balkanised, with each region passing its own laws and regulations. At times of crisis, such as after the 1998 crash, some regions even restricted 'exports' to the rest of Russia. In the Urals, there was even talk of a separate currency, supposedly to be more reliable than the rouble. The bigger and more powerful provinces, such as Tatarstan, started opening 'embassies' abroad.

Mr Putin had witnessed this – and disliked it intensely – while working in the Yeltsin Kremlin. As president, he moved swiftly to re-establish the centre's political authority, thickening the sinews of power: the prosecutors, FSB, tax police and interior ministry troops. After 2002 no regional leader challenged Mr Putin head-on. But they could still ignore him. 'Russia is big, and the Czar is far away' is an old

Russian proverb. Only under totalitarianism, it seemed, could the Kremlin reasonably hope to control life in the provinces tightly. But that changed in September 2004, when Russia suffered one of its worst terrorist attacks. Fighters proclaiming support for Chechen independence took hostage hundreds of children, parents and teachers at a school in Beslan, North Ossetia. An anti-terrorist operation killed 334 of the hostages, including 186 children. In some countries, that would have prompted a bout of anguished official soul-searching. Chechnya clearly had not been 'pacified' as the Kremlin claimed. And why had the authorities proved so incompetent? They were unable, for example, even to cordon the school off properly. Many witnesses say they saw tanks fire shells into the school, contributing to the massacre; the hostage-takers' own explosives did not seem to explain the damage caused. The authorities seemed unprepared to put out the fires that raged through the building after it was stormed. Most puzzling of all, the attack was launched *after* agreement had been reached between the then Chechen rebel leader, Aslan Maskhadov, and the North Ossetian authorities, on negotiations to end the siege. Those questions, posed only by the muffled voices of the liberal opposition, and lone journalists such as Politkovskaya, never gained a hearing. An icily angry Mr Putin gave one of his most revealing speeches. It started with a bout of nostalgia:

We live in a time that follows the collapse of a vast and great state, a state that, unfortunately, proved unable to survive in a rapidly changing world. But despite all the difficulties, we were able to preserve the core of what was once the vast Soviet Union, and we named this new country the Russian Federation.

It continued by equating the terrorists with Russia's external 'enemies', not only in the east, but – for the first time – the West.

Our country, formerly protected by the most powerful defence system along the length of its external frontiers overnight found itself defenceless both from the east and the west . . . We showed ourselves to be weak. And the weak get beaten. Some would like to tear from us a 'juicy piece of pie'. Others help them. They help, reasoning that Russia still remains one of the world's major nuclear powers, and as such still represents a threat to them. And so they reason that this threat should be removed.[18]

Shortly afterwards he announced new centralising measures – planned some time before – under which regional leaders would no longer be elected directly, but appointed by him and then endorsed by local assemblies. Every one of the special deals that Yeltsin had signed with forty of Russia's eighty-nine regions was cancelled.

The Kremlin is particularly nervous about the twenty-odd republics that are the nominal homelands of the country's indigenous non-Slavic peoples. It remembers how 'nationalism' in the Baltic states and elsewhere broke up the Soviet Union. A decade of separatist conflict in Chechnya raises the spectre of the same in other parts of the Russian Federation.[19] Many of the country's minorities have ethnic cousins abroad, most of whom are Russia's historic or even current adversaries. The Tatars and other Turkic minorities for example, look to Turkey, once a superpower that reached deep into Central Asia. Finno-Ugric minorities in places such as Komi, Mari-El, Karelia and Mordovia have linguistic and cultural ties ranging from the strong to vestigial with Estonia (described by many Russians as their country's main enemy), Finland and Hungary. All or any of these can easily be seen as a fifth column. Oil-rich Tatarstan, home of the country's second largest ethnic group after Russians themselves, had reintroduced the Latin alphabet in place of Cyrillic for writing the local language, a close relative of Turkish. That makes linguistic sense (Cyrillic works well for consonant-rich Slavic languages, but mangles almost all others). But it was quickly prohibited by Mr Putin.[20] It was not until 2007 that Tatarstan, after lengthy and expensive lobbying, won back some symbolic autonomy. A handful of other republics may now get the same treatment: limited self-rule in return for unflinching loyalty. In others local activists expect only continuing repression, and mergers with other local-government entities that will further dilute their already battered ethnic and linguistic identity. Pro-Kremlin local leaders in most of these places are therefore cutting back language teaching in the native tongues, discouraging ties with ethnic cousins abroad and cracking down on anyone seeking even the mildest forms of autonomy. As in Soviet times, Russians see their language as the gateway to world culture for those unfortunate enough to grow up speaking gobbledegook from the boondocks. Few remember the genocidal effect of Russian rule as it spread east two centuries ago; nor do they remember the especial severity of Stalinist repressions on the Soviet Union's minorities.

Such historical amnesia is a hallmark of Mr Putin's approach and part of the secret of its appeal. It pleases both the 'new Russians' of the emergent middle class, and the 'old Russians' from the parts of society left behind by the wrenching changes of the past two decades. Though Mr Putin's nostalgia for the Soviet Union strikes many outside Russia as bafflingly offensive, many Russians feel that the Soviet Union was a time of great national achievement, and are baffled that anyone would object to it (even among young Russians, more than 60 per cent agreed with their president that its collapse was a catastrophe). When they see their president being tough with the West, they feel proud.

It was possible to argue that all this was necessary. Only a tough leader could run Russia. After the anarchy of the Yeltsin years, it was time for discipline. The Russian people needed time to get used to a market economy and it was vital that they equated it with rising living standards and stability, not the looting and chaos of the 1990s. On foreign policy, the West could not expect Russia to be perpetually friendly and accommodating. Mr Putin needed to act tough, at least for internal consumption, but this could be set aside as mere posturing: on all vitally important questions, such as in dealing with Islamic extremism or nuclear proliferation, the West and Russia were on the same side. In short, if Mr Putin cut some corners, it was in a good cause. By 2008, the Russian political system would be 'consolidated'. Mr Putin would step down and be replaced by a freely chosen successor, in accordance with the Russian constitution. But those corners have been cut not in a good cause, but a bad one. It is not only that the run-up to the 2008 election gave not the slightest sign of an open, fair or free contest. The next chapter will examine the decline of political freedom in the Putin years in more detail, showing the mechanics of Russia's move from anarchy to authoritarianism – and how that trajectory is continuing.

3

Sinister Pretence: The Kremlin's Use of State Power Against Dissent

Mr Putin's personal popularity is by far the most important feature of Russian politics. It started high and has stayed there ever since. No Russian politician has ever enjoyed so much public support for so long. By the country's dismal demographic standards (the male life expectancy is fifty-nine), the president, who turned fifty-five in October 2007, is in tiptop condition, glad to strip to the waist to reveal his toned torso in carefully posed holiday pictures, or to appear in military uniform, and in manly pursuits such as skiing. Unlike most Russian men, he is abstemious and uxorious. In 2002 an all-female pop group called Singing Together had a hit song with the revealing lyrics: *'I want a man who doesn't drink,*[1] *doesn't smoke and doesn't beat me. I want a man like Putin.'* Though the personality cult is pervasive, it is also subtle and officially discouraged. Mr Putin's daily doings may lead the evening news but the coverage is usually appreciative rather than outright sycophantic.[2] Even now, eight years after he first came to political power, no statues of Mr Putin decorate Russia's squares; no streets or ships are named after him.[3]

Mr Putin claims to be a democrat, comparing himself, seemingly without irony, to Mahatma Gandhi. Mr Putin is certainly like the Indian leader in one respect: he enjoys his popularity, while feigning modesty. But the resemblance ends there. India's political system has put down deep roots since independence, not just in the formal business of counting votes fairly in freely contested elections, but in building the institutions and habits that make a country law-governed and its rulers accountable. Russia's attempt to create something similar, by contrast, has grown into a monstrous sham. The system is not avowedly dictatorial. Opposition parties are allowed to exist, albeit on the fringes of the political system. They cannot demonstrate easily. They have no significant access to the media. In a free, law-governed country, the executive power is checked and balanced from all sides: by elected representatives, by the media, by public organisations and the judiciary. All these – almost everything that could constrain the power of the Kremlin – are broken or co-opted. So too are the most fundamental political rights: free speech and free association of individuals. These are guaranteed by the Russian constitution; they flourished during the 1990s. But under Mr Putin, they have shrivelled.

The most shocking form of repression is the forcible incarceration of critics in psychiatric hospitals. Along with the Gulag system of slave labour camps, the abuse of psychiatry was a hallmark of the Soviet system's degradation and intimidation of its own people.[4] Now it is creeping back. The authorities increasingly see dissent as a sign of impaired mental health: if most people are happy with their lives, and believe overwhelmingly Mr Putin to be an almost godlike leader, surely only a mad person would challenge him – or, indeed, the system he heads? Albert Imendayev, a local politician in Cheboksary, a city on the Volga River, was planning to run in a local election in 2005. But the day before he was due to register his candidacy, he was arrested and sent off to a psychiatric hospital for 'evaluation'. By the time he was released, nine days later, it was too late to register. Sometimes the authorities mix legal intimidation with psychiatric incarceration. Another politician in

Cheboksary, Igor Molyakov, was serving a six-month sentence for libel in 2004. While in jail, he was sent to a psychiatric hospital on the grounds that his repeated complaints about corruption had made him insanely gloomy. On 23 March 2006 police raided the home of human rights activist Marina Trutko, breaking down her door, forcibly injected her with haloperidol, a drug used in the emergency treatment of schizophrenia, and took her to a psychiatric hospital where she spent six weeks undergoing a daily regimen of injections and drugs to treat what doctors diagnosed as a 'paranoid personality disorder'. It was the third time that she had been forcibly treated. The first instance was in 2002 when she was incarcerated after a courtroom quarrel with a judge.

An anonymous Muscovite called 'Yelena' made the mistake of phoning a Duma deputy, Svetlana Savitskaya, at home, asking for her e-mail address.[5] Ms Savitskaya did not like this lesson in the duties of representative government and said that she would complain to the police or have the caller consigned to an asylum. Undeterred, 'Yelena' dropped off a book by George Soros and a CD of Tibetan music with the concierge at Ms Savitskaya's home address. She phoned Ms Savitskaya to see if the package had been delivered. Ms Savitskaya again complained about the phone call. 'Yelena' then tried to deliver some more material, including articles from the press and her own thoughts about the KGB and Stalin. When she rang the doorbell, Ms Savitskaya had the guards eject her from the building. Continuing a pattern of what might well be characterised as eccentric or even tiresome behaviour, 'Yelena' then wrote to Tatyana Dmitriyeva, the director of Russia's main hospital for psychiatric medicine, describing her experience with Ms Savitskaya. She received a brush-off. She sent repeated e-mails and finally managed to telephone her at home. Ms Dmitriyeva complained to the police, who visited 'Yelena' and warned her to desist. No criminal case was brought. So far, so normal, perhaps:

important people everywhere dislike being pestered by the public and they may even complain to the police about it. But after 'Yelena' attempted to approach Ms Dmitriyeva at a public meeting, she found herself taken to the 'acute section' of a psychiatric hospital. She told a doctor she was there against her will, but a judicial hearing ruled against her, and she spent the next ten weeks incarcerated. 'Yelena' may well have broken the law. Indeed, Ms Dmitriyeva says that 'Yelena' tried to attack her. But to be locked up and forcibly medicated looks like the application of a Soviet-era penalty in the twenty-first century.

The most alarming recent case came in mid-2007 in Murmansk, with the forcible incarceration and medication of an opposition activist, Larisa Arap. She was not only involved in the opposition group led by the chess champion Garry Kasparov, the United Civic Front, but had also campaigned against the sexual abuse of minors in psychiatric care. Ms Arap wanted to renew her driving licence, and – as is normal in Russia's bureaucracy-driven system – had to get a medical note confirming that she was in good physical and mental health. But when the doctor at her local clinic noticed her name, he asked if she had been responsible for an article in a local opposition newspaper claiming that psychiatric patients had been raped. When she confirmed this, he called the police, who took her to a psychiatric hospital one hundred miles from her home town. She was given medication against her will, and started a hunger strike. After forty-six days, and following an energetic campaign by allies in Russia and abroad, she was released.

The legal framework that governs the use of psychiatry in law enforcement has been changed to a dangerous degree. Only psychiatrists from a special state-recognised register are allowed to give expert testimony. The rights of those forcibly consigned to psychiatric hospitals have been reduced. FSB interrogations of those with unusual religious beliefs increasingly include the presence of psychiatrists and involve medical-style questioning. The Moscow Helsinki Group, Russia's best-known human rights organisation, says 'everything is in place' for a return to Soviet-style punitive psychiatry. So far, psychiatric abuse is not a carefully calibrated means of repression as it was then. Local officials and medical staff categorically deny any politicisation of their actions and say that the treatment of these cases was in each case justified on medical criteria. However, if such practices are returning even occasionally, it is a dismal echo of a disgraceful past.

Far more systematic is the use of other forms of state power against political critics. Mr Gorbachev freed the last Soviet political prisoners in 1988, starting an era of freedom that lasted barely a decade. Now Russia has at least a dozen. The best-known is Mr Trepashkin, a lawyer and former FSB officer who bravely but unwisely tried to investigate the apartment bombings of September 1999. He had first come to public attention along with Litvinenko, in a group of FSB malcontents that appeared on television in late 1998 to complain about corruption and murder plots within the organisation. He was invited to start his investigation by Sergei Kovalev, a saintly ex-dissident who became the best-known human rights campaigner in Russia's parliament. Mr Trepashkin became convinced that the evidence surrounding the bombings was being doctored to divert attention from the real culprits: the FSB. But on 22 October 2003, a week before he was due to present his findings, he was arrested, and then in 2004 sentenced to a four-year jail term for disclosing official secrets. Amnesty International has made him a prisoner of conscience.[6]

Other political prisoners include two men accused of espionage: Igor Sutyagin and Valentin Danilov. Both men were academics who had passed information to foreigners; in Mr Sutyagin's case to a shadowy and now-vanished outfit working out of rented offices in London that seems highly likely to have been a front for a

foreign intelligence service. But in neither instance was it proved
that any of the material was secret. Mr Sutyagin admitted providing
the information, which consisted of compiling a press review about
military and foreign policy affairs. After a closed trial, he received a
sentence of fifteen years' hard labour. Mr Danilov had provided
information that was declassified in 1992. He received a fourteen-
year sentence. Both cases have been taken up by Amnesty, as well
as other international human rights campaigners. Whether to count
Mr Khodorkovsky as a political prisoner is much debated,[7] but the
persecution of Svetlana Bakhmina, a lawyer formerly working for
him, is a clear scandal. A mother of two children then aged two and
six, she was arrested early in the morning of 7 December 2004 and
is now serving a seven-year term for embezzlement in a high-
security penal colony. The company she supposedly defrauded,
then a subsidiary of Yukos, said it has no complaint about her
actions.

Unlike in Soviet times, the Kremlin does not need to jail all its
enemies. The effect of cases like these is chilling. If you talk to
foreigners, be careful: you risk being charged with espionage. If you
work for a business that is at odds with the Kremlin, switch sides
quick: otherwise you may end up like Mrs Bakhmina. Many cases
of harassment involve arrests after which charges are never brought,
or petty fines for 'hooliganism' and other charges. In mid-April
2007, for example, opposition activists tried to hold 'Dissenters'
marches' in Moscow and St Petersburg. The authorities reacted by
restricting travel to and within both cities, breaking up the protests
violently and detaining hundreds of participants. Journalists, too,
were arrested; thirty were beaten. Two months later, a court in
Moscow fined one of the organisers, Mr Kasparov, for 'marching in
a large group of people and shouting anti-government slogans'.
Two weeks later, the authorities confiscated 52,000 copies of an
opposition newspaper's special edition on the protests.

In March 2007 a small group of human-rights, environmental and conservation campaigners tried to hold a 'march of dissent in Russia's third largest city, Nizhny Novgorod.[8] Among their slogans were 'Give Nizhny Novgorod back to the people!' and 'Give us back freedom of speech'. The authorities initially said the march was illegal. When that failed they said it would be trespassing. Then the organisers received home visits and phone calls from officials and unidentified figures telling them to cancel it. Journalists received similar warning phone calls telling them not to cover the march, and demanding that they share with the authorities any details they knew about it. People handing out leaflets advertising the march were arrested. Some were locked up for several days, and threatened with being put in cells with common criminals who would mutilate them. Students and teachers at local high schools were warned not to join the march.[9] From the authorities' point of view, that worked well. A mere two hundred people turned up, to find an estimated three thousand interior ministry paramilitaries on the site, and many more cordoning off the outer rings of the city. Arrests started immediately, with participants being snatched from the crowd and dragged to the waiting police buses. Those roughed up included foreign journalists. Yet protests from the outside world were muted to the point of inaudibility. Mr Kasparov, a marginal figure who hardly presents a serious challenge to any candidate with Kremlin backing, fell foul of the authorities again when he tried to lead a protest at Russia's summit with the European Union in Samara in May 2007. He and his aides were prevented from travelling there, on the curious excuse that their air tickets might have been forged. Mr Kasparov, a multi-millionaire who has lived for many years in America, immediately offered to buy replacement tickets. But this was not permitted. Instead, their passports were confiscated. They were returned only after the last plane had left.

Such simple bureaucratic harassment is often enough to disrupt protests and deter participants. But the most formidable weapon in the Kremlin's arsenal is charges of 'extremism'. In a parody of the rule of law elsewhere, Russia is steadily expanding the legal basis for state violence. On 8 July 2006, the Duma passed a law criminalising extremism, including giving the president the authority secretly to order the FSB to assassinate 'extremists' at home and abroad. But what is an 'extremist'? It includes 'those causing mass disturbances, committing hooliganism or acts of vandalism'; creating and distributing 'extremist' material are criminal offences. So are 'slandering an official of the Russian Federation', 'hampering the lawful activity of state organisations', and 'humiliating national pride'. That is a useful tool for silencing both individuals and media that report their doings. For a second violation of the law on extremism, media outlets lose their licence. A new version of the law in 2007 cast the net even wider, adding crimes driven by 'political, ideological or social hatred'. Once organisations have been designated 'extremist', the media may not even mention them without referring to the ban. Conveniently, those even suspected of extremism are banned from running for public office.

The scope this gives to officials wanting to intimidate the Kremlin's critics is huge. Despite being owned by Gazprom, the radio station Ekho Moskvy has maintained its feisty journalistic tone. Its editor, Aleksei Venediktov, says that he will fire any staff he sees practising self-censorship. It broadcasts interviews with hated figures such as Toomas Hendrik Ilves, the American-educated president of Estonia, and opposition leaders such as Mr Kasparov. It is a refuge for independent-minded journalists who would scarcely gain airtime elsewhere, such as Ms Albats and Yulia Latynina. But in just two months of 2007, Ekho Moskvy received fifteen letters from prosecutors invoking the extremism law. Why was the station carrying interviews with such provocative figures? Why were Ms Latynina's commentaries so provocative? Even an editor as gutsy as Mr Venediktov, a hippy-like workaholic with a burning faith in press freedom, may not withstand such pressure for long.[10]

Ultimately, bravery in the face of threats may be futile. The authorities can also intervene more directly, by encouraging a media outlet's owner to change the editor. In 2007 Abros, a bank with close ties to the Kremlin, bought a majority stake in REN TV, a minor but independent-minded channel, and promptly installed a new editor who had previously worked at the state-run broad-caster, VGTRK.[11] Print media has maintained more freedom, at least for low-circulation outlets such as Ms Albats's New Times, and the sometimes scandal-mongering bi-weekly that Politkovskaya used to write for, Novaya Gazeta (New Newspaper).[12]

The chilly climate is bad for institutions, and worse for indivi-duals. Andrei Piontkovsky is one of Russia's best-known com-mentators: a vehement critic of Mr Putin and savagely dismissive of Mr Berezovsky, Mr Kasyanov and most of Russia's political and business leaders. He takes regular swipes at Mr Bush, at the leaders of the EU and at many others. But he is no mere gadfly. He is one of a handful of Russia's real specialists on issues of nuclear strategy, familiar with the intricacies of arms treaties and the technological difficulties of missile defence. Eloquent, witty and well informed, he would be instantly recognisable in any Western country as a punchy, heavyweight public figure (and he regularly spends time as a visiting fellow at American think tanks). It is hard to imagine any free country that would not cherish his involvement in public life. Yet in mid-2007 he received two letters from prosecutors inviting him for an 'explanatory chat'. The authorities in the southern Russian region of Krasnodar, again invoking the 'extremism' law, had charged the local branch of Yabloko, the main liberal opposi-tion party, with extremism. The inventor of Kukly, Viktor Shen-

derovich, is probably Russia's best-known satirist. Like many
others from NTV, he took refuge at Ekho Moskvy and started
a successful blog. In 2007 he too received an intimidating visit from
the prosecutors, who warned him that he was 'inciting hatred'.

In theory, print media is still free. You can start a newspaper
without too much bureaucratic trouble and try to sell advertisements
and copies. But without a powerful sponsor it will soon go out of
business. Take the example of the *New Times*,[13] pretty much the only
truly independent weekly left in Russia. Its founding editorial staff
included two of the remaining leading lights of serious Russian
journalism: Ms Albats, the country's best investigative writer, and
Raf Shakirov, fired from the editorship of *Izvestia*, once a top Russian
daily, for his stark coverage of the botched anti-terrorism operation in
Beslan. Its website carries, for example, footage of the Kremlin's bully
boys beating up opposition demonstrators – pictures that Russian
television will scarcely touch. The weekly's publisher, Irena Lesnevskaya (who in her previous incarnation helped found REN TV),
was told by a top Kremlin official that hiring Ms Albats was a 'mistake'.
Almost any other magazine in Russia would have hurried to correct
the 'mistake'. Ms Lesnevskaya politely refused. The result is that
nobody wants to advertise there. Doing so would be commercial
suicide in a business climate where official disfavour means harassment
by every state agency, followed usually by bankruptcy.[14]

The best-informed journalists are at the greatest risk if they step
out of line. Elena Trebugova, a journalist who covered the Kremlin
intimately, published two gossipy books that included embarrassing
portrayals of Mr Putin and his closest aides. She narrowly escaped
assassination and moved to London in 2007. Similarly, high-profile
individuals such as Mr Shenderovich and Mr Piontkovsky can also
expect an appreciative welcome in London, Washington, DC, or
Brussels if they need it. But for more minor figures, tangling with
the authorities means professional suicide – or worse.

Among what purport to be the world's advanced industrialised countries, Russia is one of the most dangerous places for journalists. Since 1992, a total of forty-seven have been killed. Under Mr Putin the trend has slackened: according to the New York-based Committee to Protect Journalists[15] fourteen journalists have been murdered and eight suspicious cases are under investigation. The deaths in the Yeltsin years were more numerous, but less systematic. Shortly before his death in July 2003 Shchekochikhin wrote: 'Do not tell me fairy tales about the independence of judges . . . until we have fair trials, documents will be purged, witnesses intimidated or killed, and those who try to investigate will themselves be prosecuted.'[16] Two of the paper's staff have received death threats since they started to investigate Politkovskaya's murder. Another journalist, Ivan Safronov, was probably Russia's best-known reporter of military affairs: tenacious, scrupulous and well informed. A former colonel in the Strategic Rocket Forces, he had exposed the repeated failure of Russia's most important new missile, the Bulava, and was investigating corruption in the state-run arms export business. On 2 March 2007 he fell to his death from a window in his apartment block. The authorities speedily pronounced it a clear case of suicide. His friends and colleagues could see no reason why a man in the prime of life, happy both at home and at work, should kill himself. A more likely cause of death, they said, was a big scandal that he was investigating about arms sales to Iran and Syria.

Other victims include Vyacheslav Ifanov, a cameraman at an independent local television station in Siberia. His mutilated body was found in his garage on 5 April 2007; the authorities pronounced it suicide. Paul Klebnikov, an American reporter who ran the Russian-language edition of *Forbes* magazine, was shot dead in 2004. Yevgeny Gerasimenko, an investigative business reporter, was killed in Saratov in southern Russia in 2006. His head was tied in a plastic bag and his body was bruised. An unnamed homeless man was charged with the murder and the case has been closed. Ilya Zimin, a television journalist working for NTV, was murdered on 26 February 2006 after what appears to have been a violent struggle.[17] Fatima Tlisova was a reporter for the Associated Press and other news organisations in the Caucasus. Her reporting has prompted repeated beatings and attempted poisonings, as well as harassment from the authorities. She says that men identifying themselves as FSB crushed lighted cigarettes on every finger of her right hand, telling her it was 'so that you can write better'. In 2006 her sixteen-year-old son was arrested as a sympathiser with the Chechen rebels. With her colleague Yuri Bagrov she has success-fully gained refugee status in the United States.

The message of all this is 'be quiet'. If you annoy the rich and powerful you face threats, beatings or death. Even when the Kremlin is not directly involved, its reaction to the persecution of journalists sends a clear message: if you offend the powerful, don't expect the law to protect you. In almost all cases, the investigation has been as fruitless and lackadaisical as it was in the Politkovskaya shooting.[18] As the independent voices fade, the official view becomes ever more dominant. At national television, which 90 per cent of Russians say is their main source of news, editors receive weekly or even daily instructions from the Kremlin on the 'line to take' on important stories.[19] By far the majority of airtime is devoted to entertainment, sport and anodyne feature programmes. Criticism of the authorities is allowed – but only within limits. Mr Putin likes to blame shortcomings on incompe-tent politicians and officials, while remaining beyond reproach himself.

The most telling consequence of all this is not that Mr Putin is so prominent, but that his rivals are out of sight. The presidential party United Russia (known as the party of power) is the only one that matters. It is a stripped-down version of the Communist Party of the Soviet Union (CPSU), modified for the new conditions of sham political pluralism. Its camouflage suggests that power is flowing from the bottom up, yet the real aim is to transmit power downwards. Most senior officials belong to it. It wins almost every election it contests, but unlike the CPSU, whose 'leading role' was entrenched in the constitution, its power is guaranteed by informal and bureaucratic means.

Without a free media and real scrutiny of Russia's leaders and their policies, it would be rash to take public assent for granted. In any case, turning public opinion into political results requires a system that allows the opposition to challenge the powers that be. Russian politics is rigged to make sure that doesn't happen. The electoral system systematically discriminates against outsiders. A change in the summer of 2001 made it impossible for unaffiliated individuals and informal groupings to take part in elections, and sharply toughened the criteria for party registration. Instead of ten thousand members, they now needed fifty thousand, with branches at least five-hundred-strong in at least forty-five of Russia's eighty-five regions. The new law also abolished single-mandate districts in Duma elections and raised the threshold for election from 5 to 7 per cent. That made life almost impossible for small parties, especially those without rich backers. If the authorities would prefer a candidate not to run for election, the signatures are 'checked' and enough can be ruled invalid to create a 'breach' of the 'rules'.[20] The worst recent example of this came in the March 2007 regional elections when Yabloko candidates were chucked off the ballot papers in St Petersburg, Russia's most European city. That was where the party stood the best chance of winning some seats, something that the authorities were evidently not willing to tolerate.

Yet Yabloko and the others are not outlawed. If their activists are

arrested, it is for minor public-order offences, not for treason. They
face at most a night in the police cells, not a decade in a labour
camp. Their biggest weakness is not that the authorities crush them,
but that they are so unpopular to start with. From a technical point
of view, the elections are well administered. But they are neither
free nor fair. The main international monitors said that the 2004
presidential election:

> did not adequately reflect principles necessary for a healthy demo-
> cratic election process: essential . . . standards for democratic elec-
> tions, such as a vibrant political discourse and meaningful pluralism,
> were lacking. The election process failed to meet important
> commitments concerning treatment by the State-controlled media
> on a non-discriminatory basis.[21]

That bland bureaucratic language hardly does justice to the extraordinary charade of Russia's electoral system. Mr Putin won an
overwhelming victory, with 71.2 per cent of the vote, after he
grandly declined to fight a conventional election campaign. He
didn't need to: the entire weight of the state apparatus was
deployed to discourage his opponents, promote his image and
secure the maximum result consistent with the appearance of
respectability. The two real challengers, the independent liberal
Irina Khakamada and the leftist-nationalist Sergei Glazyev, found
that local bureaucrats repeatedly interfered with their election
meetings. Typical tactics were surprise bomb scares, power cuts
or other bogus safety issues. Two supposed contenders actually
supported Mr Putin. One of them, the speaker of the upper house
of parliament, the Federation Council, explained his candidacy
thus: 'when a leader who is trusted goes into battle, he must not be
left alone. One must stand beside him.' Yabloko boycotted the poll
altogether, saying it was a farce.

Perhaps the most dangerous candidate from Mr Putin's point of view was Ivan Rybkin, a former speaker of the Duma backed by the exiled Mr Berezovsky. Mr Rybkin kicked off his campaign with a full-page advertisement in a business daily, denouncing Mr Putin as 'the biggest oligarch in Russia'. He claimed that the Kremlin was a criminal conspiracy, in which Roman Abramovich, one of Russia's most shadowy tycoons, was managing Mr Putin's ever-expanding business interests. It is worth repeating that it would be unwise to take Mr Berezovsky or his friends as champions of political freedom and clean government, and the system they are denouncing is one that, arguably, they helped create. But the questions are still interesting. What are the business interests of Mr Putin and his family? It would be astonishing if he had spent the 1990s in high office without amassing a considerable fortune.[22] No definitive proof has been presented of any wrongdoing and it may well be that Mr Putin's austere public image is matched by private rectitude. But what is clear is that none of the scrutiny that a Western country at least tries to give to its rulers' finances applies to Mr Putin. The mass media studiously ignored Mr Rybkin's allegations. Two papers owned by Mr Berezovsky reported them, as did *Novaya Gazeta*. The Kremlin did not bother with a denial, let alone a rebuttal. Similarly, serious allegations by Ms Khakamada about the authorities' cover-up of their botched handling of a terrorist hostage-taking at a theatre in the Dubrovka district of Moscow in 2002 were ignored. Like so many other incidents that have stoked public panic, and thus Mr Putin's power and popularity, the Nordost incident, in which the authorities used an anaesthetic gas to kill hostage-takers and hostages alike, is surrounded by questions that the authorities show no inclination to answer.

What happened next to Mr Rybkin seemed more like a badly plotted political thriller than an episode in an election campaign. The planned centrepiece of his campaign was the war in Chechnya.

After one abortive session of negotiations with the rebel leadership at a Moscow airport in 2001, the Kremlin has maintained the line that the separatist forces can be beaten by force alone. Mr Rybkin wanted to highlight the war's cost to Russia, tapping into the growing resentment of conscription and of the poor treatment of veterans. He slipped out of Russia to meet the underground Chechen leadership. The initial rendezvous was to be in the Ukrainian capital, Kyiv, but on the way there Mr Rybkin vanished. He appeared again five days later, in a confused state, claiming first to have taken a brief vacation, and saying that he had been in difficult talks. But in London he told Mr Berezovsky's aides that he had been drugged, and had woken up four days later to be shown a video of himself 'made by perverts'. Shortly after, he withdrew from the race. His friends say he was given the psychotropic drug SP-117, part of the KGB's blackmailing toolkit in the Cold War. Pro-Kremlin journalists were quick to denounce the incident as an attention-seeking stunt by a discredited loser. But Mr Rybkin did not seem to be using it to promote his chances. In fact he seemed rather reluctant to come back to Russia at all. Had Mr Berezovsky wanted to stoke his candidate's campaign by manufacturing a bogus threat, he could have found far more effective means of doing so.[23]

Rather than taking the risk of allowing genuine opposition, the Kremlin prefers something manageable. In the regional elections in March 2007, it sponsored a new opposition party, Just Russia. On the surface, this seemed to be engaged in a fierce contest with the Kremlin's own United Russia party. Undoubtedly the personalities in both parties were keen to win: the spoils of victory are considerable. Real differences in outlook existed. Just Russia is anti-business, avowedly socialist and also nationalistic in outlook. But the real story was different. Just Russia is not a serious contender for power, but a way of turning a potentially brittle monopoly into a more stable duopoly. Its real value is threefold.

First, it crowds out real opposition, chipping away at support for Russia's Communist Party, the main left-wing opposition grouping. Secondly, the Kremlin dislikes any strong political institution, even those that it has itself created, and competition from Just Russia stops United Russia getting overconfident. By allowing Just Russia to poll respectably – and win a handful of contests against United Russia – the Kremlin sends a message to the party barons: you may be rich, but you can still lose. It also sends a message to any regional politician with an eye to the future: sign up for one of the two main parties or book your ticket to political oblivion. The broad message is overwhelmingly clear, however. United Russia in mid-2007 was polling almost as many votes as its rivals combined.

The odd thing about this heavy-handed approach is that the Kremlin is not really facing any serious opposition. Liberal-minded opposition leaders may gain an appreciative hearing in Brussels and Washington, DC, but their parties are mostly seen inside Russia as a shambolic collection of squabbling no-hopers, chancers and freaks. Even in the Yeltsin years when it had a fair chance of winning, Yabloko got nowhere. The Communists, the only party with a claim to a real mass membership, have become a pathetic relic of a once fearsome predecessor. The party's incompetent and venal leaders consistently betray their elderly and embittered supporters.

The paradox is that so many Russians seemingly want to live in a system that curtails their freedom. As we have seen, Mr Putin's approval rating is stratospheric; the difficulties that opposition parties experience meet with clear public approval. According to opinion polls quoted in a government newspaper in 2007, fewer than 50 per cent of respondents agreed that Russia needed a political opposition at all; fewer than than 30 per cent believed the opposition had a right to push for alternative policies or take political power. Fully a third thought that the mere expression of opposition views constituted 'extremism'.[24] That may exaggerate the trend (it is certainly what the Kremlin hopes people are thinking) but it is not wholly invented. For many Russians, dissenting views and minorities of all kinds are not a vital ingredient of political pluralism, but a subversive and unpatriotic menace that is at best tolerated grudgingly, and if necessary squashed.

Such sentiments can be hard for outsiders to understand, but they make sense against the background of Russian history. When the rest of Europe was experiencing the Renaissance, the Reformation and the Enlightenment, Russia was still mired in feudalism and ruled by eccentric tyrants. Brief spasms of reform and rebellion hardly dented the autocratic rule of the Tsars. Only for a few months in 1917 under Kerensky did Russia have anything approaching parliamentary government, before it was snuffed out by the Bolshevik putsch that later became known as the 'October Revolution'. Though the political pluralism of the Yeltsin era lasted for years, not months, it also failed to put down real roots. Many Russians feel that multi-party politics failed them in the 1990s, and that their state institutions are too weak and corrupt to be trusted. Perhaps more deeply, they do not trust other Russians to vote sensibly. Handing power to a single strong leader may not be the best way of running Russia, but it may also perhaps not be the worst: at least it is easier to focus trust, attention and criticism on one man than on a bunch of greedy and self-serving politicians and bureaucrats. That argument is flawed, but while Russia's economy flourishes it will be hard to refute.

Just as political parties have atrophied, so have the institutions of state that should keep the executive branch under control. The Kremlin's human rights institutions, for example, rarely cause trouble on specific cases, though they do promote human rights in the abstract. Vladimir Lukin, a retired liberal parliamentarian and ex-ambassador, has commendably denounced Russia's endemic ethnic and religious intolerance. When news broke in 2007 of what appeared to be the use of punitive psychiatry against Ms Arap in Murmansk, he dispatched a team of independent psychiatrists to investigate the case. His office publishes reports on the rights of disabled children and similar issues. He even lambasts the authorities directly about, for example, the bureaucratic obstacles they put in the way of public protests. But his reports get little airtime: the authorities respond politely or not at all. Nothing changes. Another outfit, the pompously named Presidential Council on Promoting the Development of Institutions of Civil Society and Human Rights, is headed by a respected human rights activist, Ella Pamfilova. A third initiative is the Public Chamber, a consultative body consisting of a mixture of presidential nominees and NGO (non-governmental organisation) representatives. Such organisations are best seen as safety valves. A body like the Public Chamber can intervene, hold hearings and wag its finger when public opinion gets really heated, for example over the outrageous behaviour of official motorcades – convoys of black jeeps and limousines that drive at high speed with flagrant disregard for other road users, sometimes killing those unlucky enough to be in their way. What it does not do is make laws or hold government ministers to account.

That job, in any free, law-governed state worthy of the name, should be done by the legislature. For those who remember the *perestroika* era, the Duma is a sad disappointment. In the years 1989–91 its Soviet-era predecessor, the Congress of People's Deputies, was a raucous, gripping spectacle of pluralist politics in action. To see it at work was to see totalitarianism crumble before your eyes. Millions of Soviet citizens would stop work to watch its debates. By contrast the sight of the Duma (or the upper house) at work is not merely catatonically boring; it is downright dispiriting. The proceedings are largely a charade. Duma deputies' main interest is in their lavishly subsidised perks and in the enormous opportunities for bribes. These exist because Russian officialdom extorts pre-datory rents from every bit of human activity from birth to death, via imports, exports, taxes and endless government inspections.[25] The prosecutor-general recently estimated the total annual bribes paid at $240 billion a year – around the same size as the national budget. Having a parliamentarian on your side can be a cost-effective short cut round these bureaucratic thickets, but it is one for which he will expect an appropriate reward.

A handful of independent-minded deputies, such as the beanpole-like Vladimir Ryzhkov, will survive until the elections due in December 2007. But aside from such eccentrics, no parliamentarian takes a stand on any matter of principle. They cannot afford to. In future, almost every member of Russia's legislature will owe his (rarely her) seat to the Kremlin's whim. And accordingly they must dance to the Kremlin's tune. Their task is to look enough like a parliament to maintain the pretence that Russia is run by a legislature with real power. They act as a sounding board, for example demanding economic sanctions on 'fascist' Estonia, or any other country that has displeased the Kremlin. They can be a safety valve. In 2005, for example, amid a scandal about children adopted by foreigners who had been murdered or abused by their new parents, deputies called for a moratorium on foreign adoptions. They legislate – but only according to the script. Every law that the Kremlin backs gets through parliament. Nothing it dislikes stands a chance.

The Russian people seem unimpressed with the organs of power. Polls taken in 2007 give the Duma an approval rating of 27 per cent (with disapproval at 52 per cent). Only 5 per cent thought Duma members were working to improve the lives of the population; only 3 per cent could name any positive qualities and 44 per cent said that greed was the main motivation for seeking election. Prospects for improvement are slight. Forty-five per cent said they did not think that the parliamentary elections due in December 2007 would reflect the will of the people; only 8 per cent thought the votes would be counted with complete honesty; fully a third said they would not regard the newly elected Duma as legitimate.

Definitions of democracy vary so widely as to be almost meaningless,[26] but the foundation of freedom is justice. For all the abuses and sleaze that disfigure the advanced industrialised countries of the West, honest judges and due process are the ultimate backstop, upholding the law and transcending politics. Not in Russia. Despite some spasmodic reforms, the justice system[27] is under the control of the Kremlin. Russian courts may offer a fair trial – but only in cases where nobody powerful has an interest. Otherwise they just rubber-stamp the authorities' verdict. The problem is not just dishonest judges and pushy bureaucrats; it starts at the top. So long as the Kremlin itself is above the law, justice for anyone else is just a pretence. The International Bar Association, the OECD, the International Commission of Jurists, the American State Department and the anti-corruption group Transparency International, have all expressed concern about the fate of the legal system under Mr Putin. Independent-minded judges have been dismissed, corruption is rampant. Even one of Russia's top judges, Valery Zorkin of the Constitutional Court, says that 'bribe-taking in the courts is one of the biggest corruption markets in Russia'. A 2007 poll showed that 40 per cent of Russians did not believe that Russia was a law-governed state (30 per cent thought it was); 38 per cent distrusted the judiciary, and only 26 per cent said they trusted it. Boris Jordan, scion of an émigré Russian family from America who has become one of Moscow's most high-profile, and normally enthusiastic, investment bankers, put it bluntly at a conference in September 2007: 'Probably the single biggest thing that business in Russia today suffers from is that you can't really expect to get a proper court hearing.'[28]

The most flawed part of the justice system is not the courts

themselves, which few Russians use and fewer trust, but the
prosecutors' service. This unreformed Stalinist relic is the engine
of state illegality.[29] Prosecutors can freeze your bank account,
putting you out of business; they can have you imprisoned in a
disease-infested hellhole; they can concoct evidence that will keep
you there for decades; they can intimidate any witnesses, defence
counsel and even judges who try to stop them. With a few heroic
exceptions, the prosecutor's office is the best friend of the authoritarian bureaucrat and the well-connected gangster. The most
shameful tactic of all is intimidation of defence lawyers such as
Boris Kuznetsov, whose client list is a *Who's Who* of the Kremlin's
victims and adversaries. He has represented the Politkovskaya
family, relatives of the crew of the *Kursk*, Mr Sutyagin (the
researcher jailed on espionage charges) and many others. In
mid-2007 he fled Russia for his own safety, after being accused
of leaking state secrets. His 'crime' was that he complained to the
Constitutional Court about the FSB's illegal bugging of a client's
phone conversations. Other lawyers who take on similarly high-
profile cases say they face similar harassment, in a way that recalls
the treatment of dissidents' defence lawyers in the Soviet period.
The prosecutor's office has asked the Moscow bar association to
discipline Karina Moskalenko, a defence lawyer for Mr Khodorkovsky who has won twenty-seven cases at the European Court of
Human Rights.[30]

Intimidating those lawyers willing and able to take a case to an
international court is an ominous development. For Russians, the
best chance of justice now is not in their country's own courts, but
abroad; they make up by some way the largest number of
complainants in Strasbourg. The European Court of Human
Rights there received a remarkable 8,781 complaints by Russians
in 2005. In only two cases of the 110 that were accepted for trial
that year was no violation found. In 2006, the number of com-

plaints by Russians rose to 10,569, of which 151 were declared admissible; in only five was no violation found.[31] A recent non-political case involved four people from Cherepovets, a town on the Volga in central Russia, the lives of whose inhabitants had been made miserable by pollution from a steel plant. The court ruled that their 'right to respect for private and family life' had been violated by the contamination. The state should pay them compensation and make either the steel plant abide by environmental regulations or move it elsewhere. The Russian government paid the damages, but did nothing else. More typical are cases from Chechnya. In these, the Russian state has had to pay millions of euros in damages, and suffered repeated public humiliation for the theft, torture, false imprisonment, rape and murder carried out in its name. Unsurprisingly, perhaps, Russia has consistently blocked proposals – backed by almost every other country – to streamline the court's procedures and make it easier for citizens to use its services.[32]

So forget individual and collective protests, the media, elections, politicians and the courts. What is left is 'civil society', jargon for public-spirited people and organisations[33] that make up the political subsoil in free countries. Far more than political parties, it is their protests and endorsements that focus decision-makers' attention on matters of public concern. They include everything from anglers' groups (strong lobbyists for clean rivers) to cyclists (road safety), parents (education, conscription), pensioners or disabled people. Such activity mostly operates somewhere under the official radar: normal people only bother to engage with officialdom when they are seriously annoyed about something. It is very rarely the other way round: in a free society only when, say, a mosque is infiltrated by terrorists, or when an animal rights group turns to violence, does anybody in authority start interfering with voluntary organisations. One of the most encouraging developments of the 1990s in Russia was the growth of this kind of public-spiritedness.

It was patchy, certainly, and sometimes opportunistic and greedy – the term 'grantsuckers' was coined for those activists whose main expertise was in cadging money for fashionable causes, rather than doing any good. But it was still a vast improvement on the Soviet past, when all independent public activity was banned.[34] And it was a welcome reaction from the intense individualism and materialism fostered by the collapse of communist control. To visit tiny but inspirational charities and campaigns run from kitchen tables by devoted individuals was one of the clearest signs that Russia was slowly edging towards the European mainstream.

But now civil society in Russia is shrivelling. It is not just that any political challenge to authority is instantly deemed suspicious. Even indirect criticism is either slapped down or left exposed to extremist violence. When skinheads chanting 'death to homosexuals' attacked gay rights campaigners in Moscow in May 2007, for example, the police stood ostentatiously aside. The main weapon is to increase the burden of bureaucracy: the dull-sounding law 'On Amendment of Selected Legislative Acts of the Russian Federation' that Mr Putin signed on 10 January 2006 sets down tough registration and monitoring rules for non-governmental organisations. Even long-established outfits with headquarters overseas had to re-register with the Justice Ministry by mid-October; the documentation required included the home addresses and telephone numbers of their founders. As with many Russian laws, the drafting is so vague that it is impossible to be sure what compliance means. Organisations can be asked to provide all correspondence with outside individuals and other bodies dating back several years, and to produce detailed budgets for their forthcoming activities, with explanations for any change from the annual 'work plan'. Among those that had temporarily to stop operations were Human Rights Watch and Amnesty International.

That gives the authorities, in effect, the power to shut down any group they like, without giving a reason. In January 2006, for example, the Ministry of Justice decided to close the 'Russian Research Centre on Human Rights', an umbrella organisation that includes some of the country's most distinguished campaigning outfits, including the Moscow Helsinki Group. Nobody in officialdom seemed to see the irony: a supposedly free country was now persecuting people who had withstood the onslaught of Soviet totalitarianism. Whereas the heroes of the Cold War dissident movement had to deal with the Soviet-era penal code, the new Kremlin tactic is to find minor infringements of the law: in the case of the human rights outfit, they had, supposedly, not filed proper reports of their activities over the past five years. The Russian branch of PEN, the most venerable international campaign for writers' freedom, had its bank account frozen, ostensibly because it had failed to pay taxes. (Russia is almost unique in the severity with which it regards NGOs' tax affairs, treating their income from foreign donors as if it was, in effect, commercial revenue.) The same tactic was used against the Centre for International Legal Defence. This helps Russians sue their country in Strasbourg. Even worse: it is headed by Ms Moskalenko, Mr Khodorkovsky's lawyer.

Any organisation that tries to represent Russia's ethnic minorities can expect especially harsh treatment. Those from Muslim regions, such as Tatarstan, are immediately painted as extremists and terrorists. Anyone showing the faintest sympathy for Chechnya is risking their freedom, if not their life. Boris Stomakhin, a campaigner for Chechen independence, received a five-year sentence in 2006 for inciting hatred against the army. The Russian-Chechen Friendship Society was closed after its head, Stanislav Dmitriyevsky, was convicted of inciting racial hatred. That immediately allowed the authorities to use a legal provision that makes it illegal for an NGO to be led by anyone with a criminal conviction. The society is now registered in Finland. Lower-profile causes with an ethnic dimension attract hardly less vindictive treatment. The 600,000-strong Mari ethnic minority, for example, are a remnant of the Finno-Ugric tribes whose lands once stretched from Siberia to the Baltic. Unlike the Estonians and Finns, they have never had a state of their own. Around half live in the republic of Mari-El in northern Russia. After a brief national revival in the 1990s, they have now become the target of a vicious campaign of chauvinistic repression, spearheaded by the president of the republic, Leonid Markelov. The main aim of the Mari movement is to ensure the survival of the language, in theory officially protected but now surviving chiefly among old people and in the countryside (around 20 per cent of those calling themselves Mari admit to having no knowledge of the language whatsoever). The authorities seem to be determined to accelerate its decline. The local education authority's department for the Mari language has been closed. Television programmes in the Mari language have been cut back; few books are published. Education in Mari is patchy and mostly stops at primary level. The Mari movement's leadership is denounced as 'nationalist' and 'separatist'. Using such language is intended to associate them with the hated Chechen terrorists, and with the rebellious national republics such as Lithuania and Georgia who broke up the Soviet Union in what many Russians see as an act of inexplicable ingratitude.

For some, that disapproval means physical violence. Vladimir Kozlov, the editor of the main Mari newspaper, was savagely beaten by unknown assailants in February 2005. Later that year skinheads from a group linked to the republic's pro-Kremlin leadership attacked and beat a group of Mari musicians. A film about Mari song festivals was banned. A particular source of suspicion is Mari links with Estonia. A handful of Mari students, along with those from other places with similar ethnic ties, have received scholarships to study there. Estonia is the headquarters of the world Finno-Ugric movement – in the eyes of Kremlin propagandists a vast revanchist conspiracy set on the break-up of Russia, but in fact run by a handful of volunteers from a shabby two-room office.

Any group that has taken money from any foreign source faces grave charges of espionage or treason. Yet one of the few good things that the outside world did in Russia in the 1990s was to spray money at anyone trying to form even a half credible public organisation. It is true that this was often wasteful. It was sometimes even cynical: Western governments used such outfits as a way of collecting information about Russia, and even of influencing events there. But the Kremlin overstates the extent of this, and also regards it with paranoid suspicion. At a time when Russia could not guarantee the safe handling of nuclear waste, for example, it made sense for neighbouring countries such as Norway to help environmental groups to highlight the issue. That was not only good for Norway, but for Russia, too. But according to the Kremlin's zero-sum logic, anything that was good for foreign countries must have been bad for Russia. The immediate victims of that are state-financed foreign outfits that do not enjoy diplomatic immunity. The authorities' approach is highly selective. Germany's Goethe Institute, for example, is able to operate without difficulty, as are the Instituto Cervantes and the Institut Français. But the British Council, an organisation better known for blandness than subversion, has had a remarkably difficult time. Its Moscow offices have been raided by the tax police – on the pretext that the language lessons provided there are a tax-dodging commercial operation. In December 2006 its office in St Petersburg was closed because it had broken unspecified 'safety regulations'. In July 2007 the Council was forced to abandon its offices in Yekaterinburg on the grounds that it was not a proper department of the British Embassy. That sort of harassment of foreign cultural organisations was a hallmark of the old Cold War. Its return is a striking feature of the new one. And given that most important NGOs in Russia accepted foreign money sometime during the 1990s, almost all are under suspicion. Even the most apolitical and harmless organisations are now feeling the cold breath of official displeasure.

In 2007, the Educated Media Foundation, which has trained 15,000 Russian journalists since 1996, was forced into liquidation. In January its president, Manana Aslamazyan, accidentally broke the law by importing slightly more than the permitted amount of cash into Russia, an offence that normally goes unpunished. At most it attracts a minor fine; it is exporting undeclared cash that the authorities care about. But since then Ms Aslamazyan's foundation has been harassed by repeated police raids, and threats of prosecution for money-laundering; she fled to Paris. The foundation's plight prompted two thousand Russian journalists, including dozens working in state-controlled media, to petition Mr Putin in protest. He did not reply.[35] The foundation's real crime was not Ms Aslamazyan's mistake over the cash, or even the technical accounting errors that the investigators claimed to have discovered. It was that over the years the American government had supported it with around $8 million. That, in the Kremlin's eyes, is tantamount to treason. Mr Putin has repeatedly described foreign-financed NGOs as being nothing more than fronts for foreign espionage and mischief-making.

Such cases are not isolated examples of bureaucratic intransigence. They form a pattern. Having hollowed out real politics, the Kremlin fills the shell. An ironic shorthand term for the new phenomenon is GONGOs – 'Government-organised non-governmental organisations'. Some of these are veterans' movements and religious groups that work closely with the authorities. But the most worrying development is the growth of phoney popular movements that substitute for real public involvement. Their main role is to head off any repeat in Russia of the event that marked the nadir of Kremlin influence in the former empire in the past decade: the Ukrainian 'Orange Revolution'. This started in November 2004, with mass protests against a presidential election marked by corruption, intimidation and unabashed fraud. Tens of thousands of photogenic youngsters in orange scarves set up a tent city in the centre of the Ukrainian capital, Kyiv,[36] demanding a political change. After heavy diplomatic intervention from NATO countries to broker a deal, the stand-off ended in a rout for the pro-Kremlin candidate and the triumph of his rival, Viktor Yushchenko. The celebrations were partly premature,[37] but the protests were deeply worrying for the Kremlin. The tent city seemed spontaneous and certainly represented a large slice of Ukrainian opinion, particularly in the centre and west of the country. Few asked at the time who was paying for the tents, flags, food and sound systems. The truth was that the 'Orange Revolution' was at least in part the result of detailed planning and energetic coaching by outside activists, seasoned by experiences in similar campaigns in Slovakia and Serbia. Initially dismissed by the Kremlin as empty nonsense, the combination of youth, idealism and Western political techniques is a potentially lethal political weapon against corrupt and authoritarian regimes.

The danger of such a popular uprising in Russia may have receded now, but Kremlin officials remain convinced that American and European think tanks, with generous support from their governments, are planning something similar, or will do so sooner or later. The prime aim of the Kremlin's mass movements is to swamp any such attempt. Whereas the 'coloured revolutions' are fuelled with idealism for Western ideals, the Kremlin believes that Russian national values such as patriotism, deference and a touch of

xenophobia will prove an even more potent counter. The biggest
of these outfits is *Nashi* (Ours), run by the Kremlin and sponsored
by its associated businesses, including Gazprom. It can put thousands of uniformed young people on the streets at short notice. It
has at least 120,000 members, ranging from the idealistic to the
bored, from hooligans to opportunists. *Nashi* and its sibling organisations are partly a safety valve, giving at least the semblance of
the excitement of a real political campaign: travel, new friends and
solidarity behind a common goal. But however much it tries to
seem wholesome and patriotic, *Nashi* has other echoes. It recalls the
perks-for-loyalty approach of the Komsomol, the Soviet Union's
Communist Youth League. The unthinking nationalism and glor-
ification of Mr Putin lead some to call it the *Putinjugend* (Putin
Youth), recalling the *Hitlerjugend* (Hitler Youth) of Nazi Germany.
The ten thousand participants at the movement's 2007 summer
camp at Lake Seliger, 350 kilometres (220 miles) north of Moscow,
wore electronic tags so that the organisers could check that they
were attending the prescribed lectures and seminars. Shirkers were
expelled. Some features of camp life were bizarre: participants were
told that the mammoths had become extinct because of their low
sex drive and warned that the same could happen to Russia. Young
women were encouraged to hand in skimpy underwear, which
supposedly causes sterility, and accept more wholesome under-
garments in exchange. Others were downright nasty. Exhibits
included defamatory material about Estonian politicians (depicted
as fascists) and opposition figures (as prostitutes). The mass movements demanding freedom and justice in Ukraine and Georgia
were described as American-led stunts, with no reference to the
idealistic motives behind them or of the authoritarian, corrupt and
bureaucratic regimes they targeted. *Nashi*'s manifesto includes
lumps of regurgitated Soviet-era propaganda, praising Russians'
communist-era courage, discipline and strength. *Nashi*'s self-

described 'security service' conducts joint training exercises with the police in preparation for elections. A counter-demonstration by *Nashi* and other similar organisations can swamp anything that Russia's fragmented opposition can manage. Like the sheep in George Orwell's *Animal Farm* chanting 'Four legs good, two legs bad', it can intimidate through noise and numbers.

The two men who were at the time the front runners for the 2008 presidential election, Sergei Ivanov and Dmitri Medvedev, turned up at the camp to field questions and endorse the movement's goals and activities; later, a selection of *Nashi* members, plus others from similar outfits, had an audience with Mr Putin himself. *Nashi*'s leaders insist that its only connection to officialdom is loyalty to the president, that its money comes from donors and that its leaders are independent patriots. Yet it seems remarkably well connected. In June 2006 the British ambassador, Sir Anthony Brenton, infuriated the Kremlin by attending an opposition meeting. For months afterwards he was harassed by groups of *Nashi* supporters who interrupted his speeches, blocked his entry and exit from buildings and kept up a chorus of catcalls and abuse wherever he went.[38] Yet how did they know his movements in advance? The Russian authorities have means of finding out that sort of information, but it stretches credulity that a mere unofficial youth movement would be so well informed.

In comparison with other Kremlin-sponsored groups, though, *Nashi* looks civilised, rarely getting involved in outright xenophobia and racism. In the summer of 2007 an outfit called *Mestnye* (Locals) started distributing flyers urging Muscovites to boycott non-Russian cab drivers. These showed a young, blonde, ethnic Russian refusing a ride from a swarthy, beetle-browed driver, under the slogan 'We're not going the same way'.[39] In September 2007, *Mestnye* members organised a sting operation to catch illegal immigrants, offering lucrative work to foreign-looking people in a market on the Yaroslavskoye Shossee in north-east Moscow, a favoured location for migrant workers seeking casual work. Those who accepted the offer were driven not to the promised construction site, but to a migration service office for a document check, leading to seventy-two people being detained for immigration offences. Such unofficial xenophobia matches the official stance. On 1 April, for example, a decree explicitly backed by Mr Putin banned foreigners from trading in Russia's retail markets. Unofficial and illegal migration is certainly a big problem in Russia: by some estimates, up to 12m people are working illegally in Russia, compared to 1m legal migrants. Other countries, including America, face similar problems. But it would be inconceivable that a youth movement backed by the White House would urge Americans to boycott non-white cab drivers, or that the American authorities would ban non-citizens from a whole swathe of business life.

Depressingly for those who hoped that the first generation of Russians to grow up with no memories of totalitarianism would be liberal, the evidence points to exactly the opposite. Although explicit support for extremist and racist groups is in the low single figures, support for racist sentiments is mushrooming. Slogans such as 'Russia for the [ethnic] Russians', which was supported by no more than a third of those asked in the 1990s, now attracts the support of half of the population. A recent estimate in 2007 is that 500,000 young Russians belong to extremist youth groups.[40] The most worrying aspect is that the best-educated young Russians, far from being the tolerant cosmopolitans that Western wishful-thinkers have predicted, have unpleasantly hard-line views. In a survey carried out for the Moscow Carnegie Centre think tank,[41] the most anti-American group of young people in Russia were university-educated male Muscovites. For now, those sentiments are still channelled into official public organisations. But the danger of teaching people political agitation is that they may decide to do it on their own. By sponsoring *Nashi* and other such movements, the Kremlin may be stoking something that it cannot always control.[42] A sign of how easily xenophobes can run amok came in August 2006 in Kondopoga, an unremarkable small town in north-western Russia. A minor brawl, in which two Russians were killed, brought extremists from far afield who mounted a pogrom, in which people of 'Caucasian' (which in Russian, confusingly, is an adjective meaning from the Caucasus region, i.e. swarthy) appearance were beaten, sometimes severely, and chased from the town. The extremists torched shops and kiosks belonging to 'outsiders'. Similar movements in Moscow and St Petersburg are increasingly brazen in attacking dark-skinned people on the street. The police, notorious for their own campaigns of harassment and extortion, seem unbothered about the violence, prompting sharp protests from African and other embassies. A similar example came in mid-2007 in Angarsk, a Siberian city where environmentalists have been campaigning against a local uranium reprocessor. A group of skinheads armed with staves and clubs attacked the protesters' camp, beating one man to death.

If all domestic constraints on the Kremlin have been removed, what about pressure from abroad? Its reaction to the Litvinenko murder in 2006 shows how little the Russian leadership worries about the outside world. Litvinenko was at first sight an unlikely protagonist in an international incident. He had been a typical figure in the murky milieu between Russian business, organised crime and the security agencies. Often wrongly described as a KGB agent, he was a military veteran who became a law enforcement officer for the FSB: closer to a special agent of America's Federal Bureau of Investigation or Britain's Serious Organised Crime Agency than an operative of the Central Intelligence Agency or the Secret Intelligence Service. During the 1990s he became

disillusioned with the growing overlap between the FSB and
organised crime. In particular, he was alarmed by a plan to kill
Mr Berezovsky – a man he knew slightly. He made his complaint
public, together with Mr Trepashkin and some other FSB officers,
at a bizarre press conference in Moscow in 1999. Shortly after that
he was fired and then served a short prison sentence. On his release
he escaped from Russia, using a forged passport, and came to
Britain via Turkey. Rather reluctantly, the British authorities gave
him asylum.

Litvinenko was not a dissident in the normal sense of the word;
nor, strictly speaking, was he a defector. At the time of his
poisoning, his influence seemed minimal and his prospects poor.
He lived a troubled life on the fringes of the Russian émigré
community in London, dabbling in private security work, denouncing Mr Putin with increasing vehemence and striking up a close
friendship with the exiled Chechen leader, Ahmed Zakayev.[43] His
monthly stipend from Mr Berezovsky had been cut back. The
British authorities showed no interest in him. His limited English
and extreme views kept him isolated. He stayed busy writing
vitriolic articles for the Chechenpress website; in the summer of
2006 he denounced Mr Putin as a paedophile.[44] He co-authored a
book,[45] sponsored by Mr Berezovsky, accusing the FSB of organising the 1999 apartment block bombings. But the result was a
densely written text, a challenge even for a specialist. The full
details of his relationship to Mr Berezovsky are still unclear. From
the Russian authorities' viewpoint, Litvinenko was a traitor who
received a justly deserved prison sentence for betraying official
secrets and then fled abroad to work for a criminal and associate
with terrorists. His defenders, such as the (genuine) defector and
former KGB officer Oleg Gordievsky, say he was a hero who had
seen the menace presented by Mr Putin's Kremlin with prescient
clarity.

What is not in doubt is that he was murdered in an elaborate but incompetent way. Polonium-210 seemed to have been chosen because it would normally be undetectable. A rare radioactive isotope, it emits alpha particles, not the more common gamma radiation that standard radiological equipment would detect. Had Litvinenko died even a day earlier, the British authorities might never have identified the cause of his illness: that may have been what the assassins intended. The Kremlin did feel embarrassed enough to contest the allegation that it had ordered his killing (in contrast to its behaviour after the assassination by car bomb in 2004 in Qatar of the exiled Chechen leader, Zelimkhan Yandarbiyev[46]). Instead, it pushed the opposite explanation: the poisoning was bad for Russia, so it must have been organised by Russia's enemies, with the most likely candidate being Mr Berezovsky. It stonewalled the investigation. British detectives were not allowed to question the prime suspect, Mr Lugovoi, directly. The Russian authorities offered no help in clearing up other parts of the mystery. Instead, they adopted a tactic familiar from the last Cold War: 'admit nothing, deny everything, make counter-allegations'. Why was Britain not handing over the terrorist Zakayev and the fraudster Berezovsky,[47] they asked? Yet delivering either into the Kremlin's clutches was impossible. Russia's treatment of both Chechen insurgents and unruly tycoons had made it glaringly clear that neither man could expect even the semblance of a fair trial if they were sent back to Russia.

Exasperated, the British authorities began to focus on the FSB. It quietly expelled some London-based Russians who had been in direct contact with Mr Lugovoi. When the Russian bombast continued, the authorities went public, declaring four unnamed Russian 'diplomats' to be *persona non grata*. These officials were in fact SVR officers who appeared to have been tasked with helping with FSB operations in Britain. Russia reacted by expelling four

British Embassy officials from Moscow. International support for Britain's stance was distinctly lukewarm. America's Secretary of State, Condoleezza Rice, counselled caution. German officials said privately that Britain had 'overreacted'. The Kremlin also made a blatant attempt to dissuade the EU from showing any support for Britain. A deputy foreign minister, Aleksander Grushko, gave warning: 'Britain will appeal to EU solidarity. We hope that common sense will prevail within the EU and that its members will not give in to attempts to turn relations between Russia and the EU into a tool to achieve unilateral political goals. These have nothing in common with the EU's and Russia's real partnership interests.'[48] As Britain persisted, Russia professed bafflement. 'I don't understand the position of the British government,' a foreign ministry spokesman said. 'It is prepared to sacrifice our relations in trade and education for the sake of one man.'[49] That seemed to sum up the gulf between the Kremlin's worldview and what count as normal values in Britain. Litvinenko was perhaps not a hero. Maybe he was a nutcase, a fraud or a pest. But he was entitled to the protection of the law. Britain had failed him, but it would not forget him. Meanwhile, Mr Lugovoi became something of a media celebrity in Moscow, and was given second place in the election list for the Liberal Democrats, one of the handful of parties allowed to compete for seats in the December 2007 parliamentary elections.

That shows how flimsy outside political influence has become. The message from the Litvinenko affair is that Russia can get away with murder, metaphorically or even literally, and the response from outside will be to play down the argument and hope for better relations soon. That reflects not only Western pusillanimity, but also the removal of the final strand of outside influence on Russia: money. During the 1990s, Russia's financial weakness and desperate need for investment created at least a chance of encouraging legality and freedom. The World Bank and International Monetary Fund tried to insist on good government and reform as a condition for the billions of dollars they were lending to plug the holes in Russia's finances. That annoyed Russians, who recall (perhaps exaggeratedly) the Finance Ministry receiving faxes from Washington, DC, written in English, with instructions for immediate implementation. Even if the policies were right, they were bought at a high price: much of the money lent was looted instantly, finding its way to offshore bank accounts in Cyprus and Latvia (for the small fry) or Switzerland and Britain (where the serious money-laundering happens). But private investors, gullible at first, began to bite, too. The Kremlin knew that outsiders would risk doing business in Russian conditions only if at least some progress on property rights and enforcement of contracts was visible. The desire to please foreign shareholders and bondholders forced companies such as Yukos to mend their murky ways, clean up their corporate governance and produce proper accounts. Now all that has changed. When oil was at $10 a barrel, Russia was pitifully weak. At $75, it swaggers like a superpower. The crippling, humiliating debts that shackled the Yeltsin years have been paid off. Russia's books are not just balanced, they are bulging. Foreign companies are scrambling to open factories producing everything from cars to toothpaste. Even BP and Shell, whose prized gas fields were snatched by the Kremlin in 2007, are humbly hoping to be allowed to harvest at least some crumbs.

That also gives Russia the confidence to ignore other rules. It has sought for nearly a decade to join the World Trade Organization, the body that sets the rules for global trade. This would be a big step, at least potentially, towards bringing Russia into a law-governed international order. The WTO pushes its new members to chop back the thickets of protectionist legislation that shelters their home industries. That would have a big effect in Russia, which is notorious for both the tariff and non-tariff barriers that its well-connected domestic manufacturers have erected to keep out foreign competition. It also offers a legal avenue of complaint to those outsiders whose business falls foul of predatory or politicised customs officials. That is sensitive in Russia, too, where the customs agency is a great empire of state-run organised extortion. Membership of the WTO would also force the Kremlin to clarify its relationship with the puppet states it has created on its borders. Separatist statelets such as South Ossetia and Abkhazia (both in theory part of Georgia) and Transdniestria (a region of Moldova) enjoy customs-free access to Russia, with great potential for smuggling and money-laundering. Joining the WTO does little for the raw materials industries. But it would be good news for importers of consumer goods, and for Russian manufacturers, who face penal tariffs in some of the world's most attractive markets. It is a sign of where power lies in the Kremlin, and the mentality fuelled by Russia's energy riches, that WTO membership has become so low a priority: it would have given a hefty shock to the worst and least competitive bits of the Russian economy, and boosted the ones that will still be earning the country money when the oil and gas reserves dwindle. Russia is still trying to join in principle, but in 2007 talks seemed to be advancing at a snail's pace.

Russia's new-found wealth means that outside economic pressure on the Kremlin is minimal. The capital markets are awash with money, and Russia pays high returns. Russian companies can come to the London Stock Exchange and list their shares, regardless of whether their assets are stolen or mismanaged. Outside investors just hold their noses and explain that they cannot afford to miss out on a piece of the action. And Russia can pay for all the public investment and spending that it wishes. Moreover, the tables have been turned. Where the West once tried to use its money to speed reform in Russia, the Kremlin now uses its financial clout to subvert and weaken the political systems of other countries. As Julie Anderson, an American scholar, put it in a 2007 article:[50]

> Chekists are in position to become extremely wealthy through not only economic policies that favor their own personal private interests, but through the extra-legal takeover of others' assets . . . with this immense wealth, they can, in turn, use their significant financial resources and international contacts to penetrate foreign governments, not only through financial-based recruitment of agents and other traditional intelligence collection methods, but by gaining citizenship, starting or joining political parties, and running for political office in targeted countries. This method to political influence is complemented by the economic penetration of chekists, in league with not only foreign nationals and political figures, but also organised crime, in every region of the world, which enables them to move in and exercise influence in elite circles.

4

Why Money is Russia's Greatest Strength
and Our Greatest Weakness

Russians will, in crude terms, have become more than six times richer in the period between Mr Putin's nomination as prime minister and the end of his second term as president in mid-2008. GDP was projected to reach $1.3 trillion by the end of 2007, 6.4 times higher than in 1999. That means more cash in the pockets of the Russian people: when he became prime minister in August 1999 the average monthly wage was a pitiful $65; in 2007 it passed $540.[1] Then nearly a third of the population lived below the poverty line; now the figure is only a sixth.[2] In international comparisons, Russia's economy is no longer a weakling. It was the world's twenty-second largest economy in 1999 and the eleventh largest in 2006; in 2008 it will be in ninth place, the IMF forecasts. Investment bankers speak of the BRIC countries – Brazil, Russia, India and China – as the new powerhouses of the world economy.

Even Mr Putin's most fervent supporters do not give him sole credit for this. The oil price when he became prime minister was a mere $18 per barrel, a price at which much of Russia's oil production is barely profitable, or outright loss-making. By late 2007 it was nearing $100. Russia's oil revenues have risen more than sixfold from 1999, when Mr Putin became president, from

$30 billion then to more than $180 billion in 2006. In 2006 Russia was the world's largest gas producer and only narrowly behind Saudi Arabia in oil production. Hydrocarbons account for around two-thirds of Russia's exports, half of government revenues and around a third of GDP. Prices for other commodities have soared, too. In all, Russia has earned $700 billion in raw material exports in the past seven years. That creates a bulging war chest for politics at home and abroad. Russia's foreign exchange reserves, at around $400 billion, are the third largest in the world after China and Japan. It has paid off its public-sector debt: a crippling 150 per cent of GDP in 1998, it had fallen below 8 per cent by 2007. The government also has a colossal stabilisation fund built up from its surplus oil and gas revenues since 2004. It is not independently audited, but by the Russian government's account it is worth over $120 billion. The past eight years have freed the Kremlin from outside constraint or interference. Where outsiders once harried Russia over unpaid debts, now they are queuing for a place at the trough. Russia is one of the most lucrative markets in the world, bigger than all the other Central and East European countries combined, the same size as Brazil and slightly bigger than India. The value of Russian shares has risen by roughly $1 trillion since Mr Putin came to power. The advertising market is the twelfth biggest in the world and by far the fastest growing in Europe. Worth $8.5 billion in 2007, it will double in size within three years on current trends.

It is dizzyingly good, especially for those who remember the blizzard of bad news that marked most of the 1990s. Foreign investment aimed at satisfying the home market, and exporting raw materials, is flooding in. In 2006 it was nearly $29 billion, up eightfold since 1999. Eighty-five per cent of foreign executives surveyed by the Economist Intelligence Unit in 2006 expected double-digit profits growth in 2007. Western investment has not played such a role in Russia since the late 1920s, when companies like General Motors and Ford piled into the Soviet Union to take advantage of the attractive conditions offered by Mr Putin's distant predecessor in the Kremlin, Josef Stalin. General Motors sells so many clunky little SUVs made by its joint venture with the Soviet-era Avtovaz that it is now building a $115 million car plant near St Petersburg, joining Ford, Nissan, Toyota and Volkswagen in the Russian 'Detroit'. According to the accountancy firm PricewaterhouseCoopers (PwC), Russia will grow to become Europe's largest car market by 2011, with sales amounting to $96 billion.

Western investors bring not only money, but also ideas about management, governance, reporting and accounting standards. Like managers everywhere, the people running Russian companies want to cut the cost of their capital. That means persuading banks to lend cheaply, showing bondholders that their money is safe, and making shares attractive to outsiders. So Russian companies of all kinds are smartening up their act. They are expanding abroad, spinning off subsidiaries and trying to look like normal international companies in their corporate governance and accounting. Superficial financial transparency is the easy bit; having truly independent directors and clear ownership structures is much harder. It is easy to be rich; much harder to be respectable. Ambitious Russian managers want to be taken seriously, not sneered at as spivs in suits. The Kremlin does not help this process, by providing slush funds from the state budget to favoured companies. But it cannot stop it altogether.

The best hope for Russia lies in these ambitious, globally competitive new companies, independent of the state and of the access it grants to natural resources. Anatoly Karachinsky's IBS group is a world-class software company. Kaspersky Labs, set up by Yevgeny Kaspersky, a former KGB cryptographer, and his

wife Natalya, produces renowned anti-virus software. It is probably
the best-known brand to come out of the new Russia. Arkady
Volozh set up Yandex, which is the Russian version of Google (and
in some respects a superior product). Yet none of these are even in
the second rank of the Russian super-rich. Though software
exports have risen more than tenfold since 2000, they are still
under $1.5 billion. The whole IT sector is only 1.5 per cent of
GDP, compared with 5 per cent in America and 12 per cent in
Ireland. Research and development is only 1.2 per cent of GDP,
less than half the average for advanced industrialised countries.
Russia still benefits from a run-down but originally world-class
scientific legacy left by the Soviet Union: 3,500 research institutes,
and universities that turn out 200,000 science and engineering
graduates every year. But technological genius is not always
matched by softer skills: managing time, money, space, things,
people and projects. Intellectual property law is weak and the
courts hopelessly inexpert in judging it; if you have a good idea,
you are well advised not only to patent it abroad, but to develop it
there too. Software and music piracy (and counterfeiting of
pharmaceuticals) are still big businesses which attract little or no
official displeasure.[3] That hardly encourages local innovation in
these industries.

Andrei Illarionov is a lively-minded free-market economist who
used to be Mr Putin's economic adviser and the best advertisement
for the Kremlin's reform credentials. He resigned in December
2005, saying 'it is one thing to work in a country that is partly free.
It is another thing when the political system has changed, and the
country has stopped being free and democratic.'[4] Since then he has
become a fierce critic. From the safety of the Cato Institute in
Washington, DC, he says Russia is suffering from a synthesis of
economic mistakes from other countries, involving flawed macro-
economics, political interference and distortions caused by the

natural resource industries.[5] One component of this is the 'Dutch Disease', experienced by the Netherlands in the 1970s when booming oil and gas revenues led to an overvalued exchange rate and bloated state expenditures. High inflation and a stable rouble mean that Russia's real effective exchange rate has almost doubled since the 1998 crash, squeezing exporters of manufactured goods and stoking a boom in imports. Energy exports used to be a tenth of GDP; now they are a fifth, while the non-oil share in industrial output – which should be rising if the Russian economy were diversifying – is shrinking. Russia has also adopted a meddlesome industrial policy, rather like Argentina in past decades. The Kremlin is instinctively protectionist, and a chronic fiddler when it comes to tax regimes, import duties, special economic zones and other legal privileges for favoured industries and companies. That creates ample opportunities for kickbacks, but not robust, globally competitive companies. Since reform ground to an almost complete halt in 2003, the private sector has been eclipsed by the growth in the state's political and economic power. According to the EBRD, the share of gross domestic product created by private companies actually fell from 70 to 65 per cent in 2006. Mr Illarionov says Russia is turning into 'a rent-seeking society, where weak and ineffective people are demanding subsidies and protectionism (and receive it), and the most talented, educated and entrepreneurial people are looking for possibilities to distribute and redistribute rents'. Whereas private business used to be the preferred career choice of 78 per cent of Russian young people in 1997, that has now fallen to 42 per cent. A career in government administration and law was 30 per cent then; now it is the chosen path of fully 51 per cent.[6]

Another bad Latin American influence is the Venezuelan leader Hugo Chávez, a Putin ally and anti-American cheerleader, who has been enthusiastically nationalising his country's most important industries. History suggests taxing foreign companies usually involves less temptation for corrupt officials than trying to run the industry themselves. Russia's cheerleaders like to claim that interference in the oil and gas industries was some kind of exception. After all, do not Saudi Arabia and other energy-rich countries also insist that their resources are developed by national oil and gas companies? That is true. But private ownership tends to bring more efficient management. In 1999, 90 per cent of Russia's oil industry was in private hands. As investment poured in, production soared in Russia's clapped-out oil fields, which had been grossly mismanaged in the Soviet era and under state ownership in the early 1990s. That was a good trend, but it has stopped. Since the attack on Yukos, modernisation has halted; annual growth in oil extraction has fallen from 13 to 2 per cent. State-run giants like Rosneft spend their money on more interesting things: politics and acquisitions. After it snapped up the main Yukos asset, Yuganskneftegaz, the combined output of both companies actually fell: a case of one plus one equals 1.8. Admittedly, this is not just because of bad management: geological conditions are increasingly unfavourable, too. Efficient independent gas producers have been gobbled up by the state-run behemoth, Gazprom; its production growth over the past eight years has been a measly 0.6 per cent.

Stealthy renationalisation has been one of the sharpest economic trends in Mr Putin's second term. In 2004 the state controlled 11 per cent of the voting shares in Russia's twenty largest companies; it now controls 39 per cent. Sometimes owners voluntarily cede shares to the Kremlin's nominees at a cut price, hoping that they will at least be able to stay in business. Others simply have them taken. The tax code allows, in effect, the renationalisation without recourse of any company that the authorities covet or are displeased with. All the tax authorities have to do is to claim that ownership has been transferred with intent to defraud. The result is to distort the economy: the gigantic profits that Russia offers for those who can use political power in their personal interests inevitably suck investment and talent towards the state and companies associated with it, and away from knowledge-based industries offering advanced technology and sophisticated services.

The Kremlin has defined not only hydrocarbons, but a total of thirty-nine other industries as 'strategic'. In banking, for example, an expanding state share is holding back modernisation and the badly needed growth of lending to small and medium-sized businesses. The state's arms export company has taken over the largest car plant. It has effectively renationalised the aviation industry by merging successful small companies together with inefficient Soviet-era ones into a giant corporation with 75 per cent of shares in state hands. Gazprom has bought the country's largest machine-building company. Such state interference ensures that Russia's manufacturing industry is a weakling by world standards. Of Russia's ten biggest companies, all are in industries closely dependent on Kremlin decision-making: mostly energy and mining, and in two cases telecommunications – which depends on the state handing out access to the radio spectrum. While such big companies are doing well, small and medium-sized businesses, the bedrock of an advanced economy, are struggling. In 2000, 1,200 companies produced 80 per cent of Russian GDP. In 2006 fewer than five hundred companies are producing that share. In America, 60 per cent of GDP comes from small and medium-sized business. In Japan, 74 per cent does. In Russia the figure is only 17 per cent.[7]

The Kremlin's counter-argument to all this is that the past fifteen years show political freedom was bad for business, while authoritarian but stable rule now has proved much better. On the surface that looks true, but the claim requires careful analysis: how would

Mr Putin have fared when faced with Yeltsin's problems — and with the oil price of the 1990s? How different might Yeltsin's record have been if he had inherited an economy where private property was already entrenched, where businesses were restructuring fast to please foreign investors and where a devaluation and high oil price were boosting growth? Businessmen themselves say the great boon has been a feeling of political and economic stability. It is partly phoney: a truly stable system is also a transparent one, where people outside politics can easily see what is going on. In Russia, political decision-making is shrouded in secrecy, and abrupt changes – such as the appointment of the unknown Viktor Zubkov as prime minister in September 2007 – prompt agitated speculation about the Kremlin's real intentions. The stability is unpredictable in another way, too: it conceals arbitrary and predatory behaviour by the state. Still, many businesses feel even that is better than the wild swings and murky chaos of the Yeltsin years. The basic principles of capitalism – convertible money, property rights and enforceable contracts – may be sometimes breached in practice, but are challenged in principle by no one.

What is clear is that the islands of prosperity and modernity are small compared to other countries, and still sit in a sea of backwardness. Though cumulative foreign investment in Russia was a creditable $150 billion in mid-2007, only around half of that is direct investment; the rest is in traded securities such as shares and bonds. The stock of foreign direct investment is a modest 7 per cent of GDP, compared to 19 per cent in Ukraine, 25 per cent in Poland, 42 per cent in Georgia and a whopping 59 per cent in Estonia.[8] Exclude investment in energy, and Russia's performance looks even less impressive. Few if any companies open up shop in Russia because they want to make things there for export. Bureaucracy and the appallingly bad transport system make the costs of doing business too high. That is in sharp contrast to the other big emerging economies: China, Brazil and India. They are the workshops of the world, whereas Russia has yet to find a niche in any manufacturing export industry beyond weapons and aviation, both of which benefit from the investment and brainpower of the Soviet era.[9]

Russia is still a tough place to live: in the UN Human Development Index it was in sixty-fifth place out of 177 countries examined in 2006, one place below Libya. Since 1991, almost ten million people have left the country.[10] The economy is still remarkably state-dominated and inefficient. Fully three-quarters of property in Russia (chiefly land) belongs to the state. Seventy per cent of agricultural workers earn below the legal minimum (meaning that they work, in effect, as subsistence farmers). It is easiest to be middle class when you are single; families with children find life much harder. They are more dependent on Russia's abysmal public services, and exposed to the colossal price inflation of the housing market. The sharpest sign of Russia's underlying weakness is that decades of misgovernment have given the country one of the worst demographic profiles in the developed world, with just about the fastest-ageing population in Europe (other ex-communist countries such as Bulgaria and Georgia are in a similar mess).[11] For every 1,000 Russians there are 16 deaths and just 10.6 births. In the next decade, Russia's population will be shrinking by almost a million a year; at current rates, the UN says, it could have fallen by a third in 2050. The most glaring demographic problem, though, is not the birth rate but the extraordinarily high death rate, especially among men of working age – the twenty-second worst in the whole world. That rose from 10.76 per 1,000 men in 1989 to 15.45 per 1,000 in 2001. It has since declined only slightly, to 14.65 in 2006. (In America the comparable figure is 8.26, in the UK 10.13.) The causes are manifold: Russians smoke and drink more than almost any other people in the industrialised world. Drug abuse and sexual promiscuity are rampant among young people. That reduces fertility, as does pollution and the still-habitual use of abortion as a means of birth control.[12] The plan is to splurge. The government wants to pay higher benefits to mothers of young children, raise spending on healthcare (both by raising salaries and building new hospitals), provide subsidised mortgages, build more public housing, establish two new universities and offer more scholarships.

Though shortage of cash is no longer a constraint (with the state taking only 22 per cent of GDP in taxes and other revenues, and a budget surplus of some 6 per cent, Russia has one of the strongest fiscal positions of any economy in the world) progress on rebuilding infrastructure and improving public services is painfully slow. Russia has the worst healthcare in the industrialised world, for example. Chronic inefficiency and waste mean that big projects suffer from the same slowness and cost overruns as their Soviet predecessors did. Russia's economy undoubtedly has great potential – maybe even enough to make people feel optimistic enough to have more babies. But so long as it is subject to the greedy and incompetent interference of the Kremlin, it will not achieve it. The distorted political economy is not just a sad waste of potential benefits for the Russian people. It also – like the fundamentalist feudalism of Saudi Arabia – has a pernicious effect on outsiders who engage with it. Western trade and investment in Russia has created a powerful pro-Kremlin lobby that distorts the outside view of what is happening inside the country. Just as when business circles are dealing with Saudi Arabia (or China or Nigeria), questions of justice and freedom in Russia are brushed aside. Every time the Kremlin shows its true face, foreign businesses lobby their governments not to 'overreact'. Western businessmen show no shame in following their wallets. In the 1980s, it was communist trade union leaders who came to Russia to denounce Margaret Thatcher and Ronald Reagan as 'warmongers', and to praise the 'peace-loving' Soviet leadership. Now the fellow-travellers are capitalists, not communists. It was Britain's business tycoons who flocked to St Petersburg in June 2007 to extol the pro-business policies of the Kremlin and to denounce the 'emotional outbursts' of Tony Blair, who only a few days earlier, in one of his last statements as prime minister, had warned investors of the political risks of doing too much business with Russia.

Russia's heavy-handed rulers and their business associates are praised for the stability they represent, rather than denounced for their disregard for Western norms. Western bankers in Russia bring companies to the international capital markets, telling them just how much polish they will need to apply to attract the foreigners' cash. The world's top accounting firms make the books seem presentable; the most smooth-spoken foreign PR companies spread the word; renowned international consulting firms spruce up the management. Institutional investors in London, Frankfurt, Tokyo and New York buy the shares and bonds. Just as communist trade unionists around the world once turned a blind eye to the appalling treatment of workers in the Soviet Union, foreign capitalists now ignore the way in which the Kremlin tramples on the property rights of both Russian and foreign businessmen. In fact, they do not just ignore it, they collude in it. Take, for example, the startling role of one of the world's 'big four' auditors, PwC, in sanitising the Kremlin's assault on Yukos.

Some questioned the alacrity which PwC showed in accepting the contract to audit the company back in 1995, when Yukos's image was about as bad as a Russian oil company's could be. But the commitment of the Yukos founders to cleaning up their act arguably vindicated that decision. By 2003, Yukos had the most transparent accounts of any Russian-owned oil company (better for example, than, Gazprom, which, while delighting its shareholders with soaring returns, sheds only the minimum amount of light on the details of its costs, remuneration, acquisitions and revenues). But in June 2007, PwC said it had been mistaken, and withdrew its audit reports from the past ten years. 'PwC now believes information and representations provided . . . by Yukos' former management may not have been accurate,' it said in a statement.[13] That was a boon to the Kremlin, which used the decision as further evidence for its claim that Yukos was the Russian equivalent of Enron and that Mr Khodorkovsky had embezzled tens of billions of dollars in company funds. The aim is to have Mr Khodorkovsky sentenced to a further lengthy jail term for fraud before he becomes eligible for parole. Yet only a few months previously, PwC had been stoutly resisting Kremlin pressure, insisting that it stood by its audits.[14] That stance was bringing a severe penalty. In March 2006 police and other investigators raided its office, confiscating computers and documents. It was convicted for underpaying taxes and for abetting Yukos in what the authorities called a tax-evasion scheme. PwC protested its innocence[15] and appealed against the conviction. Prosecutors later said the firm had done no wrong. As the pressure ratcheted up, the authorities seemed set on ending PwC's ability to operate in Russia. The merest whiff of official displeasure is bad for business in Russia. Some companies, wanting to show their loyalty to the Kremlin, dumped PwC as their auditor. It even seemed as though the firm's lucrative contract to audit Gazprom was in doubt.

PwC justifies its change of position on two grounds. First, that it was misled by the Yukos management about the real state of affairs at the company in the years 2002–4. Only in mid-2007, it says, did it receive new information that three trading firms that sold Yukos products were in fact owned by shareholders in the parent company. The company's exiled management denies that: the schemes that the Russian authorities are now criticising were designed in explicit cooperation with PwC, to make sure that they were in compliance with both local and international accounting standards, they insist.

PwC denies all wrongdoing and any suggestion of bowing to government pressure.[16] That may indeed be the case, though it leaves unanswered the question of how the supposedly fraudulent Yukos schemes passed the scrutiny of auditors at the time. If highly trained and highly paid people working for one of the world's top accounting firms failed to spot a flagrant breach of the rules governing related-party transactions, they are open to charges of carelessness. If they did know, but did not object, there would be those who felt that they are open to the accusation that they helped the company evade its taxes.

If the Yukos schemes did not in fact amount to tax evasion but were, as PwC argued, legal (at least by the imprecise standards of Russian law), the explanation is still more troubling. It would suggest that PwC was bullied by the Kremlin into dumping its client. Certainly the last paragraph of the statement issued by PwC when it backtracked has a strange ring to it:

> In addition, PwC's decision to withdraw the reports was influenced by the fact that some former shareholders and management of Yukos are continuing to encourage others to rely on PwC's audit reports.

It is hard to see why an accountancy firm should have the slightest objection to a company's former (or present or future) management encouraging others to 'rely' on its audit reports. Audit reports are meant to be reliable. That is why – in normal countries, at least – they are required documentation for a public company.

This is not just about money: if the Kremlin case against Yukos is manufactured, then innocent people are in jail; some of them may die there. It is one thing for the authorities of a corrupt country to misuse the legal system to grab assets and imprison opponents. It would be dismal indeed if they were indirectly helped in this by those who are meant to be the international guardians of financial integrity.

Even stranger is when foreign businessmen connive in their own ill-treatment. Every one of the Western-financed oil and gas projects developed in the 1990s has been snatched in whole or in part by the Kremlin and its allies. Yet barely a squeak of protest can be heard. Shell and BP have both fallen victim to the Kremlin's idea that foreign capital and expertise is fine, but foreign control – and particularly foreign repatriation of sizeable profits – is not. In December 2006 Royal Dutch Shell sold a majority stake of its share in the giant Sakhalin-2 gas project to Gazprom, after the Russian government sued it for $30 billion in 'environmental damages'. It received $7.5 billion in a mixture of cash and shares, a lot less than the true value. The EBRD quietly walked away from the project. Yet Shell's boss, Jeroen van der Veer, thanked Mr Putin for solving the problem and said his company would continue to invest in Russia. Western energy companies are so desperate for a share – any share – of Russia's hydrocarbon reserves that they will do anything rather than complain. Even the largest American companies are not exempt. Exxon is the largest shareholder in a highly successful neighbouring project in Sakhalin but is also falling foul of the Kremlin. In 2006 it lost an appeal to extend its production licence. In 2007 the Kremlin blocked its plans to sell gas to China. BP's Russian subsidiary, TNK, had a licence to develop the 2 trillion m^3 Kovykta gas field in eastern Siberia. That licence committed it to producing 9 billion m^3 a year, around a third of which was for local consumers with the rest earmarked for export to China. But Gazprom, which has a monopoly on Russia's gas export pipelines, blocked that. BP was forced to sell its nearly 63 per cent stake, worth many billions, for around $800 million.[17] Again, BP presented the news as positive. It has now become a 'strategic partner' for Gazprom, and if it can help the Russian side make international investments it will be allowed to buy back a 25 per cent stake in the project.

Perhaps the most delicious irony is that one of the Kremlin's greatest champions is not only barred from visiting Russia, but faces a tax probe that could land him in jail if he went there. Charming, eloquent and dynamic, William Browder, an American-born British citizen, has defended Russia at countless investment conferences and other meetings. His persuasive argument is that outsiders must not be impatient; that economic modernisation will come as Russian companies raise their standards to suit outside investors. His investment technique – highly successful – has been to buy shares in Russian companies and then kick up a noisy and usually effective fuss about the bad habits of the management. That has usually led to at least cosmetic changes and often to substantial ones. The 'Browder treatment' might be uncomfortably bracing, but the result was almost always a higher share price for the victims. His targets included the mightiest companies in Russia, such as Gazprom and Sberbank, the state-controlled banking behemoth. Certainly investors in his firm, Hermitage Capital, have been delighted. Its value has risen sevenfold since Mr Putin became president and it is now Russia's largest investment fund. For the happy investors its hefty management charges seem more than justified. The investment he has attracted for Russia ought to make Mr Browder a national hero there, but in November 2005 he was turned back from Moscow's Sheremetyevo airport on undisclosed national security grounds: his campaign against cronyism and for investors' rights had clearly trodden on some

powerful toes. Revealingly, Mr Browder continued to insist that
Russia was an El Dorado for investors and that his own plight
was just a misunderstanding. Cheerfully extrapolating growth
figures, he maintained that Russia is heading towards becoming
one of the most prosperous countries in the world. Even when
twenty-five investigators raided his Moscow office in the summer of 2007, confiscating documents and computers, he was
undeterred, claiming that the attack was 'politically motivated'.
Several of his top executives hurriedly left the country. To an
outsider unfamiliar with the looking-glass world of Russian
business ethics, his defence might seem odd. If a top foreign
investor can be publicly humiliated by the law-enforcement
authorities for 'political' reasons, that should surely suggest that
something is deeply wrong in the relationship between politics
and the criminal justice system.

Moral myopia is not just bad for truth, justice and fairness
inside Russia. It weakens the outside world, too. Western
countries, for example, are belatedly waking up to the danger
of allowing Russia to buy downstream gas assets such as distribution networks. Combined with the Kremlin's hold on all
east–west gas pipelines, this would further strengthen Russia's
potential energy stranglehold. Gazprom's deal with Germany's
biggest energy company, E.ON Ruhrgas, has given it great
political clout in that country. Hoping to avoid the same fate,
the British government has tried to discourage Gazprom from
bidding for the country's main gas pipeline company, Centrica.
But how will it be able to refuse such a bid if it is backed by
Britain's own energy giant BP? It is as if a rape victim first thanks
the rapist for not being too rough, and then goes into business
with him. In personal relationships, such debasement would be
possible only in a world where ethics and self-respect had lost all
meaning. That is pretty much what has happened in foreign

businesses' dealing with Russia. Rosneft, for example, is in effect the Kremlin's in-house oil company. Its boss, Mr Sechin, is one of the most powerful men in Russia. Rosneft has snapped up the assets of Yukos for peanuts in a series of bogus auctions. Yet when it listed a 13 per cent chunk of its shares on the London Stock Exchange it raised $10.4 billion. Financiers such as George Soros urged Western institutions to boycott the offering; Mr Illarionov called it a 'crime against the Russian people'. If a Russian crook turned up and tried to sell stolen Fabergé eggs on the streets of the City of London, it is hardly likely that the pinstriped captains of finance would be queuing up to do business with him: handling stolen goods is a serious criminal offence. But that did not deter investors from buying Rosneft shares, or bankers from promoting them, or brokers from trading them. Their only worry – and probably a justified one – was that the political cronies and placemen in the company's top manage-ment seemed to have rather little idea about how to run a giant oil company.

Like water, money tends to flow downhill. More than twenty big Russian companies with a combined market capitalisation of around $625 billion are now listed in London. Nine of those arrived in 2007. On the New York Stock Exchange, by compar-ison, where standards of disclosure are higher, only five Russian stocks are listed. London is also a centre for Russian corporate bonds, with more than $33 billion raised in 2007, compared to only $11 billion in the whole of 2003. Britain is the second largest source of foreign direct investment into Russia, and bilateral trade, at $16.3 billion in 2006, has nearly tripled since 2001. At least the influence of Russian dirty money in Britain is limited because so many other temptations are available. Russia's billions may seem colossal to a layman, but they are dwarfed by the influence of money from elsewhere: from China, from the Gulf, from the developed world.

Although the Russian companies look big, most have only a sliver of their shares actually traded in London.

In Germany, by contrast, Kremlin Inc.'s influence seems proportionately stronger. Russia is a fast-growing trading partner: exports rose from €15 billion in 2004 to €23.4 billion in 2006. Yet only months after leaving office as Germany's federal chancellor, Gerhard Schröder, who insists that he has acted entirely ethically, became chairman of the Nord Stream gas pipeline project planned to run under the Baltic Sea (see Chapter Seven). During the Cold War, Western politicians and officials who took money from the Kremlin risked professional disgrace and even prosecution. Now business is business.[18]

That approach may work well in the context of boosting profits and the share price for the next financial year. In the longer run, it is problematic: if you believe that capitalism is a system in which money matters more than freedom, you are doomed when people who don't believe in freedom attack using money. Russia has spotted that the weakest link in the Western approach to life is inattention to the moral and ethical basis of capitalism: if only money matters, then why is the Kremlin's money worse than anyone else's? The same Westerners who regard Russia as a playground where the political risk is 'in the price' would be horrified if the same contempt for property rights and the public interest was displayed in their home countries. Yet that day is not far off. The creation of deep and liquid markets in energy is one of the best ways of countering the Kremlin's energy stranglehold in Europe. Germany's energy industries are firmly opposed to the EU's proposed liberalisation partly because it would shake up their cosy cartels and partly because Russia, their closest trade and investment partner, strongly opposes it. The German government strongly endorses that line, too. If this succeeds in derailing the EU's plans, that will mean less security, higher prices and ultimately less freedom for the citizens of Europe – and higher profits and more political clout for the Kremlin.

It would be a mistake to see this as a triumph of mere opportunism. The Kremlin approach to the West, part-cynical, part-hostile, is based on an increasingly systematic way of looking at the world: in short, an ideology. Many thought that had died with the Soviet Union. As the next chapter shows, they were wrong.

5

The 'New Tsarism':
What Makes Russia's Leaders Tick

When the Soviet Union's collapse ended the old Cold War, ideology seemed to have died with it. Seven decades of communism had left Russians highly suspicious of grand designs, and exhausted by the attempt to implement them. The radio broadcasts glorifying Marxist-Leninist ideas and the advantages of central planning to every corner of the map had already ceased under Mr Gorbachev, while the stupefying mental gymnastics of dialectical materialism, once compulsory for every high-school student, had vanished from the curriculum. Though Lenin, Stalin and Khrushchev remained etched in the national consciousness as notable leaders of the past, memories of Mikhail Suslov, the grey figure who for three decades served as the Politburo member responsible for ideology, disappeared like fog over the Moscow River. The reason was simple: communist ideology had been a total failure, while the pragmatic welfare capitalism of the West seemed an unquestionably better bet. The empty shelves in Soviet stores matched the emptiness of the ideas. If the point of the system was a better deal for workers, why did they live so much worse than their supposedly slave-driven counterparts languishing in the capitalist hellholes? Soviet-style ideology fared only little better abroad, under those who did not experience it first-hand.[1] After 1991, even

Russia's surviving communists shunned ideology, highlighting nostalgia, social fairness and order in their manifesto and denouncing greed, unfairness and chaos. Though they used the symbols and slogans of the past, few if any said they actually wanted to restore the planned economy and one-party state.

The result was that, through the 1990s, Russia was a political bazaar, where improvised kiosks offered everything from diluted communism to ultra-nationalism, via theocracy, radical liberalism and pragmatic politics on the Western European model. Proponents of the latter adopted the liberal, conservative, Christian and social-democrat labels of their counterparts. But these embryonic Western-style parties had almost no members, and their ideas put down only shallow roots in Russia. Most remained mere fan clubs for particular personalities. Money came from 'sponsors' – either powerful businessmen or rich elected officials. Still, these outfits called themselves political parties, advertised (usually lavishly) like political parties, and fought elections like political parties. Opinion polls showed their popularity rise and fall. They had anodyne names such as Our Home is Russia.[2]

It soon became clear that Western-style politics was not transplanting easily to Russia. Indeed, it was not transplanting at all. Working out what political ideas these parties stood for was hard. Most were in favour of more 'social policy' (no hard thing when millions of old people were getting their pathetic pensions paid late or not at all). Varying degrees of prickliness and xenophobia enriched the mix, as the Russian population gradually lost its initial naive enthusiasm for all things Western, and increasingly blamed its economic and social problems on 'foreigners'.[3] But it was clear on even cursory scrutiny that what these parties really believed in was getting into office and staying there. In the December 1993 elections to the Duma, the first party of a new kind broke on the scene, the 'Liberal Democrats' of Vladimir

Zhirinovsky, who won a startling 23 per cent of the vote. They were neither liberal nor democratic. Their public postures were extremist, sometimes nonsensically so. Mr Zhirinovsky promised to provide free vodka if elected, and proposed building giant fans to blow radioactive waste into the Baltic states. He later proposed that America's Secretary of State, Condoleezza Rice, would benefit from being gang-raped by Russian soldiers.[4] It was hard to decide whether Mr Zhirinovsky was a coarse clown, a real menace, a money-grabbing opportunist or all of the above. Though his public positions were highly confrontational, his parliamentary deputies almost always voted to support the Kremlin. Some wondered if his party was a creation of the FSB; others thought it simply gave its support to the highest bidder. At any rate, Mr Zhirinovsky's main role, by accident or design, was to break taboos: most other politicians appeared reasonable in comparison.

Regardless of party or label, all Russian politicians wrestled with what mixture of pride and shame the Soviet past should arouse. Expressing nothing but disgust seemed a ticket to instant political oblivion, yet finding something to celebrate was hard. Some found solace in simple nostalgia, blaming Gorbachev and Yeltsin for treachery and incompetence that had ruined a superpower. That went down well with older and less educated voters, but it was a hard sell to the rest. Pre-revolutionary Russia was the obvious alternative: pictures of the Romanovs and symbols of Orthodoxy mushroomed. But the Tsarist era resonated in so many discordant and contradictory ways: should one sentimentalise Tsar Nicholas II, or idolise his hopelessly ineffective democratic opponents? Feudal and backward, Russia then was certainly not as bad as the communists had said. Without war and Bolshevism it would have probably evolved into something better: perhaps a constitutional monarchy, certainly freer and more prosperous than the tragic experiment that succeeded it. But it required great willpower to believe that the ruthless and incompetent rule of Nicholas II was in any way admirable.

The dilemma echoed from more than a century earlier. Was contemporary Russia picking up the threads from the nineteenth-century Slavophiles, semi-mystical patriots who loathed Western materialism and individualism, or from the rationalist 'Westernisers' who longed for Russia to import the best that the outside world had to offer? Amid this confusion, Soviet revivalism competed with somewhat naive pro-Western liberalism, half-digested Tsarist nostalgia and all manner of far-fetched ideas about Russia's unfulfilled spiritual and Eurasian destiny. The Russian pantheon stretched awkwardly from the Romanovs to Andrei Sakharov,[5] via the cosmonaut Yuri Gagarin[6] and Lenin. The latter remains unburied, embalmed like a secular saint, in his mausoleum outside the Kremlin; he had, most Russians would say, been somewhat less bad than Stalin. Gulag victims could tell their stories – but guides at the FSB museum in Moscow insisted that the secret police had also suffered under Stalinism. The bombast about the Soviet Union's economic achievements vanished; lingering pride for its scientific and technological prowess remained.

Muddle was piled on muddle, because the Soviet Union's own view of the past was so contradictory, both in terms of how to treat mass murder and its perpetrators, and in how to deal with Russian nationalism. In the 1920s, the official communist line was that Russian imperialism had been a bad thing, just like Russian capitalism. Non-Russian cultures and languages such as Tatar, Mari, Komi and the like gained official status and enjoyed a few years of modest cultural revival.[7] Under Stalin, that switched sharply. Soviet communism and Russian chauvinism became almost indistinguishable. The words of the first verse of the 1944 Soviet national anthem are illustrative:

> Unbreakable Union of freeborn Republics
> Great Russia has wielded forever to stand!
> Created in struggle by will of the Peoples,
> United and Mighty our Soviet Land![8]

Under Mr Gorbachev, Russia began to look at its past more critically. Subjects such as Stalin, the Gulag and the great famine in Ukraine turned from taboo to hot topic within a matter of months. In terms of willingness to discuss history, a clear hierarchy emerged. Russian suffering could be discussed quite easily, that of other nations less so. Not that painful topics from any side were in short supply. The Red Terror unleashed by the Bolsheviks after 1917 probably killed half a million people.[9] Collectivisation in 1928–33 uprooted up to 4.5m peasants. Up to 5m people, in Ukraine and elsewhere, died of hunger. The Stalinist purges of 1937 to 1938 claimed up to 1.7m victims, of which more than 700,000 were executed without trial. During the war, nearly 1m ethnic Germans and 1.5m Chechens, Crimean Tatars and others, all of them Soviet citizens, were deported under the pretext that they were Nazi sympathisers. After the war, up to a million people were marched straight from Nazi POW camps to the Gulag.

Repression at home was matched by aggression abroad. The Bolshevik revolution quickly snuffed out the brief independence of the states of the southern Caucasus: Georgia, Armenia and Azerbaijan. They were not to rejoin the family of nations for seventy years. In a cynical carve-up with Hitler in 1939, the Soviet leadership divided Eastern Europe into spheres of influence. When the Nazis attacked Poland, Stalin joined in barely two weeks later. After Poland had been divided up and wiped from the map, 22,000 Polish officers were murdered in Katyń and elsewhere. After the war, the Kremlin snuffed out any attempt to restore freedom in the countries it had supposedly liberated. Having established brutal and

ruinous systems of one-party rule and planned economies, it put
down popular uprisings in East Germany (1953), Hungary (1956)
and Czechoslovakia (1968). In 1979, the Soviet Union invaded
Afghanistan, starting a war from which that country has never
recovered.

If dealing with that truthfully would be all but unbearable,
trying to conceal it leads to an ingrained duplicity about both past
and present. The Stalinist past still poisons political life in post-
Soviet Russia; it is the source of both the Kremlin's xenophobia
and its authoritarianism. The motto of the Ministry of Information in George Orwell's 1984[10] could hardly be more apt. 'He
who controls the past controls the future, and he who controls
the present controls the past.' And as the Kremlin increases its
power over public life, it is rewriting the past to suit itself.
Although the ramifications are huge and the details complex, the
principle could hardly be more simple. Russia is sanitising the
worst parts of its history, whereas other countries with a history of
totalitarianism and empire tend to bemoan it. In Germany, for
example, *Vergangenheitsbewältigung* is a word etched into that
country's public life. A literal translation would be 'overcoming
the past', though a more common rendering is 'coming to terms'
with it. Germany has been trying to do that ever since the Allied
occupation forces in the western zones of the defeated Third
Reich herded the population into cinemas to watch newsreel
footage of the concentration camps. The occupying powers'
intention, enforced at gunpoint, was that nobody should be able
to say that they 'didn't know', about the mass murder of millions,
or that it 'hadn't been that bad'.

It worked. Breast-beating about the past has been a hallmark of
German policy ever since. The Federal Republic paid generous
reparations to Israel and the countries of Eastern Europe.[11] History
textbooks in West German schools focus relentlessly on the Nazi

era, its origins, crimes and the disaster it brought for Germany. The anti-Nazi resistance is glorified; Willy Brandt, who had spent the war on the Allied side, became the federal chancellor.[12] But at least Germany has only to deal with twelve years of Nazi dictatorship. That can be set against much more attractive bits of history: the founding of continental liberalism in 1848; the *Zollverein*, the continent's first customs union; and many other great cultural, literary and scientific achievements in the eighteenth and nineteenth centuries. It is harder to find glorious moments in Russia's past. Germany's historical conscience may be unusually (and rightly) sensitive, but from a West European point of view, guilt about the past is pretty much the norm. Every big European country has had an empire, run it badly at times (or always) and feels bad about it, sometimes perhaps excessively so. British guilt about imperial massacres and exploitation is so embedded in the school curriculum that pupils are genuinely surprised to find out that anyone argues that the empire had redeeming features at all. Americans and Australians feel a mixture of painful emotions about their forebears' treatment of those continents' original inhabitants. Whites in the West feel guilty about racism in their own countries. Political leaders apologise on behalf of their nations for acts that happened decades, even centuries, ago, and over distant and recent crimes and shortcomings. Vietnam, apartheid, slavery, the Allied bombing of Germany – all attract the deepest scrutiny of the finest historians, novelists and playwrights. The threads – often muddled – of guilt, sensitivity, responsibility and shame run so thickly through the Western way of looking at other countries and cultures that we hardly notice that they are there.

Blind spots still exist, of course: until recently French discussion of Vichy was circumspect; Austria's view of its own history wobbles between remorse for the enthusiasm shown there for Nazism and the insistence that it was an alien import and that the country was

Hitler's first victim. Many in Britain are still only dimly aware that their country's wartime role was not unalloyed glory, at least from a Polish or Indian point of view.[13] But the blind spots grow hugely as you go east. In contrast to the Federal Republic in the west, the Soviet-occupied zone of eastern Germany did not force its people to confront their past: fascism was something imposed on Germany by outsiders (chiefly capitalists). The people of the 'GDR' were anti-fascists who had been liberated by their Soviet allies, not defeated. That did little to make the East Germans love the rapists and looters of the Red Army, but it did stop them worrying too much about what had been done to the Jews, whose suffering was all but eclipsed in the official histories in favour of Nazi atrocities against communists and trades unionists.

Russia's new attitude to the Soviet past is summed up in Mr Putin's infamous remark in his 2005 state of the nation address, that the collapse of the Soviet Union was the 'greatest geopolitical catastrophe' of the twentieth century.[14] Some supporters try to put a positive gloss on that: what the great leader meant, of course, was the loss of swathes of historic territory such as Ukraine, Central Asia and the Caucasus, plus economic and social upsets. The latter were certainly a personal catastrophe for many of the people involved. Yet a quick comparison with Germany shows the remarkable implications of the president's words. The collapse of Hitler's Third Reich also meant the loss of historic German territories such as East Prussia and Silesia. It brought colossal – indeed catastrophic – suffering to the whole German nation. But no mainstream German politician would baldly call it a 'catastrophe': first, because it was the inevitable consequence of Hitler's demented policies; secondly, because Germany's suffering cannot be seen in isolation. Hitler's downfall meant liberation for the subjugated nations of Europe, and indeed ultimately for Germany itself.

Mr Putin's words were not a casual aside that can be dismissed as part of Russia's wider confusion over its history. The Kremlin is spearheading a new approach to the past that glorifies the Soviet Union, denigrates the West and portrays the Yeltsin years as a period of disgraceful weakness and chaos from which Russia has now been rescued. The history books written in those days are therefore tainted, not least because they were published with the involvement of foreigners. 'Many school books are written by people who work to get foreign grants. They dance to a butterfly-polka[15] that others have paid for. These books, regrettably, get into schools and universities,' Mr Putin said in the summer of 2007.[16] He demanded new history textbooks that 'make our citizens, especially the young, proud of their country' and insisted 'no one must be allowed to impose guilty feelings on us'. Such textbooks are being produced; the ones he criticised are disappearing from the classroom.

The best illustration of the new approach is the way it treats Stalin and Stalinism. Outsiders – especially those whose countries suffered at Soviet hands in the Stalin era – may reasonably expect that modern Russia, by its own account a friendly and civilised country, will distance itself from the barbarism of the past. Imagine the scandal in the Netherlands, Poland or Israel if the German history syllabus presented Hitler and the Third Reich as anything other than a shameful stain on that country's past. Yet *A Modern History of Russia, 1945–2006: A Teachers' Manual*,[17] a new history teacher's guide endorsed by Mr Putin, tries to shoehorn the greatest mass murderer of Europe's past century into a familiar yet ill-fitting role: the great leader forced by circumstance to take harsh decisions. It deserves detailed study.

For a start, it makes out that the greatest victims of his tyranny were not the patriots, peasant farmers, intellectuals, religious believers and those tied to the past regime, but the Communist Party's bosses:

Practically all . . . Politburo members elected after the 17th Party
Congress [in 1934] suffered from reprisals to a certain degree . . .
The ruling class was the priority victim of the repressions in 1930–
1950.

And it was all in a good cause:

The goal was to mobilise the leadership in order to make it effective
in the process of industrialization . . . political repression . . . was
used to mobilise not only rank-and-file citizens but also the ruling
elite.

The purges created, it claims:

a new class of managers capable of solving the task of modernisation
in conditions of shortages of resources, loyal to the supreme power
and immaculate from the point of view of executive discipline . . .

In other words, it argues, Stalin was no worse than Otto von
Bismarck, the German chancellor who united his country through
Blut und Eisen (blood and iron). The guide makes tangential
reference to the extraordinary abuse of power that characterised
the Stalin era, but only by putting him alongside other Russian
leaders.

It is well known from Russian history how corrupting a long term
in power is. Biographies of such outstanding rulers as Peter the
Great and Catherine II prove it . . . Stalin followed Peter the
Great's logic: demand the impossible . . . to get the maximum
possible.

So the worst that can be said about Stalin is that he was 'controversial'.

He is considered one of the most successful leaders of the USSR.
The country's territory reached the boundaries of the former

Russian Empire (and in some areas even surpassed it). A victory in one of the greatest wars was won; industrialisation of the economy and cultural revolution took place successfully, resulting not only in mass education but also in the best educational system in the world. The USSR became one the leading countries in science; unemployment was practically defeated.

Stalin's success, by the crudest measure of industrialisation and military victory, is indisputable. But the book skates over the colossal human cost: millions of forced labourers, the elimination of whole social classes, and the famines, both intentional and those caused by negligence. It also ignores the fact that the Second World War was largely Stalin's fault. If he had not connived with Hitler in the 1930s, Nazi Germany would not have been able to attack. And had Stalin's paranoia not led him to kill the Red Army's best generals, and to ignore the warnings of impending Nazi attack, Hitler's war in the east would have been far less successful. At any time since the collapse of Soviet totalitarianism in the late 1980s, such an approach would have seemed not just misleading but sinister. Now it is treated as bald historical fact, to be fed to Russian schoolchildren. If Stalin made mistakes, so what? Lots of people make mistakes.

'Problematic pages in our history exist', Mr Putin conceded in mid-2007. But: 'We have less than some countries. And ours are not as terrible as those of some others.' He also strongly contests any attempt to put the two great mass murderers of the twentieth century on a similar footing. 'I cannot agree with equating Stalin with Hitler. Yes, Stalin was certainly a tyrant and many call him a criminal, but he was not a Nazi,' he said in 2005 in a joint interview with the then German leader, Mr Schröder, who signally failed to challenge the assertion. Mr Putin goes further, equating Soviet and Western crimes against humanity. He compared the Great Terror of 1937 to America's dropping of the atom bomb on Hiroshima.[18] The comparison is strange. A strong argument can be made that the dropping of the atom bomb ended a war and saved countless lives, including many innocent non-Japanese who deserved to die least of all. It is also quite possible to argue that Franklin D. Roosevelt and Harry Truman were mistaken, callous or reckless, overeager to see Japan defeated quickly, unwilling to consider other means of ending the war, and blind to the wider danger that nuclear weapons would pose. But unlike Stalin, they were not the direct cause of the deaths of millions of people through execution, deportation, starvation and collectivisation.

In his use of 'what about', Mr Putin echoes, consciously or unconsciously, the favourite weapon of Soviet propagandists. Asked about Afghanistan, they would cite Vietnam. Castigated for the plight of Soviet Jews, they would complain with treacly sincerity about discrimination against American blacks.[19] Every blot on the Soviet record was matched by something, real or imagined, that the West had done. Hungary? Suez! Martial law in Poland? American-backed dictatorships in Latin America! But the contrasts even then were absurd. When the American administration blundered into Vietnam, hundreds of thousands of people protested in the heart of Washington. The authorities disapproved, but did not try to imprison them. In a handful of cases the police or National Guard scandalously overreacted. The shooting of four students at Kent State University in May 1970 brought millions of students out on strike, closed hundreds of campuses, and remains a national scandal in America that is cited to this day. Yet when eight extraordinarily brave Soviet dissidents tried to demonstrate in Red Square against the invasion of Czechoslovakia in 1968, they were instantly arrested. Most were sentenced to exile or psychiatric hospital. Their names are all but forgotten.[20] The only person to protest publicly about the war in Afghanistan was Sakharov.

Russia now barely commemorates even the damage it did to itself, let alone the suffering inflicted on other people. Nothing like America's powerful and dignified Vietnam Memorial exists in Moscow for the tens of thousands of Soviet servicemen who died in Afghanistan. Russia's only museum dealing with the full horror of the Gulag is an excellent one, but it is in Perm, deep in the provinces 1,500 kilometres (900 miles) from Moscow. The handful of museums in Moscow that try to highlight the Soviet past experience official harassment, not support. It is not just a remarkable silence. Even to raise the question of the historical suffering of, say, the Poles or the Balts arouses an instant and neurotically angry reaction. Even the reluctant concessions made during the Yeltsin and Gorbachev eras are now being withdrawn. The official government newspaper, *Rossiiskaya Gazeta*, has even revived the Soviet-era lie that the murder of Polish officers at Katyń was actually a Nazi crime.[21] For Poles, who remember the combination of mass murder and official cover-up as one of the most shocking and painful episodes of the past century, that is akin to officially sanctioned Holocaust denial.

Outsiders in these historical arguments often find this hard to understand. Most West Europeans tend to share Henry Ford's view that 'history is bunk': bemoaning your country's shortcomings in a vague way is *de rigueur*, but harping on about your ancient historical grudges is taboo, a kind of primitive vengefulness usually confined to the far right of politics. So when the nations of Eastern Europe say that Russia's revisionist version of history is so scary that it threatens their very right to existence, the response from their allies is usually polite bafflement, or outright irritation.

Why should it matter if Russia claims, for example, that the Soviet Union annexed Estonia legally in 1940? Why does it matter if the territory of the Moldavian SSR included a bit of land that was (or wasn't) historically part of Russia? How badly did the Georgians behave in Abkhazia in 1991? Who does Nagorno-Karabakh really belong to? What historical and other rights do the Tatars, Russians and Ukrainians have over Crimea? Yet such seemingly obscure questions were matters of life and death for countries and people, and may yet be again. They are part of the central front in Russia's new ideological war: the desire to rewrite the history of both the distant and the recent past.

The heart of the problem is that the Stalinist version of the Second World War is now the most important myth in modern Russia's account of itself. Victory day celebrations are the highlight of the Russian patriotic calendar. To understand the Russian obsession with the 'Great Patriotic War' (as 1941–5 was termed in Soviet parlance), it may help to imagine a highly concentrated version of English nostalgia for the Battle of Britain and the Dunkirk spirit, blended with America's most rose-tinted views of the heroism of the Normandy beaches and Guadalcanal, plus every continental European country's folk memories of united resistance to Nazism, all rolled into one. It recalls an idealised world when simple national virtues of solidarity and selflessness defeated an opponent who embodied evil. Against that background of sentiment and myth, to point out that the war was largely Stalin's fault, that the Red Army behaved little better than the Wehrmacht, and that the countries in between Russia and Germany wanted not to be 'liberated' in 1944–5 but to regain their pre-war independence strikes many Russians as nothing short of blasphemous.[22] The idealisation of the Stalinist war myth, of unprovoked aggression, extraordinary sacrifice and triumphant victory, absolves Russia of any guilt, responsibility or even sensitivity about events before, during and after the war. The secret protocol of the Molotov–Ribbentrop pact, for example, was a justifiable tactical manoeuvre, and no great cause for shame.[23] History is rarely as simple as it seems, and it is quite reasonable to discuss both other pressures on Soviet policy – such as the fear of a war with Japan – and the mistakes made by Britain and France. A revisionist historian could make the argument that Stalin's deal with Hitler was no worse than Britain's betrayal of Czechoslovakia at Munich in 1938. But that would only be in the context of abhorrence, not justification. The Russian approach now lacks such crucial nuances. It blames the West for leaving Stalin no choice but to do a deal with Hitler. The practical consequences of the pact for its victims are ignored.

In the post-war period, the West and the Soviet Union are seen as moral equivalents: the Soviet Union no more 'occupied' East Germany than the United States 'occupied' the Federal Republic. NATO membership in Eastern Europe now is comparable to the Warsaw Pact's role in the past. That may sound superficially balanced; but in fact it topples the entire edifice on which not only Europe's post-war history but also the continent's current politics are based. If the Cold War in Europe stops being a struggle between freedom and tyranny, but instead becomes just an old-fashioned geopolitical tussle, then values and voters' wishes count for nothing. The former satellites were not captive nations, enslaved by an evil ideology, but mere pawns on a chessboard. The Americans subsidising the anti-communists of the Solidarity trade union in Poland is the moral equivalent of the Soviet Union helping the Sandinistas in Nicaragua. In short, communism as an ideology was a dead end, and the planned economy was a disaster; but the Kremlin's *raison d'état* survives: just like any big country, Russia has the right to determine its neighbours' future. And they have no right to complain about it.

The Kremlin's historical revisionism catches the former satellite countries in a double bind. First, the Stalin era was not that bad: if these countries suffered, so did millions of Russians, who also bore the brunt of the struggle to defeat Hitler. Second, did not the

heroic Red Army liberate Eastern Europe from the fascist yoke?
Any dissent from that must mean that they are not just ungrateful,
but hotheaded, egotistical, revanchist and closet Nazis. During a
row over a Soviet-era war memorial in 2007 (see Chapter Six),
Nashi placards outside the Estonian Embassy spelled the country's
name eSStonia, and its president as toomaSS ilveSS. The idea that
the Estonians might have good reason to regard the Soviet
'liberators' as just another occupation is seen as an obscene historical
slander.[24]

Indeed, Estonia is now one of the New Cold War's two hotspots
(the other is Georgia, of which more later). Estonia is where
Russia's geopolitical ambitions, economic muscle and historical
amnesia overlap. It is also a country determined to defend itself. For
that reason, it repays close study. If the Kremlin can crack Estonia,
the chances for the rest of Eastern Europe look bleak. At first sight,
though, it is hard to see why Russia would bother. Estonia's
population is one-hundredth of Russia's. It is of pipsqueak significance in terms of economic weight – less than 0.2 per cent of
the GDP of the euro zone. A big Polish city such as Katowice is far
more important. For Russians to identify Estonia as a serious enemy
seems little short of neurotic.[25] But Russia is right to take Estonia
seriously, and the outside world should do so, too. The country
may be small, but it is of symbolic importance to both Russia and
the West. It is the best example of a post-communist success story,
with a clean and modern public sector, and hi-tech and service
industries that contrast sharply with Russia's hydrocarbon-heavy
economy. But just as that makes outsiders moist-eyed with appre-
ciation, it makes Russia green-eyed with annoyance and envy. If
Estonia – which has, however unwillingly, shared Russia's destiny
for centuries – can succeed while playing by Western rules, it casts
doubt on the Kremlin's central argument of Russian exceptionalism. Maybe it is possible after all to combine stability and

prosperity with freedom and openness. If Estonia's success is so painfully embarrassing, then perhaps it would be better if it were not successful – or did not exist – at all.

The fight is rooted in contradictory views of history. The way the Estonians tell it, their prosperous, law-abiding country was more advanced than Finland before the war, until Estonia, along with its Baltic neighbours of Latvia and Lithuania, was obliterated by the Hitler–Stalin pact. Soviet troops marched in, under a series of preposterous excuses, including that a local foreign-language journal, the *Revue Baltique*, had published a provocative article.[26] The economy spiralled downwards. Grotesquely rigged elections produced a parliament that 'requested' to join the Soviet Union. Estonia was not to return to the world atlas until 1991. On two June days in 1941, around ten thousand of Estonia's best-educated people, including a tenth of the Jewish population, were deported to the depths of Russia – typically with a midnight knock at the door followed by a few minutes' hurried packing. Of some 2,500 children, fewer than half were ever to return. In total, more than fifty thousand people were either deported, executed or conscripted into the Red Army. Communist terror had begun.

When Hitler attacked the Soviet Union a few days later, it is hardly surprising that many Estonians were glad to see the back of the Soviet occupiers. When they returned in 1944, many Estonians fought them. That was not because they liked the Nazis: had it been American or British forces chasing out the Germans, the Allies could have counted on resolute support and a warm welcome. Conversely, had the French or Dutch shared the Estonian experience of 1940–41, and then faced not Western but Soviet 'liberators' in 1944, they too might have reacted like the Estonians. What happened next confirmed the Estonians' fears: communist terror returned with, literally, a vengeance. The Soviet authorities ruthlessly hunted down those with connections to the pre-war government. Deportations restarted, and intensified. In March 1949 they reached their peak, with some twenty thousand people, the majority of them women and minors, deported to Siberia. In all, Estonia lost around one-sixth of its population at Nazi and Soviet hands. In the name of 'breaking cultural continuity' with the pre-war republic, public and private book collections were purged of any material that might remind future generations of what they had lost. As a young man Jaan Kross, later to become Estonia's best-known novelist,[27] remembers watching a Soviet functionary outside the country's main university library, chopping up books with an axe.

Russia's version of Estonia's history is rather different. It starts off not in 1918, with the birth of the Estonian republic, but beforehand, with Peter the Great's push into the Baltic provinces previously conquered by the Teutonic Knights and then Sweden. Estonia's two decades of independence were an aberration that counts for nothing against centuries of Tsarist rule. At a meeting with journalists in 2005, Mr Putin put the Kremlin view as follows: under the peace treaty with Germany in 1918, 'Russia turned over some of its territories to Germany'. In 1939, 'Germany returned them to us, and these territories joined [*voshli v sostav*] the Soviet Union.'[28] There was therefore no occupation after the war, 'as they were already a part of the USSR'. He justified this approach by saying: 'Whether this was good or bad, such was history. It was a secret deal, the small states being a currency of exchange. Such were the realities of life, regrettably.' That allows no room to see the war from Estonians' viewpoint, while characterising the decisions they made in the harshest possible terms: the Estonians who fought in German uniforms against the returning Red Army were fascists, and those who praise their bravery and sacrifice are nothing more than nostalgic Nazis.

Estonia's tragic fate was shared almost exactly by Latvia and

Lithuania.[29] The behaviour of Soviet forces in Poland was, if anything, more scandalous. Not only did the Kremlin attack Poland in the rear in 1939, while it was already facing the Nazi war machine. They treated the population of eastern Poland so badly that many Jews chose to take their chance under the Nazis rather than face the murderous barbarity of Soviet rule.[30] In 1944, Stalin cynically ordered his troops to stand by while the Nazis crushed the Warsaw uprising. The elimination of the strongest parts of the Polish underground army, loyal to the lawful pre-war government, would make it much easier for the Soviets to install their own puppet regime. But Poland is thirty times bigger than Estonia. For now, at least, it is less of a target for the Kremlin.

The natural and civilised response to wartime Europe's catalogue of impossible choices, brutality and betrayal is to mourn the dead on all sides and vow 'never again'. That is the West European approach, refined over five decades of peace and cooperation. It is also now the approach in the ex-communist states that are in the EU or heading towards it. Intense historical animosities between Hungary and Romania, between Macedonia and Bulgaria, and between Poland and Lithuania have been largely buried. It is far more important to have neighbours that are prosperous and free than to win arguments over history. Outstanding issues are buried in specialist committees of historians, museum curators or – for example – in the thickets of philology. A long wrangle that epitomises the new style of argument is an intricate Polish–Lithuanian dispute over orthography. Poles of Lithuanian descent, backed by the government in Vilnius, want to be allowed to use letters such as ė and ų when spelling their surnames in official documents: these are part of the Lithuanian alphabet, but do not appear in the Polish one. Conversely, many Lithuanians of Polish extraction want to use their ł and ź, which do not feature in Lithuania's official alphabet. Amid such minutiae, it is hard to remember that, before the war, Polish–Lithuanian relations were at best icy and at worst violent. A Polish military expedition in 1921 took Lithuania's historic capital, the mainly Polish city of Vilnius, and kept it until Stalin returned the city to Lithuania in 1940. For that entire period, Poland and Lithuania had no diplomatic relations; in 1939, as Poland was torn apart by totalitarian superpowers, Lithuania closed its frontier to Polish refugees. During the war, Lithuanian and Polish partisans took time out from fighting the Russians and Germans to keep their old enmity alive.

Russia's approach to its neighbours could hardly be more different. Committees of historians set up during the Yeltsin era are not only dormant; their foreign members, such as the Latvian historian Heinrihs Strods, are banned from coming to Russia. Commentaries in the Kremlin-controlled media completely rewrite the historical record. It is hardly surprising that less than a tenth of young Russians think their country need apologise to the Baltic states for the Soviet occupation.

Sanitising Soviet history is one leg of the Kremlin's emerging ideology; another is rewriting the 1990s under Yeltsin. The new teachers' guide highlights anarchy, failure and weakness, while almost wholly ignoring the successes of those years, such as the growth of a free media, open multi-party elections, a lively parliamentary culture, the end of central planning and the growth of millions of small businesses. Far from being a period marked by unparalleled pluralism and political freedom, the Yeltsin years are now described as a series of disasters in which Russia's enemies tricked and humiliated the country, stoking disorder and undermining the state.[31]

It is reasonable to put the past under scrutiny, and nobody would argue that the 1990s were pleasant. But it is twisting the facts to portray, as the Kremlin does, the collapse of the Soviet Union as a disaster equivalent to the Versailles peace treaty imposed on

Germany after the end of the First World War. In that case, military defeat and international censure[32] were coupled with crippling reparations. In Russia's case, not only did it suffer no military defeat, but it was deluged with international goodwill. Far from bankrupting Russia with demands for reparations, the West was pumping in billions of dollars in loans and aid. That the result was disappointing has more to do with Russia's own political weakness, and the inevitable consequences of ruinous economic planning, than with Western bungling. Perhaps the advisers should have been less ambitious or doctrinaire in their advocacy of price liberalisation, monetary stabilisation and privatisation. Some of them may have been too close to the investment bankers who profited from privatisation and other transactions. But it is absurd to argue that they were actively malevolent. Even if Russians now think that they somehow had a raw deal, that the medicines were wrong, or would have been better prescribed in a different dosage and sequence, that is no reason for anti-Westernism. Germany and Japan suffered far worse, with outright military defeat and occupation, but became staunch Western allies within only a few years.

Such revisionist history shades right into politics: the youth wing of United Russia, *Molodaya Gvardiya* (Young Guard) organises marches under the slogan 'No return to the 1990s'. From this viewpoint, not only was the West trying to weaken Russia, but the political leaders who worked with them were selling Russia down the river. The big historical turning point is not the collapse of the Soviet Union and birth of freedom, but the end of the Yeltsin era. The new history guide's chapter on the years from 2000 states admiringly: 'We see that practically every significant deed is connected with the name and activity of President V. V. Putin.'[33]

Patriotism and historical revisionism are two of the best means the Kremlin has found to fill what Sergei Markov, one of its top advisers, calls Russia's 'ideological vacuum'. The third element is

xenophobia. According to Lilia Shevtsova of the Moscow Carnegie
Centre, one of the most lucid analysts of Russia's drift to authoritarianism, 'anti-Westernism is the new national idea'.[34] Mr Putin
has swung from citing Western countries as objects of envy to
denouncing the West for hypocrisy and arrogance. It started as
early as 2004 when he accused America of a policy on Chechnya
that was designed to destabilise the Russian Federation. In the same
year he likened America to an old-fashioned colonialist, a 'strict
uncle in a pith helmet' instructing others 'how to live their lives'
and punishing objectors with a 'missile-bomb truncheon'.[35] In his
2006 annual address to parliament, he referred to the United States
as 'Comrade Wolf', a figure who 'knows whom to eat. He is eating
and listening to no one.'[36] Over time, the rhetoric has become
harsher. America 'has overstepped its national borders in every
way . . . No one feels safe anymore,' he told a security conference
in Munich, Germany, in February 2007.[37] Later that year he
likened America obliquely to the Third Reich for its policy of
'confrontation and extremism' and 'its contempt for human life,
the same pretensions of world exclusivity and diktat'.[38] Criticising
American policy is no crime – many Americans have detested the
Bush administration since the moment it took office. But the
Kremlin's anti-Westernism creates a bogeyman that allows Russia's
rulers to sidestep any criticism of their own authoritarianism. Put
crudely, the argument goes like this: 'Democracy equals chaos and
is promoted by Russia's enemies.' Mr Putin's defenders, both in
Russia and abroad, cite all manner of slights and policy blunders by
America and Europe to justify this rhetoric, but it still seems bizarre
to compare America, a country that for decades has been a
champion of freedom, to Hitler's Germany.

For all its shaky logical foundations,[39] a sign of how well this
approach is succeeding is that the overtly pro-Western camp in
Russia has shrivelled to insignificance. Beyond a small handful of

journalists and people working at Moscow think tanks, almost no mainstream public figure is prepared to defend the EU, NATO or America against the caricature that they are menacing hypocrites out to destroy Russia. As Ms Shevtsova notes, attitudes toward the West have become a 'litmus test of loyalty to the authorities and the system'.[40]

For all the anti-Western sentiment among Russia's elite, it is hard to see an appetite yet for real confrontation. Rich and powerful Russians buy their luxury goods in the West, educate their children there, take their holidays there, stash their ill-gotten gains there. So far at least, anti-Westernism has had a mixed effect: according to polls in 2007, fully 70 per cent of Russians see Europe as a partner of sorts, even though a similar number say they do not consider themselves European. Fully 73 per cent of Russians think that the country should aim for a mutually beneficial relationship with the West; only 16 per cent think Russia should distance itself. Almost half saw the EU as a threat to Russia's economic independence; 67 per cent say they have a good opinion of it and only a third saw a long-term relationship with the EU as desirable. Such ambiguous feelings towards the West are nothing new. As Aleksandr Blok wrote in his 1918 poem *The Scythians*:

> Russia is a Sphinx. Rejoicing, grieving,
> And drenched in black blood,
> It gazes, gazes, gazes at you,
> With hatred and with love!

So far at least, anti-Westernism has been principally a political device, designed to keep power. But it may be hard to control; German intellectuals who claimed they had lost the First World War because of a 'stab in the back' reaped a bitter harvest a few years later. As Ms Shevtsova laments, 'the ruling elite has let the genie out of the bottle and it will be very difficult to put it back again'.[41]

The next element in Russia's nascent state ideology is religion, in
the form of the moral and spiritual legitimacy provided by the
leadership of the Russian Orthodox Church (ROC). Having been
a dutiful servant of the Soviet regime that in the 1930s drove it
almost to extinction, the ROC enjoyed a strong revival, at least in
terms of numbers, in the post-Soviet era. In the Yeltsin years, its
public posture was often ambiguous. Some leading figures flirted
with Russian nationalism and anti-Semitism. Others seemed more
involved in using the generous tax and legal privileges to build a
business empire – for example, in bottling mineral water, or
importing cars, tobacco and alcohol. Yeltsin's own attitude to
the ROC was dutiful rather than devout. Under Mr Putin, its
influence has soared and its profile sharpened. Whether it is sincere
or self-interested, Mr Putin's own religious belief is certainly
conspicuous. He regularly attends church services, and likes to
show his interlocutors a crucifix that he rescued from a fire at his
family home. With an approval rating of 54 per cent, the ROC is
the second most trusted institution in the country (the presidency
has 68 per cent). Yet the numbers are puzzling. Russians are still
more religious in belief than most Europeans: in a 2007 poll 58 per
cent said they believed in God, up 6 per cent from the previous
year.[42] However 59 per cent said they never attended church
services, up 4 per cent since 2005. Although church and state are
nominally separate, the church's privileged legal status has become
deeply entrenched. Indeed, Russian secularists and scientists are
becoming alarmed by the teaching of religious dogma as fact in
Russian schools, and the Orthodox hierarchy's increasingly vehement opposition to evolution. The connection is undisguised, even
with the organs of power that most damaged the ROC in the past.
The church next to the FSB's Lubyanka headquarters bears a
plaque thanking the FSB for their help in restoration work.[43]
'All power is from God and so is theirs' says a priest who leads the

service. At least some of the *siloviki* seem truly to believe that they are chosen and guided by God.

In return for state protection, the ROC provides loyal support to the Kremlin's attempt to differentiate Russian and Western civilisation. The central document of the church–state compact is a declaration issued in 2006 by the World Council of Russian People, an assembly of secular organisations that acknowledge the spiritual leadership of the ROC hierarchy. It adopted a 'Declaration of Human Dignity and Rights', a manifesto that aims to counter the United Nations 'Declaration of Human Rights', the founding document of universalist Western thinking on the subject. The head of the ROC, Patriarch Aleksei, said that the Western vision of human rights did not permit Orthodox faithful to live in accordance with their beliefs. Indeed, he said, such an approach would lead to a 'neo-pagan' revival. The Council took particular exception to the focus on individual rights, which it blamed for both moral relativism and the deprival of the interests of others. 'There are values that are no less important than human rights,' the concluding statement said. 'These are faith, ethics, [national] sacraments, Fatherland.'[44]

Reasonable people may disagree about the usefulness of human rights as a political concept. But that is not the argument at issue here: what unites both the ROC and the Kremlin is not just a shared past in the KGB but also the passionate belief that Russian civilisation is based on unique values, quite different from those in the West – an idea that fits perfectly with the notion of 'sovereign democracy'. *Pravoslaviye, Samoderzhaviye, Narodnost* (Orthodoxy, Autocracy-Sovereignty, Nationality) was the motto invented in the nineteenth century by Count Sergei Uvarov to give a philosophical basis for the rule of the reactionary and xenophobic Tsar Nicholas I: worryingly, it seems to be as potent now, in the days of modern Kremlin authoritarianism, as it was in the days of Tsarist

feudalism. The Orthodox hierarchy also shares the Kremlin's anti-
Westernism, insisting that foreign religions, particularly Roman
Catholicism, are determined to steal its flock. Vsevolod Chaplin,
the spokesman for the patriarchate, complained recently: 'After the
breakdown of the Soviet Union a great number of people in the
Roman Catholic Church decided that was the moment when it
was possible to conquer these big territories and huge populations.'[45]

Thus a distinct Russian approach to politics has been taking
shape. From the outside it seems clear that it is based on xenophobia, authoritarianism, historical revisionism and exceptionalism.
But how is it described inside Russia? Understanding that can be
tricky for outsiders, because so many of the terms used to have no
easy equivalent in English (and sometimes not in any non-Slavic
language). Take the word *gosudarstvennik*, applied approvingly to
Mr Putin and most of his associates. A possible translation would be
'statist' but that does not reflect the full meaning. Nor does the
literal 'man of state'. The state in Western political culture is the
servant of the people, and statist is a mildly derogatory term,
suggesting unaccountable bureaucracy, interference and a lack of
accountability. *Gosudarstvennik* in Russian has a ring of patriotism
about it. A *gosudarstvennik* cares about the state's prestige and
strength; he believes it to be an expression, perhaps the highest
expression, of society, culture, even of civilisation. In other words,
the Russian state exists not to serve the people, but as a project or
mission with an almost supernatural basis.[46] 'Culture is fate. God
made us Russians, citizens of Russia,'[47] says Vladislav Surkov, a
former advertising man who is now the Kremlin's chief ideologist.
That is reflected in the idea that Moscow is a 'Third Rome',
inheriting the imperial, cultural and spiritual mission of first ancient
Rome and then Byzantine Constantinople.[48] Mr Putin's desire to
restore the supremacy of the Kremlin at home, and strengthen its

reach abroad, has little or nothing to do with the will or welfare of the Russian people: their applause is welcome – and indeed expected – but the motivation is a transcendent not a practical one. The point is to promote Russia's *derzhavnost* – an untranslatable word meaning, roughly, 'great-power-status'. That means the state throwing its weight about abroad, with behaviour sometimes called *derzhavnichestvo* (great-power-ishness); and also at home. The latter involves another crucial if misleading phrase: *diktatura zakona* (dictatorship of the law). Much used by Mr Putin in the early years of his rule, it sounded superficially like a plea for Russia to become a *Rechtsstaat*, the German term for a state where the rule of law is supreme. That is certainly the case in other free countries: where the law is the servant of the people, not the other way round (elected representatives can, over time and with a big enough mandate, rewrite any law, and even the constitution). In Russia, however, *diktatura zakona* has turned out to mean not the subjection of the executive power to the abstract values of an independent judicial system, but the executive branch's untrammelled use of legal sanctions against its opponents – including, for example, defence lawyers.[49]

The final phrase in this short political glossary is the *vlastnaya vertikal* (power vertical). Unfamiliar to outside ears, this has strong connotations of order and stability in Russia: its partial Western counterpart might be the British phrase 'joined-up government'. But whereas that in a Western country means different institutions working sensibly together, in Russia the idea is rather different: that orders given at the top are carried out below. The first clear ideological element that emerged from the Kremlin was the need for Russia to be a strong centralised state. Mr Putin himself says it is in the country's 'DNA'.[50] The decentralisation of the Yeltsin years he dismisses as anarchy, something that gave comfort to those foreigners who want to break Russia up into more manageable units. The idea of vertically integrated power might seem un-exceptional, as what happens in a well-organised bureaucracy anyway. But Russia does not have, and has never had, a well-organised state administration. It is riddled with not only incom-petence, waste and laziness, but also favouritism and special inter-ests. In its 2006 report on Russia, even the normally cautious Organisation for Economic Co-operation and Development (OECD) could barely restrain its language:

> The state bureaucracy is inefficient, largely unresponsive to either
> the public or its political masters, and often corrupt. It is cited by
> foreign and domestic investors alike as one of the principal obstacles
> to investment in Russia today. It poses a particularly heavy burden
> on small and medium-sized enterprises, which are often less able to
> defend themselves against the bureaucracy than are large compa-
> nies. Moreover, the poor quality of the state administration im-
> pinges on structural reforms in almost every other field, since it
> limits the government's ability to implement any policies that
> require administrative or regulatory capacities of a high order. It
> also imposes significant costs on citizens engaged in such routine
> tasks as registering property transactions.[51]

This is not new. When fuelled by terror and slave labour in the Stalin era, the bureaucracy managed to industrialise the country quickly, though at enormous human and other costs. Since then, the Soviet bureaucracy reverted to something that would have been all too familiar to the great nineteenth-century Russian novelists like Gogol: functionaries paying lip service to their orders from above, while concentrating on the main jobs, of shirking responsibility, dodging blame, enriching themselves and helping their friends. That, ultimately, helped dissolve Soviet power. Left unchecked, the same misrule could also destroy Russia. A strong *vlastnaya vertikal* is the supposed antidote to the corrosive swamp of state administration: it is a culture of discipline and respect in which orders are carried out, money is accounted for and the state's interests are served, not betrayed.[52] In Western countries that happens, more or less, thanks to the professional pride of bureaucrats, the scrutiny of the citizenry and the media, the pressure from other public institutions, and scrutiny from elected representatives. But almost none of these function in Russia. Indeed, the Russian language lacks a word for 'public servant' or 'civil servant' – the usual translation, *chinovnik*, would be better rendered as 'placeholder'.[53]

The practical result of the ideology of centralisation is to concentrate power at the very top, where it becomes unaccountable, unpredictable and inefficient. As Ms Shevtsova points out, the system created by the Kremlin has four structural weaknesses. First, personalised power and the electoral calendar are inherently risky as they require the regular manipulation of elections. That is a potential source of popular discontent. Secondly, the regime wants both stability and to redistribute resources in its own favour. That undermines property rights and unnerves investors. Thirdly, lack of legitimacy means that succession is fraught with difficulty. It involves regular disruptive purges, where the new placeholder, and his superior, blames the previous incumbent for all past failures. Finally, the destruction of political pluralism removes the main social safety valve. The last point may prove the most important. History suggests that highly centralised societies do not work very well, and Russia is proving no exception. The signature of the 'First Person' (as Mr Putin is sometimes known), or the lack of it, can make or break a career, a deal or a life. As a result, taking initiatives is risky; hoarding information makes sense; obedience matters more than results. The Kremlin may not have consciously wanted to end reform, but it can be no surprise that the ideas of the brightest and best people in Russia have been sidelined, seemingly indefinitely.

Mr Putin's fondness for at least the appearance of tight control may stem from his repeated difficulties in establishing it. For someone ostensibly so powerful and so popular, his grip has often seemed surprisingly fragile. The first year of his second term, for example, was ill-starred. It started in May 2004 with the murder of his hand-picked collaborationist leader in Chechnya, Akhmed Kadyrov. Hardly an ornament to Russia's political life, his notoriously brutal henchmen matched even their terrorist opponents in scandalous disregard for life, property and the laws of war. But Kadyrov's assassination by separatist fighters was a sombre reminder that the claims that armed resistance had been crushed were simply false. Then came Mr Putin's one and only attempt to make a serious and painful reform to Russia's wasteful and obsolescent system of social payments. The idea was a simple one: to replace benefits in kind with cash. Instead of providing cheap housing, free transport, subsidised medicines and so forth, the state would pay the recipients instead. That is the way most countries organise social welfare. Subsidised goods and services encourage monopolistic thinking among the providers, reduce choice and cause waste. But in Russia, that is not the worst outcome. In any system involving cash transfers, the money can simply be stolen by anyone powerful enough to cover their tracks. Pensioners' right to free travel on public transport, by contrast, exists simply by virtue of age, which is visible and cannot be cancelled or stolen. As a result, Russians believed, probably with good reason, that they would end up paying the full price for something that they had previously got for free. Spontaneous demonstrations mushroomed across the country, prompting a hurried and humiliating climbdown. Since then, serious reform has been a dead letter. The year got worse: the 'Orange Revolution' in neighbouring Ukraine in the late autumn showed people power at its most romantic and compelling – and highlighted the rigid and sterile politics of Russia, and the dispiriting apathy of the population there.

The Kremlin's response to that was not to loosen up, but to tighten still further. Russia was 'at war' with its terrorist foes, Mr Putin said. That justified almost any restriction on political liberty. The urgent need was to make Russia stronger, and therefore safer. Michael Yuryev, a businessman close to the Kremlin, in 2004 gave[54] an illuminating list of what he regarded as truly essential freedoms on which the 'national idea' should never infringe. They boiled down to private enterprise and the right to travel. He explicitly excluded from the list the requirement to obey constitutional provisions on electoral terms, the right to form political parties and the freedom of privately owned mass media. Mr Yuryev used to be seen as an extremist eccentric who believes in an irreconcilable clash of Russian and Western values, and wants Russia to be both isolated and explicitly imperial in outlook. His recently published book, *The Third Empire. Russia As It Must Be*[55] describes a world in 2053 when Russia has defeated America in a nuclear exchange. That may just be unpleasant fantasy. But Mr Putin has repeatedly adopted both his phrases and his ideas.

The new ideology that has taken shape since 2004 has a name, the anodyne-sounding 'sovereign democracy'. This elides two key concepts enshrined in the preamble to the Russian constitution. But 'sovereign' clearly counts for more than 'democracy'. As Masha Lipman of the Carnegie Center notes, the phrase conveys two messages:

First, that Russia's regime is democratic and, second, that this claim must be accepted, period. Any attempt at verification will be regarded as unfriendly and as meddling in Russia's domestic affairs. And sovereignty also implies that outside (i.e. western) norms do not apply.[56]

The new ideology includes a surprising dose of what in Western countries would be called 'New Age' thinking. That might seem surprising at first sight: the tough, greedy world of the Kremlin could hardly be more different from the herbs, healing crystals and hogwash beloved by devotees of the 'Age of Aquarius' and similar notions. But according to Mr Surkov, 'Russian cultural conscious-ness is clearly holistic [and] intuitive and opposed to [the] mecha-nistic [and] reductionist'. He continues:

> Synthesis prevails over analysis, idealism over pragmatism, images over logic, intuition over reasoning, general over particular. This naturally does not mean that the Russians lack analytical thinking and people in the western countries [lack] intuition. The issue here is the ratio. Let's put it like that: the Russian person is more interested in the time than in the blueprint of an alarm clock.[57]

So what stems from this 'intuition' about how a society should best be organised? Mr Surkov continues:

> First, it is the aspiration for the political wholeness through the centralisation of power functions. Second, idealisation of the goals, pursued by the political struggle. Third, personification of political institutions. All these phenomena exist in other political cultures, however, their presence in our political culture exceeds the average level.

That may sound vague to an outsider, but it has clear practical effects, which nudge Russia in the direction of what might easily be called fascism. The first and third ideas combined mean that no institutions matter outside the presidency. Power flows from the very top. That means that parliament, the judiciary, the police and the civil service – all the institutions whose complex interrelation guarantee individual freedoms – are subordinate to the will of the man at the top.

Whether or not this should even be called an ideology is contested. Mr Surkov is widely described as the Kremlin's head of ideology, a designation he does not reject. His colleague Dmitri Medvedev, however, has said he dislikes the term 'sovereign democracy' and called it an 'ideological cliché'.[58] At any rate it is not the ideology of Suslov's day. Mr Surkov is a lively-minded figure with an easy, populist touch. Suslov was regarded as dull even by the narcolepsy-inducing standards of the Soviet politburo. Mr Surkov uses little jargon; Suslov used nothing else. Mr Surkov was a successful businessman in television, advertising and public relations before he moved to the Kremlin in 2004 (his biography suggests he may have worked for the GRU in the 1980s); his career, spanning the worlds of high state office, media, espionage and private business, is the embodiment of Russia under Mr Putin. Suslov embodied the Brezhnev-era Kremlin; it is hard to imagine him in any role other than as a communist functionary. But the similarity is still striking. In both cases, the aim was to explain the difference between the ideal and the reality. Suslov had to explain why the CPSU deserved to stay in power even though the utopia it promised showed no sign of arriving. Mr Surkov has to give a justification for Russia's new political system, of authoritarian state capitalism. Like Mr Suslov, he also has to explain why questioning the system is not just mistaken, but treacherous.

The big question for the West is how to deal with it. Some argue that this is all better than nothing. Vlad Sobell, a Russia expert at the London offices of Daiwa, a Japanese investment bank, says that Mr Surkov is developing a 'fresh, post-totalitarian application of liberalism'.[59] Russia has its own political culture, so it needs its own political philosophy, the argument goes. Better to have something home-grown than import misunderstood ideas from outside, such as Marxism. Secondly, Russia is also right in rejecting the idea that global stability depends on America playing the role of 'global teacher–cum–policeman'. Multi–polarity will be more stable than a unipolar world dominated by America. Others simply want to rebut 'sovereign democracy' in both its premises and its arguments. Certainly much of it is based on exaggerations and misapprehensions. The outside world was not trying to weaken Russia in the 1990s (indeed, one of the big fears of that era was that Russia might disintegrate, or prove too weak to control its nuclear weapons). This administration has overstretched America's military power and shredded its reputation. But the idea that America is threatening the world is a bogeyman. Bogged down in Iraq and Afghanistan and scrambling to cope with the rise of China, the supposed global hegemon is too weak to fulfil the tasks it faces, not too strong. America's 'democracy promotion' efforts may be ill-judged or hypocritical on occasion, but the isolationism that America-bashers seem to want would have a high price: it would mean, in effect, agreeing to leave the world in the hands of dictators.

Russia certainly has the right to its own political culture: every country does. And the aftermath of totalitarianism may mean tolerating some unpleasant features, at least for a time (Germany in the 1950s was very different from Germany now). Mr Surkov is right on that. But he has not made a persuasive case for reinventing the wheel: the basic means by which a free country works are universal: the rule of law, separation of powers, independent media and fair elections. And the clear sign from the Kremlin is that these elements of political life are not just optional, but outright undesirable.

The most telling point, though, is not to rebut the Kremlin's criticisms of the West, which may in some cases be accurate and merited. It is to point out that other countries' shortcomings do not justify Russia creating new ones of its own. Violent abuse of power by the state is bad, regardless of what other countries are doing. Whether it is snatching assets from well-run private companies,

locking up opponents, stifling criticism or hollowing out supposedly independent public institutions of state, the Kremlin is doing
a disservice to the people of Russia, in whose name it supposedly
governs. The novels of Fyodor Dostoyevsky include powerful
criticisms of the West in the nineteenth century. But that did
not mean that the brutalities of Tsarist autocracy such as the use of
the knout, serfdom, censorship and deportation to Siberia were a
better way of governing the country.

So why does the Kremlin promote this ragbag ideology, which
alienates outsiders and promotes misgovernment of the country?
The crudest reason is that it is an easy way of staying in control.
Portraying Russia as a fortress besieged by malevolent hypocrites is
a handy way of explaining to the population why its sacrifice of
freedom is necessary. Secondly, intimidating the outside world is a
good starting point for fending off their interference. Talking
toughly was a standard approach of Soviet negotiators during
the Cold War. Terrifying rages and frosty silences would melt
without explanation with the prospect (usually illusory) that the
thaw would continue if only the other side would see reason and
back down. But the most worrying explanation of all is the
simplest: the Kremlin adopts an ideology based on Soviet nostalgia
and xenophobic rhetoric because it partly or even wholly believes
in it. It makes it all the more worrying that the outside world still
seems so unbothered.

6

How Eastern Europe Sits on the Front Line of the New Cold War

'A quarrel in a faraway country between people of whom we know nothing' is how Britain's prime minister Neville Chamberlain dismissed Czechoslovakia's struggle for survival before flying to Munich in September 1938 to seal that country's dismemberment by Nazi Germany. Then the fate of the continent was being decided in Central Europe. Nearly seventy years later the story is the same, but the threat is from Russia, not Germany. The countries concerned are the largely the same, too, those covered by the Molotov–Ribbentrop pact, stretching from the Baltic coast to the Black Sea. Chamberlain's sentiments are alive today, too. Should, say, German households pay more for gas in order to safeguard the interests of faraway Estonia? That may seem as absurd a linkage as the notion in 1938 that Chamberlain found so 'horrible, fantastic and incredible': that British citizens were trying out gas masks because of disputes over the Sudetenland.[1] In fact it is a topical and practical one. Disdain for the interests of the East European states betrays ignorance of both the defeat the free world suffered in the 1930s, and of the route to victory in the old Cold War.

The first lesson is that division among strong countries means the destruction of their weaker allies. If Germany, America and France cannot agree on, say, how to defend Georgia, Moldova or any other small nation now being menaced by the Kremlin, then their chances are little better than those of Czechoslovakia in the late 1930s. The second and more recent lesson is that strength of ideas may matter more than military capability. NATO won the last Cold War partly because it could outspend the Kremlin, and partly because planned economies and one-party states are inherently prone to decay. But the other ingredient – and perhaps even the most important in retrospect – was 'soft power'. Highlighting the contrast between the prosperity and freedom of the 'capitalist camp' and the backwardness and repression in the 'socialist camp' dissolved the totalitarian glue that held the Soviet empire together. In effect, the messianic communism of the 1920s, which believed that the masses in every country needed only to hear the message to support it, went into reverse. Fewer and fewer people in the capitalist world wished they lived in the communist one, and the more they learned about it the less they wanted it. By contrast, most people living under communist rule wished things to be different. The more they learned about the West, the more they liked it, and the less they believed their own rulers' propaganda. That process did not stop with the collapse of communism: after 1989, the same soft power consolidated the West's victory. Having thrown off dictatorship, the nations of Eastern Europe soon decided that they wanted 'Euroatlanticism'. That is convenient shorthand for the advantages offered by the American-backed security umbrella of NATO membership, and the good government and economic advantages associated with the path to membership of the EU.[2]

Euroatlanticism is not an easy ride, but it is clearly a beneficial one. Joining the EU means a commitment to cleaning up all the debris of totalitarian rule.[3] It means everything from making the courts and police honest and efficient to ensuring solid property rights and strong anti-monopoly laws, introducing internationally recognised education and environmental standards; and sticking to the stable macro-economic policies necessary to adopt, eventually, the euro. Admittedly, the details are often messy. It is easy to ridicule pedantic food hygiene standards, and to complain about tiresome and costly regulations that protect inefficient farmers or clog up the labour market. The rules are not only sometimes silly, but may be applied hypocritically or inconsistently. Some countries are much better at promising reform than doing it. But the results speak for themselves. The expansion of the EU has been a great success. The new members are growing fast, spectacularly so in some cases. Even their often weak and incompetent governments do not affect foreign investors' confidence. And unlike Russia's distorted, petro-fuelled economic growth, the new members' prosperity is based on manufacturing, services, and – increasingly – high technology. The eastwards expansion of NATO has had a similar beneficial effect.[4] Demoralised, sprawling Soviet-style bureaucracies and excitable, amateurish militias in the former captive nations have reformed. In some cases, such as Poland, they are becoming modern and flexible armed forces.

While Euroatlanticism has continued a deep and seemingly irresistible advance, the story for the Kremlin for most of the years since 1989 has been of retreat and defeat. It is salutary to note what was regarded in 1992 as the irreducible minimum that Russia could accept. Igor Rodionov, then head of the military staff college (and later Yeltsin's defence minister) said Russia would insist on:

> The neutrality of East European countries or their friendly relations with Russia; free Russian access to seaports in the Baltics; the exclusion of 'third country' military forces from the Baltics and non-membership of the Baltic states in military blocs directed at Russia; the prevention of the countries that constitute the CIS from

becoming part of a buffer zone aimed at separating Russia from the West, South, or East; maintaining the CIS states under Russia's exclusive influence.[5]

That has been a fairly spectacular failure. All the Soviet Union's Warsaw Pact allies – Poland, the Czech Republic, Slovakia and Hungary, as well as Romania and Bulgaria – have joined NATO; so too have the Baltic states, which Russia terms 'ex-Soviet republics'.[6] 'Georgia is pressing to join the alliance, too. Russia has lost its access to the Baltic seaports in a failed attempt to exert economic pressure on Estonia, Latvia and Lithuania.

Not only was the Soviet Union's hard power – military and economic muscle – no longer available after 1991 but Russia's soft power was weak, too. Russia offered little to rival Euroatlanticism: its friends were a diminishing number of dictatorships; incompetent, unattractive and unsuccessful. In Slovakia, for example, Russian security services and business circles cultivated close links in the 1990s with the strong-willed and heavy-handed prime minister, Vladimír Mečiar. That stoked intense opposition from most local opposition parties, strongly helped by European and American think tanks and activists. A cross-party anti-Mečiar movement stormed to victory in the 1998 parliamentary election, kick-started reform and turned the country from an isolated backwater to a foreign investors' darling.[7] Similarly, the Serbian strongman Slobodan Milošević enjoyed strong Russian support in his wars with Western-backed Croatian, Bosnian and Kosovar adversaries. But the economic and political consequences of his nationalist rule, and the sanctions they brought, were ruinous; in 2000 he, too, was toppled.[8] In Lithuania, two politicians with close ties to Russia have left office in unhappy circumstances. Rolandas Paksas served as president for fourteen months. He was impeached in 2004 and banned from running for public office in future after the country's security service complained publicly about his alleged ties (which he vehemently denied) to Russian intelligence and organised crime. The leader of Lithuania's Labour Party, Viktor Uspaskich, fled to Russia and successfully gained political asylum there in 2006. His personal book-keeper had revealed to the Lithuanian authorities what appeared to be some Russia-linked irregularities in the party's finances (Mr Uspaskich, a wealthy businessman, strenuously protests his innocence and returned to Lithuania in autumn 2007 – and to house arrest).

The coloured revolutions in Georgia in 2003 ('Rose'), Ukraine in 2004 ('Orange') and Kyrgystan in 2005 ('Tulip') highlighted the failure of Russia's approach to its neighbours. In each case they displaced a corrupt and authoritarian regime; in the latter two cases, it was one that the Kremlin had found easy to deal with. A possible lesson from this was that people in the ex-Soviet region have a strong appetite for clean government and freedom. But the Russian reaction was a mixture of bafflement, and renewed resolve to find better tactics. That determination has begun to bring results.

Two things have happened. First, the Euroatlantic tide has stopped flowing eastwards. Appetite for expanding the EU and NATO has waned as disappointment with the new members has grown in Brussels. Secondly, Russia's own power, hard and soft, has started increasing. The first examples came from Central Asia. The Uzbek dictator Islam Karimov, after a brief flirtation with America after 2001, is now one of Mr Putin's closest and most dependable allies.[9] The Uzbek regime appreciates Kremlin help in its ruthless suppression of Islamist opposition forces, and in countering intermittent outside criticism of its deplorable human rights record (though the latter, at least from Britain and America, is muted: they too find Uzbekistan a useful ally in the 'war on terror'). The West has also lost influence in Kazakhstan, ruled by its president-for-life Nursultan Nazarbayev. Despite rampant corruption, the country is the most advanced and impressive in Central Asia. But Kazakh foreign policy is ultra-cautious, reflecting the president's domestic priorities: economic growth and education. Mr Nazarbayev's regime is steadily building stronger relations with the West, and with China – but wants on no account to quarrel with Moscow. A glance at the map shows why: the Kazakh–Russian border is the longest land frontier in the world. Northern Kazakhstan is largely populated by ethnic Russians, roughly a third of the population. For now at least, Kazakhstan could only lose from a confrontation. Irresolution and division in the West make the Kazakhs despair: why should they take a Euroatlantic option seriously, when it is not offered seriously?

The Kremlin's power is greatest in Tajikistan, a poverty-stricken narcostate wholly dependent on Russia for its financial and military survival. Russian troops ensured that Emomali Rakhmonov, the country's leader, won a five-year civil war that ended in 1997; they have kept him there ever since. Remittances from Tajik migrant workers in Russia are an economic lifeline for the impoverished population. In Kyrgyzstan, Russia has bounced back. That country flirted with an idealistic pro-Western orientation under its first post-Soviet leader, Askar Akayev, who said he wanted it to be the 'Switzerland of Central Asia'.[10] When his rule mired in autocracy and corruption, a popular uprising in 2006 seemed to presage a Ukraine-style revolution. As in Ukraine, that proved premature. Kyrgyzstan is the uneasy host to both an American and a Russian airbase. The oddball of the region is Turkmenistan. With gas reserves second only to Russia's in the former Soviet Union, it is the most mysterious of all the post-Soviet countries. For the first fifteen years of independence it was run by its former communist boss Saparmurat Niyazov, an eccentric megalomaniac who re-named himself Turkmenbashi (Father of the Turkmen), closed down public services and instituted a terror-based personality cult.

His replacement, Gurbanguly Berdimuhammedov, has relaxed some of the most odious features of Niyazov's rule, but has also weakened the country's determined isolationist stance, which seems to be allowing Russia greater influence.

Specific conditions in the Kremlin's two European allies, Armenia and Belarus, have so far made them almost immune to the pull of Euroatlanticism. Armenia enjoys by far the most political pluralism of any of Russia's allies; it is also one of the biggest per capita recipients of American aid in the world. That makes it an unlikely member of the Kremlin camp. The main – and probably sole – reason for its orientation is its need for support against neighbouring Azerbaijan.[11] Belarus is on paper the Kremlin's closest ally. Heavily Russified in the Soviet era, it lacked the strong alliance between patriots and freedom-lovers that pulled neighbouring countries such as Lithuania and Poland out of the Kremlin's orbit. After coming to power in 1994, the Belarusan president Alyaksandr Lukashenka[12] suggested merging his country with Russia to form a Russian–Belarusan Union, sometimes known as the union state. Paradoxically, this project, seemingly the only Russian foreign-policy venture with a clear chance of success, has proved a complete failure.

The main reason is that both sides' enthusiastic pan-Slavic rhetoric concealed wildly contradictory aims. The power-hungry Mr Lukashenka saw the union state as a chance to strut on a much wider stage: in the declining Yeltsin years he was (and not only in his own eyes) a possible hard-line candidate for the presidency of the new entity. In the meantime, he hoped that the economic merger would mean continued supplies of gas for his country's old-fashioned industry at Russia's subsidised domestic price, and the chance to piggy-back the weak Belarusan rouble on the much stronger Russian one. Yeltsin disliked his Belarusan counterpart's dictatorial ways, but appreciated the convivial atmosphere of their meetings. Mr Putin took a different view. He loathed the waffle and boondoggles such as customs fiddles associated with the union state. His suggestion was that Belarus should simply join Russia, with Mr Lukashenka's presidency either being abolished or down-graded to a purely ceremonial position. He also drove a much tougher bargain on energy supplies. In January 2007, Belarus agreed to sell Russia half its national pipeline company, Beltransgas, for $2.5 billion; in exchange Gazprom merely doubled the gas price, rather than quadrupling it as threatened. Belarus also gained a six-month delay in paying the new rate, and scrambled to try to borrow €1 billion on international markets to plug the gap.

Faced with Mr Putin's visible disdain and repeated public snubs, Mr Lukashenka has reinvented himself as a patriot, adopting the language of national independence and a distinct Belarusan iden-tity. This was remarkable, given the sometimes lethal forms of persecution his regime had adopted towards the country's nation-alist opposition in the past. He has put out strong feelers in 2006 and 2007 about the possibility of a radical change of direction. The West, particularly America, is enthusiastic about this, but insists that a score of political prisoners be released first. After that it is prepared to discuss the restoration of political freedoms in exchange for a safe and dignified exit from power for Mr Lukashenka and his close colleagues. This is already a big step, given that the regime has murdered at least four of its critics.[13] But it seems that it is a step too far for Mr Lukashenka, or for the people who advise him.

The Kremlin has also revived the organisations Russia has set up in the former Soviet Union. The first of these was the Common-wealth of Independent States, which includes the twelve former Soviet republics (but not the Baltic states). In one sense, the CIS has been a startling failure. Of its dozens of documents and agreements on economic and political integration, almost all have proved entirely meaningless. A supposed free trade zone, to have been launched in 2005, has been repeatedly postponed. Even more limited attempts to promote cultural cooperation, or to free the movement of people, capital, goods and services are still bogged down by predatory customs regimes and bureaucracy. The main residual purposes of the CIS are as a source of sinecures,[14] for providing rival teams of election monitors to rebut outside claims of ballot-rigging, and as a means of scheduling meetings with ex-Soviet leaders whom the Kremlin might not want to invite for a bilateral visit to Russia. But it is still a useful backstop. Though Georgia, Ukraine and Turkmenistan have all announced their withdrawal in whole or in part at different times, no member country has actually left altogether.

Other, newer, organisations have a narrower membership and more closely defined goals, chiefly in security cooperation. In 2001 Russia's most loyal allies in ex-Soviet Central Asia, Kazakhstan, Kyrgyzstan, Tajikistan and Uzbekistan, joined along with China in the new Shanghai Cooperation Organisation (SCO).[15] This was originally conceived as a coordination organisation to deal with the evil trinity of post-Soviet politics: 'terrorism, separatism and extremism'. It was paralleled by the Collective Security Treaty Organisation (CSTO),[16] a Kremlin-led version of NATO, with embryonic joint armed forces. In 2005 the SCO widened its focus, adopting a sharply anti-Western and anti-interventionist tone (see Chapter Eight). Forming a joint front on security has proved easier than securing real economic integration. The much-touted Eurasian Economic Community and the Common Economic Space, both intended to be Kremlin-led rivals to the EU, have been conspicuously if unsurprisingly unsuccessful. Integrating open, law-governed economies is hard enough; doing the same for those run by closely allied bureaucrats, tycoons and spooks is much harder. Having shored up its allies, Russia is now projecting its power into the enemy camp. The first and most conventional means for this is old-fashioned politics and diplomacy, involving a mixture of schmoozing, sulks, tantrums and arm-twisting very familiar from the days of the last Cold War.

A big battleground for this is the Organisation for Security and Co-operation in Europe (OSCE). This is the successor to the Conference on Security and Cooperation in Europe (CSCE), which played a big role in projecting Western soft power into the Soviet bloc in the days of the Cold War.[17] After two years of talks in Helsinki, countries on both sides of the Iron Curtain signed the 'Helsinki Final Act' in 1975. The West accepted Europe's current frontiers.[18] In return the Soviet side agreed to respect universal human rights. The Soviet leadership thought this would be merely a paper concession. In fact it allowed campaigners in the east, such as Czechoslovakia's Charter 77 and the Moscow Helsinki Group, to complain that their governments were violating international commitments. That revived the dissident movement and proved a potent propaganda weapon. After the collapse of communism, the CSCE renamed itself the OSCE. Russia used to be a strong supporter, seeing it as a useful alternative to NATO. Now it treats it as a battleground. Russia is determined to throttle the OSCE's election-monitoring arm, the Office for Democratic Institutions and Human Rights (ODIHR, pronounced, aptly enough, 'oh-dear'). For example, it has said that it will accept only the same level of election monitoring that the OSCE extends to countries such as Turkey and America. It repeatedly urges the OSCE to investigate the rights of Russians in the Baltic states (something that it has done, and pronounced satisfactory). More fundamentally, it wants the organisation to return to its original mission, as a place for discussion between nation states, and to stop 'interference' on its own behalf. It wants the secretariat to be strictly accountable to the member states – which, given the OSCE's consensus-based structure, means that it will be able to do almost nothing.

It is a similar story in other international organisations dealing with the ex-communist world. At the Council of Europe, which sponsors the European Court of Human Rights, Russia is blocking reforms that would streamline the submission of complaints. This would particularly benefit Russian citizens, who are the biggest group of plaintiffs. Russia wants the Council of Europe to change its priorities, moving away from human rights towards migration policy, cultural work and crime-fighting. At the EBRD, Russia is blocking projects in pro-Western countries, while insisting on extensive support for Russian companies and infrastructure projects, and the lending of respectability to Kremlin-backed banks that want to approach international capital markets. In the United Nations Development Programme, it has furiously objected to the hiring of Estonia's former prime minister and flat-tax pioneer, Mart Laar, as an adviser to Georgia.

The Kremlin does not find that any kind of multilateral diplomacy comes naturally. Its main political approach is to find bilateral differences and weaknesses and exploit them. It keeps alive, for instance, lingering disputes over ex-Soviet borders, refusing to clear up border disagreements with Estonia and Latvia. Both countries lost small amounts of territory during the Soviet occupation. Both have renounced any claim to them now. But the Kremlin wants to confirm its victory by removing any reference to either country's pre-war frontier. The fiercest tussles are still in the darkest corners. The prime example of this is Moldova, the poorest, weakest and probably most obscure country in Europe. It also has probably the flimsiest historical claim to statehood of any ex-Soviet country.[19] Some, like the Baltic states, had decades of independence in living memory. Others such as Ukraine and Georgia clearly existed as separate countries in the more distant past. But Moldova is an arbitrary creation of the Molotov–Ribbentrop pact, which annexed Romania's eastern provinces to the Soviet Union. After the war the northern and southern extremities were handed over to the 'Ukrainian Soviet Socialist Republic'. The middle bit, plus a strip of mainly Russian-speaking territory on the east bank of the Dniestr River, formed the 'Moldavian Soviet Socialist Republic', under wholly arbitrary boundaries. The usual Stalinist terror ensued. Well-educated people and anyone suspected of Romanian nationalist sympathies were deported to Siberia. The language was rewritten in Cyrillic characters, and declared to be not Romanian but 'Moldovan' (although the spoken versions of both languages remained almost indistinguishable). When the Soviet Union began collapsing, opinion in Moldova divided three ways. A vocal minority simply wanted reunification with Romania, arguing that if the Molotov–Ribbentrop pact was illegitimate, then its consequences must be reversed everywhere. A second, larger group wanted independence for a multi-ethnic Moldova, including both the Romanian-speaking part and the Russophone region of 'Transdniestria' (which happened to be home to all the republic's industrial enterprises). A third group, based in Transdniestria, were Kremlin loyalists and claimed that 'Romanian nationalists' were planning discrimination and reprisals against local Russian-speakers.

With common sense and careful negotiation, the differences between the three sides could have been settled. But such qualities were in short supply in 1990–2. Transdniestria declared independence, and beat back (with extensive support from Russia) a Moldovan government attempt to re-establish control. Since then, the two sides have maintained an uneasy ceasefire. No other country – not even Russia – has formally recognised the Transdniestrian regime. Its narrow strip of territory has become a centre for lucrative smuggling rackets and covert arms sales – businesses in which well-connected politicians in Russia, Ukraine and even Moldova have developed lucrative interests. Russia maintains a force of 'peacekeepers' in Transdniestria, who are also in charge of a colossal conventional weapons dump left over from the days of the Warsaw Pact. Russia was supposed to have withdrawn this by 2001 but claims, implausibly, that the local population will not permit it. It is true that 'spontaneous' demonstrations have blocked the railway tracks near the barracks and depots but it is hard to believe that the otherwise loyal and efficient Transdniestrian security service would not be able to disperse them if necessary.

In theory, five outside powers – America, the OSCE, Russia, Ukraine and the EU – are trying to bring the Moldovan and Transdniestrian sides together, and promote the 'three Ds': the demilitarisation, democratisation and decriminalisation of Trans-dniestria.[20] In practice, these talks, like those in other frozen conflicts, have proved unsuccessful. The Kremlin's bilateral efforts to persuade Moldova to accept a confederation with Transdniestria have come closer to success, though so far American and European intervention has managed to prevent Moldova actually signing up for any Russian peace plan. The real reason why the West is losing in Moldova is not military, however, but the country's own political and economic weakness: the product of corrupt and clueless government. More than almost anywhere else in the ex-communist world, the Euroatlantic option lacks credibility and impact. Almost nobody in the current Moldovan government, for example (the foreign minister included) speaks English. Ro-mania, which should be Moldova's bridge to Europe, is seen as an unpredictable and chauvinistic threat, not a helpful neighbour. On the economic front, Moldova's industry is mostly based on low value-added products such as cheap wine and unprocessed fruit. That makes it vulnerable to the trade sanctions imposed by Russia in 2006. Other ex-communist countries have responded to these by reorienting their exports to Western countries. Moldovan firms seem to lack the ability or willingness to do this. Russia has also squeezed the Transdniestrian economy by raising gas prices and cutting credits. That presents the Moldovan leadership with the tempting prospect of an immediate deal, if they will only drop their remaining ambitions for European integration.[21] If events proceed in this way, the result will be a striking defeat for the Euroatlantic forces in the post-communist world. A combination of timidity and inaction will have allowed Russia to use a mixture of economic, political and military levers against an almost defenceless adversary. In return for sacrificing a few Transdniestrian pawns, Russia may win back a country into its sphere of influence for the first time since the collapse of communism.

In Georgia, by contrast, the exact opposite is happening. Ties with Russia, once regarded as irreplaceable, are shrivelling. Integration with Europe, once a distant dream held only by wild optimists, is a reality. Admittedly, Georgia had a highly unpromising start. With no living memories of lawful life, freedom or statehood to look back on, Georgia's path to independence was rocky. Russia had ruled the Caucasus already for a century before the Bolshevik revolution. It snuffed out the infant Georgian Democratic Republic in 1921. In the 1930s, Stalin applied a reign of terror that the Baltic states and other wartime captives would find all too familiar ten years later. Tens of thousands of people were deported or murdered.

As communist rule crumbled in the late 1980s, nationalist leaders such as the erratic philologist Zviad Gamsakhurdia, backed by enthusiastic nationalist militias, faced an almost impossible task, running a country with no secure borders and no tradition of statehood. They showed little interest in the mundane tasks that were occupying the Estonians, such as stabilising the currency, attracting foreign investors and establishing a modern civil service. Instead they fought civil wars with the country's two main ethnic minorities, the Ossetians and the Abkhaz. Both of these enjoyed a degree of autonomy under Soviet rule, and disliked the idea of

Georgian independence, particularly if based on Mr Gamsakhurdia's swaggering and eccentric ethno-nationalism. The results were appalling. In the Abkhaz capital Sukhumi, anonymous arsonists torched the national library, museum and state archive. It was as if Washington, DC, lost the Library of Congress, the Kennedy Centre and the Smithsonian in one blaze. The Abkhaz,[22] with strong support from both Russians and Chechen extremists who disliked the Georgians even more than the Russians, triumphed. Two hundred and fifty thousand ethnic Georgians – around half the population – fled.

That difficult birth nearly proved fatal for Georgia. For almost a decade, it was written off by Western allies as a hopeless basket case. Mr Gamsakhurdia was deposed in 1992 and Eduard Shevardnadze, who had been Mr Gorbachev's foreign minister, took over. He brought stability, but no reform. Crony capitalism took root: the Shevardnadze family had an eye for profit, but no sense of how to build lasting economic growth. Russia maintained troops in Georgia, and occasionally used them. Reform was skin deep.[23] All that changed in 2003 when the Georgian population, almost Italian in its love of good company and dislike for organisation, rose up against the incompetent and increasingly authoritarian Shevardnadze regime. That put in power Mikheil Saakashvili, an American-educated, *Economist*-reading lawyer, determined to reform Georgia at warp speed, with Estonia as his explicit model. Though nobody would cite the country as a model of freedom, pluralism and good government, progress has been astonishing. Foreign investment is pouring in. Public services are improving, taxes are flat, the economy stable and booming. Whole government departments, such as the notoriously corrupt traffic police, have been simply abolished.

The result is to reverse Georgia's magnetic polarity. It no longer repels. It attracts. The first region to shift allegiance was Ajaria, a semi-independent region that had become a magnet for international organised crime under its leader, Aslan Abashidze. His popularity – genuine in the early years of his regime – was based on having spared his people, Georgian-speaking Muslims, from the miseries afflicting the rest of the country. But as that chaos and poverty turned into economic growth, stability and political freedom his hold weakened. In a putsch in spring 2004, Mr Abashidze was forced out by popular protests and fled to Moscow. Ajaria has become a Georgian showcase, attracting foreign investment and tourism from the whole Black Sea region and beyond. Mr Abashidze had been a strong supporter of Mr Putin's, but his departure was a minor blow compared to the effect that Georgia's prosperity had on the weaker of the Kremlin's two puppet states in Georgia, South Ossetia. The Ossetians' historic homeland straddles the Caucasus mountains. On the north side, the Ossetians, orthodox by religion, find themselves stranded in Russia's worst-governed region amid increasingly restive Muslim populations in the neighbouring republics. South Ossetia was an autonomous region of Soviet Georgia; it has retained a phoney independence, Kremlin-backed but unrecognised elsewhere, since 1992.

Initially, Mr Saakashvili tried force, sending his interior ministry troops in an abortive attempt to seize control of South Ossetia. That brought widespread international censure and underlined the Georgian leader's sometimes alarming approach to decision-making. Since then, he has tried a different tactic, exploiting the Kremlin's crude imposition of its own stooges in place of the native South Ossetian politicians who led the fight against Georgian nationalism in the early 1990s. These founding fathers have formed a government-in-exile that strongly backs reintegration with Georgia. Georgia's economic prosperity dwarfs the effect of South Ossetia's only industry: smuggling. Significantly, some of the seventy-thousand South Ossetian population have even started commuting to work to jobs in Georgia. They find there not the autocratic ethnocracy depicted by Kremlin propaganda, but a thriving and tolerant society. Despite increasing levels of Kremlin subsidy, the South Ossetians' historic sympathies to Moscow may be shrivelling.[24]

All this is good news for Georgian citizens of all ethnicities and a sharp contrast to the position on the other side of the Caucasus mountains. But it is bad news for the Kremlin, which sees successful neighbours as a problem, not a benefit. For Mr Saakashvili does not want just to reform his country's domestic arrangements. He wants to anchor it in the Euroatlantic economic and security structures that have served other countries so well. Enthusiasm in NATO and the EU for admitting Georgia has been minimal. But it is growing, and the main reason is the same as stoked the Baltics' case for admission. This country is in some respects already recognisably European. And it is visibly under threat from Russia. Trouble started brewing in 2006, when from March to May Russia imposed an escalating series of import restrictions, first on wine, vegetables, and fruits; then on sparkling wine and brandy, finally Georgian mineral water[25] – at the time one of the country's most important exports. The ostensible reason was concerns over hygiene, although no such concerns were raised by other countries. On 8 July Russia abruptly closed the only legal land border crossing, allegedly for some construction works. That halted, in effect, all Georgian exports to Russia. On 27 September 2006, Georgia arrested four officers of the GRU. They had been planning a coup, Mr Saakashvili insists. His American-trained counter-intelligence service had warned him that they could no longer keep track of all the Russian spies and thugs who were hard at work trying to sabotage reforms and undermine the authorities' hold on power. That prompted a remarkably angry response from the Kremlin. Mr Putin compared the Georgian action to the policies of Stalin's KGB chief Lavrenti Beria.[26] A more cool-headed Georgian leader might have quietly deported the men. But Mr Saakashvili, whose charm is matched only by his temper, ordered them to be paraded in front of the television cameras as they were handed over to the Russian authorities. Russia recalled its ambassador, and cut postal, phone and banking links with Georgia. Gazprom said it would double the gas price it charges Georgia, from $110 to $230 per thousand m³.

More sinisterly, other bits of Russian officialdom such as the tax police, immigration authorities and school administrators started harassing people with Georgian surnames. Russian officials singled out Georgians as illegal immigrants; police in Moscow started carrying out spot checks of documents of people congregating near places such as the Georgian Embassy and church. At some schools in Moscow, the police demanded lists of children with ethnic Georgian surnames. This would be as absurd as trying to round up Irish citizens in Britain or America simply on the basis of surnames such as Donnelly or O'Reilly. Grigory Chkhartishvili, for example, is a successful author of detective stories under the pen name Boris Akunin. He has only the most distant family connections to Georgia. Seemingly for no reason other than his distinctive surname, his publisher's officers were raided by the tax police.[27]

On 6 October, the Russian authorities began deporting the detainees. According to a report by Human Rights Watch,[28] some 2,380 Georgians were expelled in the next two months, while some 2,200 others left by their own means after receiving deportation orders. An unknown number of other Georgians simply decided it would be better to leave. Some Georgians were indeed in Russia illegally, but those deported included Russian citizens of Georgian ethnic background, and Georgians with valid visas and work permits. Those detained had little right of appeal or access to lawyers, and either 'perfunctory' court hearings (in the report's words) or none at all. Conditions during the deportations were often harsh and sometimes abominable. According to Human

Rights Watch, some detainees were deprived of food and water for extended periods of time, or told to drink from the toilet bowl. Medical care was routinely denied, leading to at least two deaths, those of Manana Jabelia and Tengiz Togonidze. Though the anti-Georgian campaign ebbed as quickly as it swelled, the way in which Kremlin-sponsored xenophobia has leached into so many corners of Russian life was alarmingly clear. Russia seemed to expect Georgia to buckle. But as so often with economic sanctions imposed by the Kremlin, the attempt to exert political pressure through Soviet-era trade ties proved counter-productive.[29] Georgian exporters raised quality and packaging standards and started to export to new markets. Mr Saakashvili, who had long been urging his country's entrepreneurs to shed their dependence on Russian customers, said he was grateful. Georgia's growth rate lost at most a couple of percentage points as a result of the Kremlin sanctions. And the country's morale soared.

The tactics used on Georgia and Moldova exemplify the Kremlin's use of 'hard power'. This is not principally military force (though the threat of that plays a role). It is chiefly the use of economic and legal levers, and, most of all, the use of the pipelines inherited from the Soviet Union. In 2003, the Kremlin shut off shipments to the Latvian oil terminal at Ventspils, in the hope of forcing its sale to a Russian oil company. When in 2005 Lithuania sold its oil refinery at Mažeikiai, the most important industrial installation in the Baltic states, to a Polish company, rather than to the Russian bidder preferred by the Kremlin, Russia shut down the ill-named *Druzhba* (Friendship) pipeline that supplied it.[30] Russia's official explanation was that the pipeline needed repairs. That was a blatantly political move. A Lithuanian offer to examine the nature of the problem, and to help with the cost of dealing with it, was abruptly declined. 'Sorry, guys, you sold the refinery to the wrong people,' a visiting Russian parliamentarian confided to his Lithuanian counterparts. Russia now says that the pipeline is so old that it is not worth repairing at all. Lithuania is importing oil to Mažeikiai from its coastal terminal at Butingė. That is profitable while oil prices are high; when they fall, Mažeikiai risks bankruptcy. After a row with Estonia over a Soviet-era war memorial in 2007 (see below in this chapter), Russia cut oil shipments. 'Business will develop where the situation is comfortable and profitable and where the moral and political climate is favourable,' said the transport minister, Igor Levitin.[31] Yet the immediate casualty of the move was not Estonia's booming economy, which was growing at a headlong 10 per cent annual rate, but the shareholders of its empty oil terminals – mostly ethnic Russians.

As a study[32] by Robert Larsson of Sweden's Defence Research Institute shows, Russia uses the energy weapon with surprising frequency, while at the same time insisting that it is an ultra-reliable supplier. The secret of this apparent paradox is that supplies to West European countries are rarely interrupted, and never deliberately. The targets are invariably the former satellite states that – unlike their Western counterparts – typically have no other independent source of supply. The simplest approach is to cut supplies off, while blaming sabotage or natural disasters. Power lines to Georgia, for example, fell victim to mysterious and simultaneous bombing attacks in 2006. Russia not only refused to allow Georgian investigators to see the evidence, but also declined any offer of help to speed the repair work. The other means is sharp price rises, which often seem to bear no relation either to geography or history. However, like the Kremlin's other tactics, the energy weapon so far has proved not only blunt but ineffective. It also sharply underlines the case for diversification: Georgia, for example, managed to restore a decrepit Soviet-era pipeline to bring gas from Azerbaijan. What works rather better is to create economic dependence through friendly economic ties, creating a strong business lobby that wants good relations with Russia no matter what. When the Estonian government convened a high-level seminar to discuss energy security, it invited as a matter of course a representative from the national gas company, Eesti Gas. The invitation was accepted – but then an embarrassed company official phoned back so say that it would not be taking part on instructions from a shareholder: Gazprom.

The hardest form of 'hard power' is military sabre-rattling. That mainly involves military exercises and minor irritants. A classic Russian tactic is to send unauthorised flights into another country's airspace to test its defences. If it complains, Russia huffily contests the fact that the infringement occurred, or says that it was a simple misunderstanding and that the targeted country is overreacting. For countries such as the Baltic states and Georgia, which have no air defences of their own, such probes are a humiliating reminder of their vulnerability. All three Baltic countries, for example, are dependent on a squadron of borrowed NATO fighter planes whose record in reacting to Russian intruders has been less than impressive. War games send a similar message. The Russian forces in Pskov, for example, just across the border from Estonia and Latvia, practised the recapture of the Baltic states in 2007. Details of the exercise are sketchy, but it seems to have involved an inter-vention to protect the rights of 'Russian-speakers' threatened with violence by local 'nationalists'. The aim of the exercise was to see how easily the Russian invading forces could capture the airfields and ports, thus preventing NATO from reinforcing its allies.

Sometimes the games are real: on the night of 11 March 2007, a fleet of helicopters spent two hours firing cannon, rockets and an anti-tank missile at three villages in the Kodori gorge, a region of Abkhazia where the Georgian authorities have recovered control and set up a parallel administration. Luckily, nobody was killed in the helicopter attack, as, quite by chance, the buildings hit by the rockets were unoccupied. Russia denied any responsibility. When UNOMIG, the United Nations force that monitors the uneasy ceasefire in Abkhazia, began an investigation, Russia repeatedly stonewalled, declining to provide aviation logs, or trace the origin of a missile whose parts were recovered after the attack. But it was hard to avoid the facts: more than fifty witnesses said they heard helicopters; no other country in the region has helicopters with night-fighting capabilities; the munitions used were Russian-made. Russia insisted that there was 'no definitive evidence' about the origin of the attack and argued that Georgians were the likely culprits: after all, if the attack reflects badly on Russia, then Russia's enemies must be the most likely perpetrators.[33] A Kremlin spokes-man said, 'Observers have noticed lots of actions of a provocative nature from the Georgian side.'[34] It is, of course, far more likely that the attack was meant to warn off the Georgians from extending their reach into Abkhazia. Many outsiders shrugged their shoulders, and thought the whole incident was just a baffling but isolated affair. It was not: on 6 August 2007 a Russian-made Raduga Kh-58 anti-radar missile, fired by one of two Sukhoi Su-24 jets in Georgian airspace, landed in a village near Tbilisi.[35] Its 150kg warhead failed to explode. Again, the facts point in one direction only: Georgia's air force has no Su-24s, while Russia's has hun-dreds. Georgian radar produced records showing that they had tracked the intruders entering the country's airspace from Russia. The most likely planned target was nearby, a new NATO-com-patible radar station. It is possible that the Russian pilot panicked, or that the missile misfired, or the whole thing was intended merely to test outside reaction to an aborted attack. If the latter is the case, the Kremlin will have drawn a striking conclusion: that Georgia's allies are largely unwilling to speak out in its defence, or to push for international organisations to investigate. Only the Baltic states came out quickly with strong statements supporting Georgia;

Sweden joined them later. Most other countries said they were 'concerned', or appealed to 'both sides' to 'exercise restraint'. An OSCE investigation said that, given the conflicting accounts, it was hard to say what had really happened. Russia said this backed its own stance, that the whole thing was a stunt cooked up by the Georgians to gain international sympathy. It is hard to imagine a more powerful signal to the Kremlin that military adventurism in the former empire comes with no political price attached.

The more hard power is used, the less it can be defended on moral and legal grounds. That means that it can be counter-productive. Western governments may not wish to complain directly, but their enthusiasm for close ties with the Kremlin cools while Russia's critics gain more ammunition and former satellites' desire to break away is fuelled. The use of hard power usually involves the conspicuous rejection of international norms, including those to which Russia is publicly committed, such as territorial integrity, peaceful settlement of international disputes and free and fair elections. The Kremlin's clumsy intervention in the 2004 Ukrainian election, for example, helped ignite popular discontent and gave the organisers of the 'Orange Revolution' a handy extra foreign villain to add to the panoply of domestic ones.[36]

Using soft power, by contrast, may be less conspicuous and costly. The simplest feature of the Kremlin's rhetorical counter-attack is an appeal to national self-interest (or, more accurately, the self-interest of national elites). Konstantin Kosachev, chairman of the Duma foreign affairs committee, terms it 'absurd' that ex-Soviet countries should shun the benefits of cooperation with Russia and instead want to 'enter the straitjacket of European institutions and fall under the diktat of Brussels'.[37] In other words, countries that throw in their lot with the Western camp, far from gaining freedom, lose their sovereignty and are forced to accept an alien set of values. 'Sovereign democracy' not only allows rulers to run their country as they like but also contrasts with the sometimes onerous international obligations of Euroatlanticism.

The most effective manifestation of this is in the Kremlin's own version of 'people power', both in the form of mass public movements and phoney NGOs. Here the main asset is ethnic Russians, up to 25m of whom were living in other bits of the Soviet Union when it collapsed. Although that number was probably exaggerated, and many millions have since returned to Russia or changed their ethnic self-description, those that remain form both a powerful reservoir of support for pro-Russian and anti-Western policies and a pretext for Russian intervention, ostensibly to defend their rights. Before 2000, interest in this subject among politicians in high office was patchy. It was mainly expressed as a populist concern by ambitious contenders for power, such as the mayor of Moscow, Yuri Luzhkov. One reason for this was the philosophical conundrum posed by supporting Russian separatists in places such as Nara in Estonia, Crimea in Ukraine or the breakaway enclave of Transdniestria in Moldova. Their leaders loudly proclaimed their desire to break away from their titular governments and join Russia. That sat oddly with the Kremlin's official denunciation of 'separatism' in places such as Chechnya or, potentially, Tatarstan.

Mr Putin has given a sharp new edge to Russian concerns on this issue. As early as April 2000, he endorsed a new military doctrine that defined 'discrimination' against its citizens abroad as one of the military threats facing Russia.[38] In his 2001 address to the upper house of parliament, the Federation Council, he widened that to include not just Russian citizens, but 'compatriots', a loose term that can be used to include any Russian-speaker with a pro-Kremlin orientation. In 2002, in a speech to diplomats, he again underlined the importance he attached to the subject. Russia set up new bodies to encourage migration back to Russia, to simplify the procedures for gaining Russian citizenship, and – most importantly

– to funnel cash and other support to pro-Kremlin organisations outside Russia. Tougher visa regulations for Georgians, Azeris and others accentuated the choice: without a Russian passport it became much harder for them to study, work or trade.

An early example of Kremlin-driven 'people power' came in the largely Russian-populated Ukrainian region of Crimea, where communist and pro-Moscow groups won an overwhelming victory in regional elections in March 2006. Aided by FSB and GRU officials, and family members linked to the Russian naval base at Sevastopol, pro-Kremlin Crimean politicians organised highly successful mass demonstrations against NATO exercises planned for June of that year. These exercises, involving drills for peace-keeping and emergency relief, had taken place in Ukraine since 1997 without attracting significant opposition. The protests spread to other Russian-speaking regions of eastern Ukraine, which declared themselves to be 'NATO-free zones'. Supporters of the defeated candidate in the 2004 presidential elections, Viktor Yanukovych, began to copy the tactics of their 'orange' adversaries, adopting the colour blue and organising rallies featuring pop music, celebrity endorsements and other razzmatazz.[39] The Crimea protests added an extra political burden to the already flimsy chances of forming a pro-Western governing coalition at national level in Kyiv. As soon as that coalition's chances collapsed, paving the way for a different, more pro-Russian administration, the protests abruptly stopped.

Elsewhere, Russia is using a new, subtler and more effective weapon: NGOs. Financed by Western think tanks, charities and (sometimes) government agencies, these have proved the most effective way of organising and financing popular movements for political freedoms in ex-communist countries. In the Kremlin's eyes, they are little more than fronts for foreign intelligence agencies. If their work results in more influence for America,

Britain and Western Europe in the region, then it clearly must be sponsored by the CIA, MI6 and the like. The idea that the peoples of Eastern Europe might genuinely want to be in alliance with the world's largest free countries is dismissed as sentimental nonsense. Nikolai Patrushev, head of the FSB, said in 2005: 'NGOs must not be allowed to engage in any activity they like.' He suggested a CIS-wide legal code be brought in to regulate their activity 'before the wave of Orange Revolutions spreads'.[40] Now Russia is trying to use the same tactic. Kremlin-financed think tanks have been set up in Ukraine, the Caucasus and Moldova, coupled with media outlets, internet websites and networks of academics. A senior Kremlin official, Modest Kolerov, who heads the department for 'interregional and cultural ties with foreign countries',[41] is in charge of this network, which includes phoney news sites on the internet that peddle distorted or outright invented versions of events. Sometimes these are so preposterous that it is hard to imagine anyone believing them. In 2005, for example, the now-defunct www.news24.ru reported that the riots in suburban Paris had been incited by 'Estonian nationalists'. When Estonia's justice minister Rein Lang marked his birthday with a private performance of a satirical play about Hitler,[42] Russian websites reported this as if the minister had celebrated his birthday by staging a Nazi rally.[43]

The most elaborate disinformation efforts are mounted in English, with a polished presentation that belies their origins. The *Tiraspol Times*, for example, pumps out propaganda on behalf of the separatist regime in Transdniestria. It purports to be a normal newspaper, with an online edition that carries pictures of a printed version and a glossy weekly review. Anyone looking at it would think it was another one of the many English-language papers to be found throughout Eastern Europe, where eager-beaver tyros straight out of journalism school scratch a living under the direction of hard-bitten locals. The truth is rather stranger. None of the journalists who purportedly work in the 'newsroom' seem to have any verifiable existence outside the paper's webpages. The paper publishes no address or phone number. No real-world journalist in either Transdniestria or Moldova has ever seen a representative from the *Tiraspol Times* at any public event – even those that are reported, seemingly first-hand, in its pages. Nor, indeed, has any Western embassy or other official source I contacted in the region ever seen a physical copy of the paper: it appears to exist only in online form. The paper's finances are mysterious: it carries very little advertising, and does not appear to take any subscriptions. Its publisher is an elusive Irishman called Des Grant with his own (real-world) media business in that country and a longstanding connection to Transdniestria. He says the paper gets money from 'sponsors' but declines to provide any further details. A bit of internet detective work shows that the website is registered at a real address in the Transdniestrian capital, Tiraspol – but on inspection this proves to be shared by a hotel and the headquarters of one of the main local political parties. At neither place does anyone know anything of the *Tiraspol Times*.

Still stranger was the 'International Council for Democratic Institutions and State Sovereignty' (ICDISS), which claimed to be a heavyweight think tank based in Washington, DC. It had an impressive website, and had produced a heavily footnoted report, seemingly authored by distinguished international lawyers, that backed the Transdniestrian regime's case for international recognition. It even had a Wikipedia entry, cross-referenced to other real-world organisations.[44] Russian-language media in the region gleefully took up the report, arguing that it showed that international opinion was shifting in the Kremlin's direction. On closer examination, this proved little more substantial than the *Tiraspol Times*. The ICDISS's 'officers' proved to be just as elusive as the inhabitants of that paper's 'newsroom'. Nobody was willing to talk on the phone; e-mails provided only a series of ever more evasive excuses. The published report – which seemed to be the only one ever produced by the organisation – had lifted large chunks of a quite different document, dealing with a different international legal issue. The international lawyers cited in the report angrily denied having had anything to do with it; shortly afterwards, the document disappeared from the ICDISS website. It was hard to avoid the conclusion that a sophisticated disinformation exercise had been tripped up by its own overconfidence.[45]

The exercises of Kremlin soft power in Moldova and Crimea have so far been mere sideshows, however. The big argument is in the Baltic states. In a narrow sense it is about history; more widely it rages over the right of these countries to determine their own cultural and linguistic future. The central issue is the fate of the Soviet-era migrants (mostly Russian-speaking but not all ethnic Russians) who were brought to Estonia and Latvia in the Soviet era to boost the industrial workforce and to dilute the occupied countries' national identity.[46] Deeply resented under Soviet rule, this became a central political issue once independence was regained. In Estonia's case, 88 per cent of the population had been ethnic Estonians before the war.[47] By 1989 that had shrunk to 61.5 per cent. The Estonian language was pushed out of public life.[48] On regaining independence, Estonia said citizenship for occupation-era migrants and their descendants would be conditional on a basic knowledge of Estonian language and history.

That struck many as harsh. After all, around half of these people had been born in Estonia. They had not chosen to come there. It would be unfair to leave them as stateless, casting the shadows of suffering and injustice still wider. Still less would it be fair to discriminate against them in the workplace. Lithuania gave automatic citizenship to all Soviet citizens living on its territory at the time of independence: that included less than a tenth of the population who described their ethnicity as Russian, and a similar number calling themselves Polish. But Estonia's and Latvia's predicament was different. Migration, mainly of ethnic Russians, during the Soviet era had been far larger. Many of the 'illegal immigrants' who had arrived during this period were deeply opposed to Estonian independence. They mostly spoke no Estonian and had no desire to learn. Indeed, if addressed in Estonian, they would object. If Estonia set no conditions for citizenship, the chances that the new arrivals and their descendants would integrate seemed slim. Estonia and Latvia gave automatic citizenship therefore only to the citizens of the pre-war republic and their descendants. Estonia made an exception for a limited number of Russians who had actively supported the Congress of Estonia, a shadow parliament set up during the struggle to regain independence; they were entitled to citizenship on demand. Everyone else had to apply for naturalisation.

Many outsiders thought that was dangerously mistaken. The wars in ex-Yugoslavia showed how quickly newly independent countries could alienate minorities with disastrous results, requiring outside intervention, with a terrible cost. But in the Baltics, these fears proved groundless. One reason was that the local Russian leaders were a deeply unimpressive lot: Soviet has-beens and never-weres. Another was economics: the Baltic states were thriving while Russia was in chaos, meaning that few Russians decided to take advantage of resettlement grants and go home to the motherland. Some that did soon tried to return. In fact, Estonia's citizenship and language laws (like the broadly similar ones in Latvia) have proved successful. Although Russian remains widely spoken, the national languages have regained unquestioned prominence. By mid-2007, nearly 84 per cent of the population held Estonian citizenship, up from 68 per cent in 1991. As of mid-2007 around 8 per cent were citizens of other countries (mostly Russia) and a similar number were still stateless. Several thousand people a year continue to receive citizenship by naturalisation. Some international organisations make occasional suggestions about tweaks to the law – such as cutting the cost of language lessons. But in Europe and America the principle that Estonia and Latvia award citizenship to those who make a conscious choice and show the necessary commitment seems established.

Russia, by contrast, contests the citizenship policy both in principle and in practice. From the Kremlin's point of view, all Soviet citizens living in Estonia at the time of independence deserve the same treatment. The Estonians' policy is discrimination, pure and simple, based on the crudest form of ethnic nationalism. The West's collusion in this is an act of gross hypocrisy. If true, that would be a grave charge. Estonia's counter-argument, though, is a strong one: citizenship is given on historical, not ethnic grounds. Nearly a tenth of the population of the pre-war republic were ethnic Russians. Any who are alive today, and any who can prove descent from them, get citizenship automatically. The same is true in Latvia. Furthermore, Estonia has now relaxed its citizenship law, creating exemptions for those who have finished an Estonian-language school, and for the elderly or mentally handicapped. Non-citizens were allowed to vote in local elections, and, assuming they spoke the national language sufficiently, were able to hold all jobs except those involving national security. But the Kremlin keeps up a constant barrage of criticism, claiming that the rights of Russians are being abused and demanding that the outside world do something about it.[49]

People power and conventional political pressure combined in late April 2007 in the Kremlin's reaction to an Estonian government decision to move a Soviet war memorial, and some nearby graves, from central Tallinn to a military cemetery. Though the memorial had become a magnet for extremists on both sides, creating a minor policing problem, it was not a national security threat and many in Estonia and abroad regarded the decision to relocate it as precipitate and unwise. Although Estonians disliked the statue, as a symbol of the renewal of a hated Soviet occupation, in the eyes of many Estonian Russians it was 'Alyosha the Liberator' representing the heroism and sacrifice of the struggle against Hitler.

On the night of 26 April, as the Estonian authorities cordoned off the statue and prepared to move it, a mob looted the centre of Tallinn, breaking windows and torching bus shelters. Chanting 'It's all ours', 'Fuck Estonia' and 'USSR for ever', the mainly young and often drunken protesters were to many Estonians a sign of Russians reverting to type. The truth was less alarming: although the majority of Estonian Russians objected to the decision to move the statue, only a tiny minority of them expressed their views violently. What was truly worrying was that the Kremlin not only did not condemn the violence being perpetrated in the name of Russian patriotism, but endorsed it, praising the looters as youthful patriots who were protesting about Estonia's 'fascist' vandalism of a sacred edifice. The Russian media portrayed those arrested as political prisoners; the one fatality of the night of 30 April, an ethnic Russian stabbed in a fight over looted property, was portrayed as a victim of police brutality. Estonia initially found itself in perilous diplomatic isolation. Other countries mumbled excuses and banalities, saying that Estonia and Russia should sort out their differences peacefully. Only Poland, itself no stranger to the attacks of the Kremlin propaganda machine, came out at once with forthright support.

Luckily for the Estonians, Russia grossly overplayed its hand. *Nashi* and other organisations attacked Estonia's Moscow embassy. They defaced the embassy's outside walls and placed loudspeakers against them, blasting round-the-clock military music from the Stalin era into the building.[50] They jostled the

Estonian ambassador, Marina Kaljurand, when she tried to give a press conference (the child of a Latvian–Russian mixed marriage, she was hard to demonise as the champion of neo-Nazi revanchism). The pickets – without any legal authority and with the supine cooperation of the city's normally officious police – blocked the street, checked the documents of passers-by and organised the noisy and sometimes violent protests, including the threat to 'dismantle' the embassy.[51] When the Swedish ambassador visited in a sign of belated solidarity, the pickets tried to overturn his car. All that was a clear breach of the Vienna Convention (something that the Kremlin insists be meticulously observed when Russian embassies attract protesters). A Russian delegation invited to Tallinn, echoing the language used by Stalin's emissary Andrei Zhdanov in 1940, demanded the resignation of Estonia's government and a criminal investigation into the repression of 'anti-fascists'. That was a big mistake. Had the Kremlin stayed in the background, Estonia would have suffered heavy damage to its reputation. Western pressure for a change of citizenship and language policies would have increased. Quite possibly the government would have had to resign. But by overplaying its hand, the Kremlin made even the exercise of soft power at an easy target ineffective and counter-productive. Any queasiness that the outside world felt about Estonia's seemingly cavalier treatment of a war memorial was counter-balanced by outright nausea at Russia's response. Statements of support began flooding in. Estonia's president, Mr Ilves, was invited to the White House. In turn, the Russian media became almost hysterical. *Komsomolskaya Pravda* (Young Communist League Truth) printed an astonishing piece of doggerel looking forward to the day when the Russian armed forces might retake Estonia by force. The final extract reads:

The Pskov division is not far off,
A short forced march and Tallinn falls.

They may say public opinion will be against it
Now that Estonia is in NATO.
So what? Who in NATO cares?
I will not hang on their every word.
So what if they call it an occupation?
They will grumble and grind their teeth
Saying freedom's flame is doused again.
But we will settle with those greedy swine
Who would sell their mother and father for gas.
I am not scared to tell you, Estonians,
The EU will not be able to help you . . .[52]

The Kremlin's activities in its former empire are mainly organised
from the shadows. As well as Mr Kolerov, the mainstream external
intelligence services have been given lavish resources and unlimited
political backing since Mr Putin came to power. In a speech in July
2007, he said the foreign intelligence service, the SVR,[53] should
'permanently increase its capabilities'.[54] The FSB, which was once
restricted to dealing with security threats inside Russia, now has a full
legal licence to operate abroad. As well as promoting disinformation
and manipulating public life, these two agencies and the GRU all try
to penetrate the central institutions of state in the ex-Soviet
countries. Counter-intelligence officers note with alarm their success
in recruiting and placing agents and informants in the criminal justice
system, the armed forces, the security and intelligence services, the
foreign, defence and interior ministries and elsewhere. According to
a Western intelligence officer in a particularly vulnerable ex-Soviet
country: 'Nothing happens here that the Russians don't know
about, and nothing happens that they don't like.'[55]

During the Estonia crisis, Russia opened a new front: cyberwarfare. National security experts have been worried for years about
the internet's potential for disruption, subversion, criminality and
espionage. Sometimes the perpetrators are gangsters, sometimes
terrorists; sometimes they have the backing of a nation state. In
Estonia's case, the attacks seemed to mix all three factors. The
technicalities of cyberwarfare are shrouded in jargon. But the one
word outsiders need to remember is 'botnets'. These are remotely
controlled networks of computers that have been hijacked, usually
by means of virus-infected e-mails, and then are used to swamp the
target by deluging it with internet traffic: imagine a website that
normally handles a few hundred visitors a minute, which then
experiences thousands every second. Luckily, Estonia's internet
capabilities are excellent. The only point at which lives could have
been endangered was when, for a brief period, the cyberattacks
managed to knock out the telephone number for the emergency
services. But they did not succeed in disrupting electric power, or
making sewage pumping stations run backwards, or any of the
other nightmarish scenarios that preoccupy cyberwarfare experts.
The main effect was to disrupt Estonia's links with the outside
world. Important government websites were unavailable – including those, such as the foreign ministry, that were most needed to
counter the Kremlin propaganda offensive. Tracing the source of
the cyberattacks was tricky. The infected computers were in
botnets that spread all over the world. It is possible, though
unlikely, that cybercriminals in Bulgaria and Australia suddenly
decided for reasons of their own to try a systematic assault on
Estonia. It seems far more probable that somebody paid the owners
of botnets to mount the attacks: the most likely culprit by far is
someone in the Kremlin or close to it.[56]

The 'bronze soldier' row is unlikely to be the last time that Russia
tries to exert influence on the Baltic states. Russian-speakers,

particularly in Estonia and Latvia, are still dangerously unintegrated and open to incitement or provocation by extremist movements. In the 1990s, security services in all three Baltic states found links between local ultra-nationalists and Russia's secret services. Persuading local skinheads to attack Russian cultural, social or historical landmarks, or ethnic Russians in person, would give the Kremlin the perfect excuse to demand that the rights of 'compatriots' be protected. Another potential vulnerability is the transit agreements across Lithuania to Kaliningrad. Although Russia now transports most of the sensitive military traffic to its western bastion by ferry, it retains the right to send sealed trains across Lithuanian territory and also has an air corridor available on request. Lithuanian 'extremists' blew up this railway in 1994 but luckily no casualties resulted. It could easily happen again. Sabotage to the power generation network could lead to blackouts in Kaliningrad, again giving the Kremlin the pretext to intervene to stop an economic 'blockade'. Russia may also turn attention again to the Crimea, where its new tactic appears to be to stoke radical Muslim sentiments among the region's indigenous, but now marginalised, Tatar population. That would allow Russia to complain that Islamist terrorists were threatening the security of its naval base at the Crimean port of Sevastopol, home to the Black Sea Fleet, thus creating a pretext for intervention.[57]

Such threats lie in the future. Russia's biggest chance now lies in the failure of the ex-communist countries to make the most of the chances of the past decade. Admittedly, their starting point in 1989 was intimidatingly difficult. They had been cut off from the outside world, their economies distorted by communist rule and public-spiritedness obliterated. The habits of how to live in a free society were distant memories, not practical skills. They had to be re-learned, and at a time of wrenching economic change. It is easy therefore to see why many of the most sophisticated foreign-policy thinkers in Western Europe saw the collapse of communism not as a triumph, but as a tragedy. By keeping the backward nations of the Soviet bloc locked up behind totalitarian bars, the way was clear for the more civilised and advanced countries of Western Europe to consolidate their successful economic and political integration. The old EU could absorb occasional new members, but the difficulties presented by integrating Greece, which joined in 1981, made many feel that the outer limits had already been reached. The fall of the Berlin Wall turned the comfortable life of the West Europeans upside down. 'This is the biggest catastrophe to hit my country for decades,' a thoughtful Finnish diplomat told me in 1991, just after Estonia had regained independence. Little seemed left of the newly re-emerged country's pre-war charms: it was all too easy to imagine its future as a poverty-stricken gangster land, riven with ethnic conflicts and run by strange bearded men with bad teeth and eccentric ideas. Finland and Estonia shared a linguistic and cultural heritage – but little else. 'There is no way we can abandon them. There is no way we can protect them. There is no way that we can civilise them,' he moaned. His worst nightmare, he explained, was that Finland would sooner or later inevitably be drawn into a row with Russia on Estonia's behalf.

Austrians felt similarly, seeing only threats, not opportunities, from the end of their carefully structured and highly profitable neutrality between NATO and the Warsaw Pact. Germany's weekly *Der Spiegel* ran a cover story in 1990 on the tens of thousands of refugees from hunger and chaos in the former Soviet Union who would inevitably head westwards.[58] Germany imposed stiff tariffs on Polish exports that threatened its 'strategic' industries. These included shovels and garden gnomes. Such sharp fears soon seemed passé. The EU grudgingly decided that, in principle if nothing else, it had to expand to include at least those ex-communist countries that would swallow whole the Union's voluminous rulebook. That set the stage for a lengthy and often mind-numbing series of wrangles marked by disingenuous behaviour on both sides. Applicant countries would sometimes actually meet standards in full, but more often merely pretend they had. EU inspectors would fume and produce cross reports about the backsliders, always aware that their objections might be overruled for political reasons.

By 2004, it seemed as though the historic journey of the ex-communist countries was all but over. They were not only anchored in the main Western clubs, but the nightmarish memories of communist rule were fading. The magnetic effect of EU membership had forced them to accelerate economic reform. Foreign investment was flooding in, economic growth was rocketing. Joining the euro was only a matter of time. Public administration, although still deplorable in many cases, was slowly modernising. Perhaps most importantly, it was a condition of joining the EU and NATO that ancient historical quarrels were forgotten. But since 2004, things have started to unscramble. The sacrifices and discipline needed to join a club are usually greater than those required to stay in it, and the EU and NATO are no exception. Reform has stalled, and continuing economic growth means that politicians see little need to take painful but necessary decisions. Corruption is rising again, as is the political temperature. The staid consensual politics of old Europe disappear quickly when you cross the old Iron Curtain. The rule is minority governments, sharply polarised politics, and a heavy diet of scandal, usually involving some mixture of corruption, organised crime and misbehaviour by the intelligence services.

Another ingredient is in some countries a sharp disregard for what Western Europe sees as the elementary values of a liberal society at home and abroad. Poland in particular has attracted criticism for its clumsy and abrasive diplomacy. The country's president Lech Kaczynski, for example, scandalised Western opinion at an EU summit in 2007 by arguing for greater voting weights for Poland, on the grounds that, had it not been for Germany's actions in the Second World War, his country's population would now be 50 per cent larger. That may be true, but it is a world away from the polite and tactful tones in which EU meetings are normally conducted. Such behaviour confirms the world-weary West European stereotype that the new members of the EU are prickly and unpredictable – in short, perhaps not quite as civilised as the 'old' members.[59] That is reinforced by startlingly different ideas about social norms, especially on equal rights for homosexuals. In both Poland and Latvia, government politicians have endorsed protests against gay marches, in some cases ones that have turned violent. Ex-communist countries have been slow to protect their most vulnerable citizens. Conditions in children's homes, for example, remain dire, while Roma (Gypsies) live in dreadful conditions throughout the region. Their plight attracts much international hand-wringing, but usually little more than lip service locally. A third example of weak government that worries West Europeans is overmighty spooks. In almost every country (Estonia is a rare exception) the military intelligence and domestic security forces operate with a lack of political control and disrespect for the law that would be a scandal in most Western countries.

Public services in the new EU members are still poor by European standards: healthcare, the criminal justice system and public administration are particularly unimpressive. But that has not produced strong political pressure for good government. People prefer to vote with their feet than wait for their votes to be counted. Millions have emigrated, for the short or long term, to Western Europe. Britain has gained up to a million Poles; Romania has lost nearly two million people, chiefly to work in Spain and Italy. The size of this migration is still hard to document, though it is clearly the biggest in Europe since the end of the Second World War. The motives for leaving are multiple. Wages may be two or three times higher in the rich countries of Europe, though the cost of living is high and separation from family and friends has its cost. That benefit may erode over time. Harder to bridge is the gap in public services. It is hard for people who have not lived in an ex-communist country to understand the demoralising – literally – effect of persistent rudeness and corruption in public services, which leaves the user constantly feeling that he is a supplicant, not a client (let alone a valued customer). Medical treatment in almost every ex-communist country involves a series of carefully calibrated payments to doctors, nurses, anaesthetists and therapists. The education system in many post-communist countries is riddled with corruption, including both payments for 'special lessons' from teachers, incentives to secure admission to a sought-after university, and even backhanders to ensure good exam results. Simply renewing a driving licence or applying for minor bits of official paperwork can be lengthy and humiliating. Government bureaucrats have inherited the communist-era idea that the outsider is always wrong; his time is free; and arbitrary decision-making is the privilege of office.

The effects of the migration, positive and negative, are still unfolding. Economic growth in Britain is higher, and interest rates lower, as a result of the influx of hard-working and inexpensive East Europeans. Conversely, the East European countries are in greater danger of overheating. Wages are soaring – by as much as 30 per cent a year in some industries such as construction. If that continues, it threatens competitiveness; if it stops sharply, it could cause a painful crash. In theory, the migrants will eventually return home to use their new skills in a market where they have a competitive advantage. Politicians should be worried by emigration, the clearest vote of no confidence a citizen can pass on his country. But in practice it has eased, not stoked, the pressure on the complacent politicians of the ex-communist world: if the most discontented people have left for abroad, they are less likely to vote at home.

Why should this matter in the context of the New Cold War? Because it is just this idea, that the new EU members are somehow second-class members of the club, that Russia is trying to promote. It would be fanciful to say that the Kremlin is masterminding every diplomatic hiccup and slip in economic policy from the Baltic to the Black Sea. But it is certainly true that bad government and diplomatic isolation make it much easier for Russia to exert its influence. West European politicians say privately that they despair of some of the new members. The old EU featured hard bargaining, and sometimes spectacular rows. But its core members felt united by a common purpose that now seems to be lacking. That is stoking demands for a 'two-speed' Europe, probably based around membership of the euro zone, which includes most of old Europe, but excludes most of the new member states.

It would be nice to think that nothing much would change: the single market would hang together, and that the baker's dozen of countries on the eastern periphery of the new core would at least remain part of a thriving free-trade area, as Norway and Switzerland do today. But the unravelling would most likely go much further. The EU already finds it hard to make Poland, for example, abide by European competition law. Without a seat at the top table in Brussels, Polish governments would find it hard to justify allowing foreigners to buy up big companies. The single market in capital would be the first to go. It would be quickly followed by restrictions on labour mobility, and soon on free trade in goods and services. The ex-communist states' wobbly finances are propped up in part by the financial markets' confidence that they will join the euro eventually. If that belief erodes, the halo effect of proximity to rich stable Europe evaporates. Slow-lane Europe's bad government, backwardness and weakness will stand starkly revealed. And who will pay then?

Worse, even the remnants of common policy towards Russia would go, too. The new 'core Europe' would be dominated by France, Germany and Italy (assuming Britain, as usual, dithered). These countries tend to see rows with the Kremlin as costly distractions. They will continue striking bargains with Russia on energy and anything else, over the heads of the countries in between. The Nord Stream gas pipeline is a foretaste of what Poland and the Baltics can expect if a two-speed Europe takes shape. Moreover, the already withered carrot of enlargement would look much less appealing. Today the EU can still hope to make the politicians of the western Balkans keep talking rather than fighting by dangling the distant prospect of full membership. But who is going to lift a finger to join the slow lane to nowhere in a two-speed Europe? Serbia's flirtation in late 2007 with the idea of political ties with Russia rather than the EU is an early sign of what to expect. The prospect of being second-class citizens of Europe should therefore be a terrifying scenario for the new member states: the rational response would be for them to smarten up their act, by hastening to adopt the euro, by restoring their reputation as reformers and by pushing for adoption of the EU's constitutional treaty. But they aren't.

The paradox is that these ill-governed, tetchy and intolerant countries are the front line that the West is trying to defend. So far, the record is patchy, but becoming slightly more encouraging. At the EU–Russia summit in Samara in May 2007, the EU's leaders batted aside Mr Putin's claim that their policy was being distorted by the 'egocentrism' of the new member states. Russia's attempt to isolate Poland on the issue of meat exports (which Russia has banned on hygiene grounds) proved utterly unsuccessful. After years in which every meeting had produced an upbeat communiqué and launched a plethora of new initiatives, this time the two sides simply agreed to disagree. By EU standards, this was a startlingly bold and tough-minded approach. Ms Merkel, representing the EU presidency, coolly informed Mr Putin that if he had a problem with one EU country, he had a problem with the whole EU. She publicly rebuked him for the Russian authorities' harassment of Mr Kasparov and other opposition activists trying to lobby the summit.[60] A foreign ministers' meeting in Portugal in September 2007 brought even tougher language.

One reason for this is that the Kremlin has systematically overplayed its hand. Another is that the unholy trio of West European leaders willing to cut special deals with Russia, Mr Schröder, Silvio Berlusconi and Jacques Chirac, have all left office. Mr Schröder's closeness was matched only by Mr Chirac's, who hoped that a Moscow–Berlin–Paris axis would be a powerful counter-balance to American hegemony. His successor as president, Nicolas Sarkozy, has spoken out against Russia's backsliding, as has his foreign minister, Bernard Kouchner; whether this principled stance survives the intense interest French companies are showing in the Russian market remains to be seen. In Italy, the government of Romano Prodi seems likely to follow any EU policy led by France and Germany, although Italy's own policy seems quietly Russia-friendly. But such solidarity will fray unless the new member states show that they are able to give solidarity as well as take it. The Kremlin needs only to create enough division within the EU – for example, by nobbling a handful of countries such as Greece, Austria and Latvia – to be able to say that it is pointless negotiating with a paralysed Commission in Brussels. For really important issues, dealing with the big countries is simpler – and more profitable. The most glaring example of this is the subject of the next chapter.

7

Pipeline Politics:
The Threat and the Reality

The Kremlin's aims in the politics of energy are no secret. They are outlined in the country's energy strategy, approved by Mr Putin in the summer of 2003, which puts energy policy at the centre of Russian diplomacy. It echoes a point made by Mr Putin in what purports to be his economics dissertation,[1] written in the 1990s and presented in 1997. The topic was a mouthful: 'The strategic planning of the reproduction of the mineral raw materials base of the region under conditions of the formation of market relationships'. But the message was clear: the management of Russia's natural resources is too important to leave to private business. The few published extracts of the thesis make no reference to globalisation or market forces. They argue that the aim of the natural resource industry is to boost the geopolitical strength of Russia. In practice, that means four things. The Kremlin wants to prevent European countries diversifying their sources of energy supply, particularly in gas. It wants to strengthen its hold over the international gas market. It wants to acquire 'downstream assets' – distribution and storage capability – in Western countries. And it wants to use those assets to exert political pressure.

As Ariel Cohen of America's Heritage Foundation think tank rightly notes,[2] Russia's policies are usually camouflaged by stealth, gradualism and apparent reasonableness. But since 2005, all four aims have been proceeding with remarkable speed. The contest resembles a battle-hardened chess grandmaster playing against a bunch of inattentive and squabbling amateurs. Europe's fundamental weakness in dealing with Russia is that it is not a single energy market. It is a series of energy islands, each administered and regulated by a national government. Naturally enough, each government thinks about its own interests, trying to ensure cheap energy for its consumers and jobs for its producers. Nobody wants to tell voters they have to make sacrifices in order to help out some other country. Unsurprisingly, given the EU's failure to create deep, liquid and competitive energy markets at home, it has also failed to get Russia to agree to liberalise its own monopolistic practices. In Mr Putin's words:

> The gas pipeline system is the creation of the Soviet Union. We intend to retain state control over the gas transport system and over Gazprom. We will not split Gazprom up. And the European Commission should not have any illusions. In the gas sector, they will have to deal with the state.[3]

Were those pipelines carrying vodka, or even oil, it would not matter. Europe can make its own vodka; it can import oil from anywhere in the world by tanker. But gas is different. Pipelines are not only by far the cheapest and most practical way of delivering gas. Europe is already dependent on imported gas from Russian pipelines – a dependence that is set to increase. Of Europe's gas consumption, 60 per cent is imported, nearly half of that via Russia. Over the next twenty years, at least according to some projections, the imported share will rise to 80 per cent, as Europe's own gas production falls and demand rises. For some European countries such as Britain, this is still not too serious: a mixture of imports of liquefied natural gas (LNG)[4] and supply from the North Sea mean that Russia is unlikely to dominate the market. Further east, it looks different. The following table shows selected European countries' dependence on imported Russian gas:

Switzerland	13%
Netherlands	17%
France	23%
Italy	32%
Germany	40%
Slovenia	51%
Romania	63%
Poland	63%
Czech Republic	75%
Hungary	77%
Austria	78%
Greece	84%
Bulgaria	100%
Slovakia	100%
Finland	100%
Estonia	100%
Latvia	100%
Lithuania	100%

Source: Eni World Oil and Gas Review 2006[5]

European policymakers see the problem, but have so far been able to do little about it. An EU–Russia 'energy dialogue', launched in 2000,[6] was based on the idea that Russia would progressively liberalise its energy markets. Instead the reverse has happened, and Mr Putin has repeatedly[7] made it clear that Russia will not ratify the Energy Charter, which would among other things de-monopolise its oil and gas export pipelines. The hope was that Russia would accept this in return for a free trade agreement.

However, as Russia's exports to the EU chiefly consist of raw materials, this proved an unattractive offer. Instead Russia demands 'reciprocity' in energy dealings with the EU. This does not mean a legal framework that applies equally to both sides; rather, it means allowing European countries to invest in oil and gas fields in Russia only if they sell to their Russian partners distribution networks and other assets of equal value in Europe. That sets the stage for a fundamental clash between the EU's liberal, market-based system and the dirigiste and monopolistic approach of the Kremlin in which, so far, Russia is winning hands down. The EU may bleat, but nothing stops British, German, Dutch and Italian companies (to name only a few countries) from doing their own deals with Gazprom and Rosneft. Gazprom, for example, now has investments in at least sixteen out of twenty-seven EU countries; in Britain, Italy, Germany and France among others, it has won direct access to at least some consumers, with all that implies.[8]

That would not matter if Gazprom were just another publicly traded, law-governed energy company. But it is not. Western companies that deal with it insist they do not wish to condone theft, censorship and thuggishness, and see no sign of such things in Russia. But the fact is that Gazprom is the gas division of Kremlin Inc. and is, for example, directly linked to the end of press freedom in Russia: it has bought up troublesome media outlets such as NTV and bent them to the Kremlin's will. Deals with Gazprom also raise a question about Europe's own rules: as the Kremlin does not allow any competition in its core business (such as export pipelines) at home, why should it respect the rules of the European market? It is more likely that it will try to change them. Gazprom certainly does not like the slightest scent of EU scrutiny of its activities. In October 2006, Europe's leaders asked the EU's competition directorate, which polices the internal market against cartels and monopolies, to investigate Gazprom's growing role in the EU.[9] Mr

Putin complained sharply. German diplomats say that their country's federal chancellor, Ms Merkel, told him that Gazprom should find it 'an honour to be treated like Microsoft'.[10] If the EU is able to start serious liberalisation of the energy market, unbundling distribution, sales and imports, Gazprom will have more than that to worry about. The thirty-year contracts it has with ENI in Italy, BASF in Germany and Gaz de France may need to be redrafted, at least to exclude its direct access to end users. The EU is also considering new rules that would prevent Russian and other state-backed buyers taking control of downstream energy assets such as distribution networks and refineries. That could include giving the EU power to block outside investments that damage common strategic interests.

Such moves would be welcome, but they are a long way off and subject to sabotage by Russia's allies in Europe. So far, the stage has been set perfectly for the Kremlin's favourite tactic: divide and rule. Its success can be seen most clearly in the tale of two pipelines. Nord Stream – backed by Russia – aims to take gas under the Baltic Sea to Germany.[11] Nabucco – backed by the EU – aims to take gas from Central Asia and the Caspian to Europe.[12] In reality, neither pipeline is likely to be built, but the political wrangling around each highlights the West's weakness, and Russia's strength.

Nord Stream is the child of the most notorious diplomatic alliance in Europe's modern history, between the previous German government headed by Mr Schröder and Mr Putin's Kremlin. It was blessed with a secret €1 billion loan guarantee issued just days before the German leader left office – shortly to become chairman of the pipeline consortium. Mr Schröder is prickly and litigious, making it hard to discuss his activities in public. In 2006 he successfully sued Guido Westerwelle, the leader of Germany's liberal party, the FDP, who drew a connection between Mr Schröder's behaviour in office and the benefits he has reaped once out of it. Though Mr Westerwelle was forbidden by the court from repeating a particular formulation of his criticism of the former chancellor, he continues to do so in other terms. After losing the case Mr Westerwelle said he continued to believe that Mr Schröder's behaviour was 'distasteful and questionable'. Tom Lantos, the American congressman and Holocaust survivor, went further, saying that he wanted to call Schröder a 'political prostitute' but that the sex workers in his constituency objected.[13]

The biggest shareholder in Nord Stream is Gazprom – in effect the Kremlin. The other shareholders, with 24.5 per cent each, are Germany's biggest energy companies, E.ON Ruhrgas and Wintershall, part of BASF. The pipeline, 1,200 kilometres (750 miles) long, will be the most expensive ever built. Originally supposed to cost €4 billion when announced in 2005, Gazprom raised the estimate to €5 billion in 2006 and €6 billion in 2007. Outside estimates are that the real cost will be nearly double that by the time it is completed. The supposed completion date of 2010 looks unrealistic too:[14] the deadline for bidding to supply pipes was postponed by several months in 2007. The drawbacks are formidable. Underwater pipelines are far more expensive than their land-based counterparts. The Baltic seabed is littered with munitions from two world wars. Every other country on the Baltic littoral dislikes the plan and has raised a plethora of environmental objections. Finland wants the route shifted away from its coast, strengthening Estonia's bargaining position. Poland wants it moved closer to the Danish coast. Sweden objected to a planned compressor station to be built on a sea platform near its island of Gotland. That had worried security-conscious Swedes who thought it might be used for electronic espionage[15] or allow the Kremlin to intervene on the pretence of an 'anti-terrorist' operation to protect the platform. In mid-2007 the pipeline consortium said it might not build the platform after all, though this would increase still further the project's technical difficulties and cost. Despite all these difficulties, Nord Stream's advantage for the Kremlin is clear. Russia's two existing gas export pipelines to Germany go across other countries – Belarus and Poland in the north, and Ukraine, Slovakia and the Czech Republic to the south. That means that deliveries to Germany are hostage to those transit countries' goodwill; put another way, if it tries to punish those countries, its more important customers further west may suffer.

The most striking example of this came at the end of 2005, when Russia tried to raise the price of natural gas deliveries to Ukraine.[16] Ukraine certainly had its gas cheap in the past, at a mere $50 per thousand m^3. In one sense, Gazprom has the right to charge what it likes; moreover, higher gas prices would be a good thing everywhere in the former Soviet Union, where energy is still used astonishingly wastefully. Indeed, Western countries had been urging Russia to stop subsidising domestic gas prices as a condition for its membership of the WTO. Still, given Russia's monopoly hold on Ukrainian gas supplies, a responsible country would have used its pricing power carefully, avoiding unpredictable moves and any suspicion of politicisation. Russia did exactly the opposite, doubling the price at short notice. The strong suspicion in Ukraine and in the West was that Russia was punishing its southern neighbour for the Orange Revolution: if you won't vote for our candidates (and allow them to rig elections) then don't expect us to sell you cheap gas. When Ukraine refused to pay, Russia cut the supply, with the result that Ukraine then diverted for its own needs deliveries meant for Germany. That was not wholly Russia's fault; but its credibility in Western Europe as a reliable partner was badly dented.

Nord Stream offers the Kremlin a chance to sidestep such problems by delivering gas independently. It can raise prices for deliveries to Ukraine, Belarus or Poland; if they do not pay, it can cut them off, without worrying about supplies to its customers further west. The advantage of gas-based diplomacy is that Russia does not actually need to do anything practical: the mere knowledge that it could do so increases its political and economic leverage. In fact, the Kremlin has already strongly increased its hold over both Ukraine's and Belarus's pipelines by use of this approach. Even before a drop of gas flows through Nord Stream, the effect of its construction on the politics of land-based gas transit may have rendered it unnecessary. Nord Stream is also of symbolic importance, highlighting the German–Russian axis and thus intimidating the smaller countries in between, which find the idea of the continent's future being stitched up between Berlin and Moscow distasteful or outright scary. Radek Sikorski, then Poland's defence minister, described it in 2006 as the energy version of the Molotov–Ribbentrop pact.[17] That prompted claims that he was exaggerating, but the parallels were striking: both were German–Russian deals drafted in secret for the mutual benefit of the two continental superpowers, against the interests of the countries in between. Though Nord Stream's backers insist that the project is business pure and simple, this would be easier to believe if it were more transparent. The company is based in Zug, a tax haven in Switzerland, a country noted for its banking secrecy laws. Despite this respectable Western front end, the pipeline itself will be designed, built and operated by Gazprom. Nord Stream boosters also claim that the EU supports the project. This does not appear to be the case. It is true that the EU gives its blessing to many projects that diversify its gas supplies, but the EU energy commissioner, Andris Piebalgs, has said firmly that the European commission does not support Nord Stream 'over other options'.[18]

The Nord Stream project highlights many of the most troubling aspects of German–Russian relations in the Schröder era. The German chancellor developed a close friendship with his Russian counterpart, spending Christmas and other holidays together, at a time when Mr Putin was systematically reducing political freedoms in Russia.[19] Mr Putin's German friend and his wife have adopted two orphans from St Petersburg – in seeming contradiction of both Russia's ban on foreign adoptions and of German rules that would normally prohibit a couple of their age (over sixty and over forty respectively) adopting young children. Suspicion was also stoked by the project's choice of Chief Executive Officer, the head of Dresdner Bank in Russia, Matthias Warnig. He had been a senior officer in the *Stasi* in the Soviet-occupied zone of Germany, the 'GDR', and is believed to have met Mr Putin during his service with the KGB in the East German city of Dresden. Mr Warnig now claims that he met his Russian friend only in St Petersburg in the 1990s.[20] Dresdner has already attracted controversy in connection with the dismemberment of Yukos.

Gazprom itself is even more controversial. Its standard mode of operation is to export via intermediary companies with murky ownership structures, meaning that the profits can be diverted to unknown beneficiaries. The most conspicuous of these used to be Itera, a company whose role seemed to consist solely of buying Russian gas cheaply and selling it to export customers at a hefty mark-up. Itera's shareholders, as far as could be discovered, were relatives of the senior management of Gazprom. Itera was swept aside during Mr Putin's first term, to the delight of Gazprom's Western shareholders. But similar structures soon returned. In the case of export to Ukraine, the first lucky beneficiary company of gas export business via Russia (in fact, largely Turkmen gas) was called EuralTransGas (ETG). Like Itera, it had no pipelines, compressors, storage facilities or indeed any other assets. It employed only thirty people. Yet in 2003, its only full year of operation, ETG had revenues of $2 billion, though it declared a profit of a mere $220 million. Aside from $425 million paid to Gazprom (for the gas) it was unclear where the rest of the money went; presumably its senior staff were adequately rewarded for their demanding jobs.[21]

EuralTransGas then gave way to RosUkrEnergo. This is registered in (no surprises here) Zug in Switzerland. Half its shares are owned by Gazprom; the rest are held in a trust by Austria's Raiffeisen Bank on behalf of two controversial businessmen, Dmitriy Firtash (who has 90 per cent) and Ivan Fursin (10 per cent). Both the chairman and deputy chairman of Ukraine's national gas company, Naftohaz Ukrainy, have served on Ros-UkrEnergo's board. Raiffeisen – set up by one of Austria's greatest philanthropists – seems to feel no need to clarify matters. Raiffeisen's association with RosUkrEnergo has given rise to lurid speculation. The bank, along with all others concerned, vehemently denies any wrongdoing. But it is hard to argue that the interests of gas customers, or for that matter those of shareholders in Gazprom and taxpayers in Russia, are best served by secrecy about the company's activities and business model. A further issue is the ultimate beneficial ownership of RosUkrEnergo. The company's shareholders strenuously deny ties with Semion Mogilevich, a Ukrainian-born businessman with Israeli citizenship, believed to be living in Russia, who is on the FBI's wanted list for racketeering.[22] He denies these charges as well as any links with RosUkr-Energo. But the connection between Mr Mogilevich and RosUkrEnergo was suggested in 2005 by the then head of Ukraine's security service, Oleksandr Turchynov. An investigation into this issue in Ukraine has stalled, amid claims of Kremlin pressure.

Gazprom's own shareholding structure is, of course, unclear; so is its contribution to the Nord Stream project. As a privately held company, Nord Stream publishes no financial data. It gives only the scantiest details of the project: $7.5 billion will be invested, and it will be profitable.[23] More than that, nobody is saying. But even on the data available, the case for Nord Stream looks questionable. The cited cost of €5 billion is between a third and a half of the likely real total. Costs for operation, maintenance and decommissioning are not included. It would be possible instead to double up the existing land-based pipelines for less than half the stated €5 billion. It is unclear if Nord Stream's gas will really be needed. The consortium cites projections from the International Energy Agency that show Europe's demand for imported gas soaring. It does not take account of energy conservation, a switch to imported LNG, or to other sources of fuel, such as nuclear power. It is unclear both where the 55 billion m³ planned for the pipeline's annual through-put is coming from (Russia is facing a gas shortage) and where it is going to (the destination countries are still to be decided). Even the route is unclear. Nord Stream may go in Sweden's economic zone; but – if Estonia, Finland, Latvia and other countries agree – it may also take a different (and somewhat less expensive) route on the eastern side of the Baltic Sea. Other branch pipelines may go to Denmark, Poland, the Netherlands and Britain.

It is even less clear how Nord Stream's gas will be saleable in what may well by then be a liberalised European energy market. If Nord Stream's shareholders try to force-feed expensive gas from their pipeline to Germany's power stations, rather than, for ex-ample, cheaper LNG from Britain or even Norwegian North Sea gas, it will be open to strong legal challenge under EU competition laws. Such worries are mainly for energy specialists. But even those utterly uninterested in the intricacies of energy economics are alarmed by something else: the military dimension. The Kremlin has given Gazprom, a private company, the unusual right to recruit and operate its own military forces to protect its overseas pipe-lines.[24] Russia is also beefing up its Baltic fleet in order to help prospect the seabed, and protect the pipeline once it is built.

So far, the picture is clear. The Nord Stream project, with all its associated controversy and uncertainty, suits the Kremlin and worries its former satellites. The big question is why it suits Germany, which has on other fronts been a strong supporter of the ex-communist countries' freedom and security.[25] A strong personal relationship in the past between two top politicians is hardly enough to explain the strong support it has gained across a wide section of that country's politics and business. The partial answer is that Germany's special relationship with Russia goes back centuries. Catherine the Great invited German farmers to come and settle in the Volga basin. German nobles ran the then Baltic provinces of the Tsarist-era Russian empire. The royal families intermarried. Germany was one of the biggest investors in pre-revolutionary Russia; some machinery from that era can still be found in good working order, nearly a century later. In both world wars, the casualties on Germany's eastern front dwarfed those in the better-known battles in Western Europe. A mixture of guilt, resentment and fear makes Germans flinch at any kind of public confrontation with Russia. Restoring diplomatic ties with the Soviet Union was a prized achievement of Konrad Adenauer's Christian Democratic Union (CDU) government in 1956, and every government since then has tried to improve relations further. During the Cold War, many Germans felt they were paying a heavy price to be in the front line of someone else's conflict. Although the foreign-policy elite in the Federal Republic of Germany consistently supported the Atlantic alliance, the public's viewpoint was more anti-American. In many eyes, the Soviet Union and United States were seen as equal partners in the division of Europe – and of Germany.

Mr Gorbachev's arrival in the Kremlin in 1985 came at a time when German–American relations were strained by the issue of medium-range nuclear weapons.[26] Mr Gorbachev's arrival in the Kremlin fuelled that sentiment further. To many Germans, he was a far more attractive figure than Ronald Reagan. That era of 'Gorbymania' was entrenched by the Kremlin's relaxed attitude to the collapse of its puppet regime in eastern Germany. Under Chancellor Helmut Kohl, West Germany was able to negotiate reunification with astonishingly little resistance. Mr Gorbachev agreed to withdraw Soviet forces and to allow the united German state to be a member of NATO; Yeltsin honoured the bargain, withdrawing the remaining troops to Russia. Mr Kohl's ties with Yeltsin were closer than those enjoyed by any other Western leader. Germany provided billions of Deutschmarks in financial support for Russia; German companies were early investors; by 1998 they had invested DM2 billion, behind only America and Cyprus (the latter being mostly recycled money from Russia).[27] In 1997, Germany and France started regular trilateral summits with Russia.[28] The aim was to make Russia feel that it was not excluded from European decision-making. But East European countries, at that stage not yet in either the EU or NATO, regarded that with concern.

When Mr Schröder came to power in 1998 he denounced his predecessor's 'Sauna-diplomacy'. But in his friendship with Mr Putin, the new German leader soon exceeded even the sweatiest personal ties of the Kohl–Yeltsin era, visiting Russia dozens of times on both personal and political business. He proved a staunch defender of Mr Putin's human rights record, and gave Germany's strong support for grand schemes of integration, especially in energy. From 1998 to 2006, trade rose threefold, from €15 billion to €50 billion. Russia sells mostly energy to Germany. German exports to Russia, once mainly food and consumer goods, now include industrial machinery and chemicals. The number of German companies active in Russia has doubled in five years, to 4,500. At the heights of the German economy, ties with Russia are particularly close. Oleg Deripaska, the Kremlin's favourite oligarch, has bought a stake of nearly 10 per cent in Hochtief, Germany's biggest construction company, and is trying to buy more. His holding company Basic Element has bought 30 per cent of Strabag, Europe's largest tunnel and bridge builder.[29] Germany's biggest energy firm, E.ON Ruhrgas, owns 6.5 per cent of Gazprom; the two chief executives sit on each others' boards. It is perhaps the only outside shareholder that the Russian gas behemoth treats with respect. The connection is highly profitable for both companies. E.ON provides extensive technical assistance to Gazprom in modernising that company's rickety compressors and leaky pipelines. Gazprom provides cheap and reliable gas supplies.

That exemplifies the problem. It is hard to fault German companies for acting in the interests of their shareholders. And it is hard to fault their combined lobbying of the government. The *Ostauschuss der deutschen Wirtschaft* (Eastern Committee of German Industry) promotes and protects trade and investment in a highly promising market. Its chairman, Klaus Mangold, is an eloquent critic in private of Russia's political shortcomings while striking a publicly optimistic note about the country's development.[30] As Russia hurries to modernise its dilapidated infrastructure and worn-out industrial plant, Mr Mangold rightly sees great opportunities for German companies, which are world-beaters in both machine-building and construction. But this ignores the wider picture – one that is in sharp focus for Mr Schröder's successor as federal chancellor since 2005, Ms Merkel.

Brought up under communist rule in the 'German Democratic Republic', Ms Merkel is the first – and probably last – leader of a big industrialised European country in this century to have first-hand experience of adult life under totalitarianism. Unlike Mr Schröder she speaks Russian, and has friends not in that country's power elite, but in the liberal intelligentsia. Privately, she regards Mr Putin with the deepest suspicion. Since taking office, she has

presided over a sea change in Germany's stance towards its eastern
neighbours. Whereas Mr Schröder described Mr Putin as a
'*lupenreiner Demokrat*' (flawless democrat), Ms Merkel repeatedly
and publicly raises embarrasing questions about political repression in Russia. Mr Schröder shunned Russian human rights
activists; Ms Merkel makes a point of seeing them. In October
2006, Mr Putin offered Germany a one-off deal on access to one
of its most tempting unexplored gas reserves, the offshore Shtokman field. Russia had just broken off negotiations with other big
world energy companies, saying it would develop the field alone.
But Ms Merkel declined to discuss this, citing the common EU
energy policy. She also criticised the Kremlin's treatment of
investors at the Sakhalin project in Russia's Far East, saying, 'If
Russia creates obstacles to European investment, it shouldn't
object to reciprocal measures.'

Ms Merkel has also made a point of meeting senior politicians
from Poland and other former Soviet satellites both before and after
her meetings with Mr Putin (which number more than ten since
taking office). The aim is both to put forward their views, and to
report back to them afterwards. That has already gone a long way
to dispel suspicions about Germany's real intentions. The same goes
for her officials. In the Schröder era calls from Baltic officials in
particular went either unreturned or received only a cursory
answer; now the response is speedy and helpful. That, at least,
is the change of tone in the federal chancellery. But the acid test is
how far Germany's policy actually changes. German–Russian
relations are still marked by pragmatism and by what seems to
many outsiders as rather too much mutual goodwill. The key
concept is still *Annäherung durch Verflechtung* (rapprochement
through interdependence). Ms Merkel heads a coalition government in which views on policy towards Russia differ widely. Her
own foreign minister, Frank-Walter Steinmeier, was one of Mr

Schröder's closest ministerial colleagues and continues to push his policy hard. He and other members of the junior coalition partner, the Social Democrats (SPD), have echoed Russia's complaints about Polish and Czech willingness to host bases for a planned American missile-defence system. Many in the SPD are so viscerally opposed to the current American administration that they regard Mr Putin as a more congenial ally. That view is shared by German public opinion, which shows a surprising tendency to sympathise more with the Kremlin than with the current American administration.

So Ms Merkel is fighting on two fronts: against the anti-American left and the pro-business right, both of which are willing to overlook the Kremlin's shortcomings for reasons of their own. For all Ms Merkel's efforts, the fact remains that Russia has unparalleled influence in Germany, which seems to survive even a sharp change of political tone at the top. That Germany after 2012 will be importing two-thirds of its gas from Russia has rung not alarm bells but a dinner bell. Gas companies in other countries are scrambling not to be left behind. Gasunie of the Netherlands, for example, has bought a 9 per cent stake in Nord Stream. In return it is offering Gazprom a share in an undersea pipeline to Britain.[31] In 2006 Gazprom gained a 50 per cent share in Wingas, the energy trading unit of the BASF subsidiary Wintershall, positioning it well for any future energy liberalisation in Europe. The two companies have set up a 50:50 joint venture, Wingas Europe, to market Russian gas in Germany and other European countries. Gazprom also wants a share in Wintershall fields in the North Sea and Libya.[32] In exchange Wintershall gained a 25 per cent stake, worth roughly $500 million, in the largely undeveloped Yuzhno-Russkoye gas field, plus an extra 10 per cent in non-voting shares in a company that will develop the field.[33] Yuzhno-Russkoye's reserves are equivalent to fifteen years of Russian gas exports to Germany at current rates. As this becomes more valuable, Gazprom is asking E.ON to hand over stakes in its businesses elsewhere in Europe. E.ON offered its businesses in Hungary, but Gazprom dismissed that as too little. It wants a stake in Ruhrgas's vast electricity and gas distribution businesses in Germany. In August 2007 it asked E.ON to hand over its electricity generating business in Britain.[34]

In Latvia and Estonia (where Gazprom is well entrenched thanks to its stake in the local gas companies) governments have eyed participation in the Baltic pipeline, too. Latvia hopes that Russian investment will make a profitable concern of its large and unexploited underground gas storage capabilities. Estonia's government originally hoped to make some money from allowing the pipeline to cross its territorial waters or seabed economic zone. Mr Schröder, indeed, was heading to Tallinn to discuss this when the row over the 'bronze soldier' war memorial broke. Only his remarkably unwise comment that the Estonian decision to move the statue 'offended every form of civilised behaviour' forced his hosts to cancel the trip. Estonia now says that the pipeline may not cross its maritime economic zone. Gazprom also hopes to extend the pipeline into the North Sea and use Belgium as a 'regional hub' for gas transmission to nearby countries, including Britain. It has signed a twenty-five-year deal with Fluxys, a Belgian gas firm, to build a storage site at Poederlee and plans a seabed pipeline from Zeebrugge to the English coast. However, a Belgian anti-monopoly regulator, CREG, has blocked this, saying it gives Gazprom an unfairly exclusive deal over too long a period.

If Nord Stream demonstrates Russia's ability to push its pet pipeline forward, the story of the other important pipeline, Nabucco, demonstrates Europe's inability to do the same. A glance at the map[35] on page ix shows why Nabucco is necessary.

Supposedly to be completed in 2012, the project would bring a planned 30 billion m^3 of gas to Europe from four possible sources:

Iraq, Iran, Azerbaijan and Central Asia. Crucially, it does this by running across Turkey and the Balkans, not Russia. It is hard to overstate the importance of this. Although Nabucco would not carry large quantities of gas – only around a tenth of Europe's needs – it would have huge effects. First, it would free countries such as Turkmenistan and Kazakhstan from total dependence on Soviet-era pipelines: this allows the Kremlin to dictate the price and quantity of their exports. Second, it would allow European gas companies to bargain with Gazprom from a position of greater strength. Perhaps most importantly of all, it would signal to the Kremlin that Europe is able to deal jointly with energy security in a serious way. That is entirely the right approach – in theory. But Russia's victory has been near-total and deeply humiliating: by mid-2007 it seemed not just to have checkmated Nabucco's backers, but to have swept the pieces from the board and gone home.

Problems have arisen at every point. For a start, the vital linchpin in the plan, Turkey, is increasingly estranged from both America and the EU, and snuggling closely up to Russia, with which it built the $3.7 billion Blue Stream pipeline across the Black Sea. To this day it is not clear what, to whom or how much Gazprom paid in Turkey to get the pipeline built. Although Turkey is a member of NATO, its military and security services – with their commercial allies – are a law unto themselves. But this astonishing feat of deep-water seabed engineering is used only to less than a third of its capacity; it would therefore make sense from a purely commercial point of view for Turkey to exploit Blue Stream fully, rather than to build new pipelines. That sentiment is not counter-balanced by any political support in Turkey to help out its traditional allies. The refusal to support the war in Iraq, plus the creation of an American-backed semi-independent Kurdish state in that country's north have severely strained both ends of the American–Turkish strategic partnership.

Turkey thinks America is soft on Kurdish separatism and terrorism; America that on a crucial issue of international security, Turkey failed to show solidarity. But those difficulties are minor compared to the strain on Turkish relations with the EU. Talks on Turkish membership risk being postponed indefinitely, with both Mr Sarkozy and Ms Merkel publicly opposed to it in principle.

Even worse is that none of the potential sources of gas are easily available. Relations with Iran are in the deep freeze, thanks to the Tehran regime's determination to pursue (with Russian help) advanced nuclear technology. Gazprom has effortlessly checkmated Iran's only attempt to export large amounts of gas so far, via Armenia, by investing a wholly unnecessary $2 billion in a refinery and power plant there. The deal came with one condition: Armenia could build a small gas import pipeline from Iran, freeing itself from any potential blockade by Georgia and Azerbaijan, its northern neighbours. But it was to abandon any plans to export Iranian gas northwards. Most other sources for Nabucco look fanciful, too. The failure to bring peace and security to Iraq means that that country's potential as a gas exporter is still purely theoretical. The failure to reach a Middle East peace settlement, instability in Lebanon and Syria's continuing pariah status mean that nobody is going to invest money in Arab transit pipelines to Turkey in the foreseeable future.

That leaves the Caspian, where the West's hopes rest on the flimsy chances of persuading two dictatorships, ultra-cautious Kazakhstan and impenetrable Turkmenistan, to take the risk of snubbing Moscow and selling their gas westwards. Unsurprisingly, in the battle for the Caspian Russia has so far outwitted the West at every turn. The chances never looked good. Russia regards the Caspian Sea as a lake. Under international law, the countries round a lake have a power of veto over the economic exploitation of the land under it. Russia can therefore block any attempt to build a

pipeline on the Caspian seabed linking Turkmen and Kazakh gas
fields to Azerbaijan's existing pipeline westwards. To underline its
legal case, it has also been building up its naval forces in the
Caspian. But, in fact, Russia used an even more powerful weapon
than either gunboats or international lawyers: simple diplomatic
clout. In May 2007 Mr Putin signed a deal with the leaders of
Kazakhstan and Turkmenistan to build a new gas export pipeline
skirting the northern shore of the Caspian and taking the region's
gas riches to Europe via Russia.

Nabucco was thus kyboshed on two fronts. But Russia has added
two more. First, it has suggested building South Stream, a $5.5
billion westwards extension of Blue Stream, landing in Bulgaria
and bringing 30 billion m^3 annually of Russian gas to Europe
through the Balkans.[36] That would mimic Nabucco's route – but
with the crucial difference that the pipeline would be built, filled,
maintained and operated by the Kremlin. Like Blue Stream, it
would be built jointly with Italy's giant energy firm ENI. One spur
will go to southern Italy via Greece, the other to northern Italy via
Romania, Hungary and Slovenia. It may also reach as far as Austria.
This was potentially devastating news for policymakers in both the
EU and America. The economics of gas pipelines are simple:
whoever builds the first one has a big advantage. It can offer
the cheapest gas, making it impossible for a newcomer to attract
investors. Russia's final move has been to stitch up the European
countries that are shareholders in Nabucco, and would in theory be
its biggest beneficiaries. It starts with Bulgaria, where the ex-
communist government is deeply influenced by Russian business
interests. The Russian-owned refinery at Bourgas is Bulgaria's
single biggest private-sector taxpayer. Russian economic – and
some say criminal – circles are deeply connected with Bulgarian
decision-making. Although Bulgaria is militarily a loyal American
and NATO ally, on the energy front it is in Russia's pocket.

Much the same is true of neighbouring Romania, where the Atlanticist president, Traian Basescu, has lost control of the country's foreign policy to a business-friendly government that is keen to make the country the energy hub of the Balkan region. In August 2007, the country's biggest oil company, Rompetrol, sold a 75 per cent stake to Kazakhstan's KazMunayGaz. On the surface, that could strengthen Romania's energy independence. But at any time in the future the new Kazakh owner may find it convenient, or necessary, to sell Rompetrol on to Russia. Russia is also back in business in ex-Yugoslavia, a region that is a prime candidate for integration into the rest of Europe, and where Western influence has long been predominant. It was American arms, air power and diplomatic pressure that allowed Croatia to break away successfully from Yugoslavia. Bosnia owes its precarious unity and independence to the intense and energetic involvement of both the EU and the United States. Yet the mere sniff of Russian money seems to have turned the geopolitics of ex-Yugoslavia upside down. At an energy summit held in the Croatian capital Zagreb in mid-2007, all six former Yugoslav republics, plus Greece, Bulgaria, Romania and Albania, gave a crawling welcome to Mr Putin, who announced a series of new oil and gas initiatives that leave the Western efforts in tatters. Mr Putin pointed out that in 2006, 73 billion m^3 of gas – half of Russia's gas exports to Europe – went to countries in the southern and south-eastern parts of the continent.[37] He offered not only Russian investment in infrastructure (transit, storage and distribution) but also in modernisation of energy generation. That was a powerful message in an energy-starved region of Europe, where countries such as Macedonia and Albania experience infuriating power cuts and where the EU-forced closure of Bulgaria's ancient nuclear power station at Kozluduy is regarded as almost insanely insensitive and damaging. Russia's investment, said Mr Putin, would form an electricity 'ring' around the region. If it creates overwhelming energy dependence on a monopoly supplier, that ring may turn out to look more like a chain.

The *coup de grâce* for Nabucco may be a lack of commitment to it in Austria and Hungary, the countries that should be the pipeline's destination, and thus its greatest beneficiaries. At the commemorations in Budapest marking the fiftieth anniversary of the 1956 Hungarian uprising, Mr Putin delivered some words of guarded apology. That was a coup for the Hungarian prime minister, Ferenc Gyurcsány, who is engaged in a vigorous internal political battle with opponents who try to draw a direct link between his social democratic party's communist origins and the Soviet crushing of the revolt. Mr Gyurcsány's government seemed to have shifted against Nabucco. 'We don't need dreams. We need projects,' he said in early 2007. That was understandable: the effect of Europe's weak energy policy has been to leave all those concerned with the firm belief that Brussels is talking merely about notions, whereas the Kremlin is talking business. But in September 2007, Mr Gyurcsány wobbled again, insisting that his country was still a strong supporter of Nabucco.[38]

That may reflect Hungarian crossness about the Kremlin's increasing influence in neighbouring Austria, where the main oil and natural gas company, ÖMV, is meant to be coordinating the Nabucco project. When Mr Putin visited Vienna on 23–24 May 2007, he promised to make Austria a 'hub' for Russian exports of natural gas – including, ironically, much of the Central Asian gas that was supposed to flow through Nabucco. In 2006 Austria had signed a long-term contract under which Gazprom will supply 80 per cent of Austria's gas requirements over the next twenty years.[39] During Mr Putin's visit, he celebrated the start of work on a big underground gas storage installation near Salzburg. With a 2.4 billion m^3 capacity, the €260 million facility will be the second largest of its kind in the region. In return for the long-term supply contract, Austria has allowed Gazprom to buy a share in gas distribution businesses in some of Austria's biggest federal states. Gazprom is also to acquire a stake in Austria's gas transit business and will build a joint gas transit management centre with ÖMV, the largest in Europe.[40]

Gazprom appears to have been trying to create competition between the Hungarian and Austrian energy industries over which will have the closest ties with Russia. In the summer of 2007 ÖMV, in what was believed to be a joint move with Gazprom, launched a surprise hostile bid for its Hungarian counterpart, MOL, raising its stake from 10 to over 18 per cent. That included €1 billion it paid for a 6 per cent stake in MOL originally acquired by a controversial Russian tycoon, Megdet Rakimkulov.[41] The takeover looks odd for several reasons. It makes little business sense other than in sheer scale. MOL is in many ways the stronger company, having done better than ÖMV in acquisitions in the former Yugoslavia and Italy. ÖMV is only slightly larger than its target and is having to borrow €13.5 billion from Barclays and JP Morgan Chase to pay for the takeover of MOL. The aim is to lever open Austria, Hungary and Slovakia to Russian acquisitions. This will probably happen once EU competition laws make ÖMV sell one of MOL's top refineries, most likely Slovnaft, near the Slovak capital Bratislava. This would be almost certain to fall into Rosneft's hands, as it can operate only on Russian oil, flowing along a Russian-owned pipeline. As its part of the deal, ÖMV is likely to get shares in upstream assets in Russia in return for downstream assets in Central Europe.

Unsurprisingly, this manoeuvring seems to have alarmed Hungary, and outweighed the influence of the lobby there that concentrates only on cheap gas and high profits. In the 1990s, Hungary had already fought off an attempt by a shady Russian-backed company to build up a stake in MOL, the country's largest company. The question, however, is how far Hungary will be able to resist. In April 2007, the EU forced the Hungarian state to sell its 'golden share' in MOL, meaning it no longer has a veto over the future of MOL. Not for the first time, the EU's liberal and market-based principles are proving an ideal framework for the illiberal, anti-competitive polices of the Kremlin's gas business. So is the desire of individual managers, officials and politicians in the West to further their own careers.[42]

For all that, Nabucco is not, yet, quite dead. Russia may have had a triumphant year in the gas wars, but European and American diplomats insist that they still have some cards to play. Turkey, they argue, does not want to be dependent solely on Russian gas. Many outsiders said that the Baku–Tbilisi–Ceyhan oil pipeline, which brings Azeri crude to Turkey's deep-water Mediterranean port, would never be built. Thanks to strong American pressure, it was not only built, but turned into a big success. Last year it pumped 143m barrels of crude oil. It may be possible to bring Turkmen gas to Turkey via Iran, instead of across the Caspian, or indeed buy Iranian gas. That would require the West to turn a blind eye to a deal that would be highly beneficial to the regime in Tehran, at a time when international pressure is supposed to be weakening it. It would also depend on Russia being unable to block it, either through its own links with the Iranian regime, or through pressure on Turkey. A gas pipeline from Turkey to Greece and Italy is still possible, whatever the other reverses in the Balkans. Brave talk and ingenious schemes are plentiful. But the champions of Western interests look out-gunned. Europe is disunited, and America far away. Mr Piebalgs conspicuously lacks the backing of big EU member countries such as Germany, Italy and the Netherlands, all of which prefer bilateral deals with Russia. The impressive figure of Matt Bryza, an up-and-coming diplomat who is America's 'Deputy Assistant Secretary of State for

European and Eurasian Affairs' can hardly expect to counter a policy that has the explicit backing and concentrated attention of Mr Putin and his senior officials, as well as the world's largest gas company.

These pipeline wars may prove the first act of the drama. The plot of the second act concerns the Kremlin's attempt to stitch up the world gas market, rather than just the European one. The main vehicle for this plan is a body, founded in 2001, called the Gas-Exporting Countries' Forum (GECF). It has no staff, headquarters, fixed membership, budget, charter, legal basis or even – at the time of writing – a website: in effect, it is a meeting with a label. Some countries who turn up are not exporters, and important exporters (including the main Western producers: Australia, Canada, the Netherlands and Norway) are not members. However, the fifteen countries that regularly attend its meetings account for 73 per cent of the world's gas reserves and 41 per cent of production. At its meeting in Doha, Qatar, in April 2007, the GECF decided to set up a High-Level Group, coordinated by Russia, to research markets and discuss how gas prices should be determined. That will report back to the GECF meeting in Moscow in 2008. The meeting did not endorse demands by Venezuela, Bolivia, and Iran to set up a cartel immediately. But it may have a powerful effect nonetheless. The key Kremlin aim is first to prevent the development of a liquid international market for gas, such as already exists in oil, and secondly to stop countries diversifying their gas supplies. Instead, Russia wants to carve up the world markets by area, so that gas suppliers do not undercut one another. It wants a common approach by GECF participants on new pipelines (thus further weakening customers' attempts to diversify); and 'joint' exploration, development and liquefaction plants. 'Joint' in this case is code for 'Russian-backed'.

That may sound ambitious, but it will be quite straightforward for GECF members to stop LNG – the best hope for energy

independence in both Europe and America – being traded on the
spot market. In other words, the GECF will become an umbrella
organisation for regional cartels, such as the one that already exists
in South America. In Europe, that will mean Russia strengthening
its commercial and political ties with other gas exporters, and
making sure that any independent-minded customers' room for
manoeuvre is as constrained as possible. An early example of what
this might mean is Gazprom's growing relationship with Algeria's
state company Sonatrach, which is the second largest gas exporter
to Europe, providing 10 per cent of the continent's consumption
compared to Russia's 25 per cent. A debt swap in 2006, coupled
with a big arms purchase from Russia, prompted Mr Piebalgs, the
EU energy commissioner, to give warning of a growing regional
gas cartel. The deal put 69 per cent of Italy's gas supply, in effect,
under Gazprom control and gave the Russian side access to
Algeria's LNG technology, something that it is has so far lacked.
Italy's main energy company, ENI, already a close Gazprom ally,
helped bid for Yukos assets, which it promptly sold on to its
Russian friends.

Russia's energy policy means that insiders gain and outsiders lose.
That is a potent weapon. But is it loaded? Few worry as much as
they should about whether Russia will have enough gas to meet
the demands of the next decades, and what that means for
counterparts and customers. At first sight it seems preposterous
that a country with 47 trillion m^3, the world's largest proven gas
reserves, could be running short. But it is. Vladimir Milov, an
outspoken former energy minister who now runs an independent
think tank in Moscow, says that both oil and gas extraction are
facing a 'crisis', with gas in a worse state than oil. The figures are
stark and simple. Gas production has stalled and is likely to decline.
Demand is going up – by roughly 50 billion m^3 a year in Europe.
According to Mr Milov,[43] the gas deficit between Gazprom's own

production and what it can import from Central Asia, and what it needs to supply to domestic and foreign customers, will be 132 billion m³ in 2010. The International Energy Agency reckons that the deficit by 2015 will be 200 billion m³. By 2020, all Gazprom's production would be needed for the Russian market, leaving none for export. And these are the conservative, optimistic projections.

There are two reasons: waste and theft. Russia uses gas (like all other forms of energy) with colossal inefficiency, consuming more than twice as much energy per unit of output than other big industrialised countries such as Canada or Germany. This is not surprising, given how little industry pays for gas: around $50 per thousand m³, compared to four or five times that paid in the West. Ex-communist countries that pay world prices have sharply increased their energy efficiency; Poland, for example, has doubled the amount of output it gets from a unit of energy. Russia's efficiency has hardly budged from the dismal levels of the Soviet Union. That may change if the Kremlin will stick to the price hikes agreed last year that double the domestic gas price by 2011. Russian consumers will have seen nothing like this before: subsidised gas is one of the last remaining elements of the Soviet planned economy. Given the Kremlin's timid reaction to the public protests about the limited welfare reforms in 2004, it is questionable whether it will back these much more painful price rises to the end. The problem is not raising prices, but cutting off those who will not or cannot pay them. In a country where the temperature drops below −30° Celsius in winter, that is a matter of life and death. Faced with a choice of whether to freeze voters or hurt its export customers, the Kremlin is likely to choose the latter.

Even if gas becomes more expensive and is used more thriftily, problems are looming elsewhere. Russia's strong economic growth means more demand for electricity, which in turn creates more demand for gas. Russia's creaking power sector urgently needs to

build more gas-fired capacity: it will face a deficit of 20,000
megawatts by 2012 if it does not. Worse, Russia is pressing ahead
with 'gasification' – the supply of gas to domestic homes for heating
and cooking. This is as politically popular as it is economically
insane. It involves building 12,000 kilometres of new pipelines at a
cost of $1.3 billion – and creates another 9 billion m^3 of demand at a
time when Gazprom is already struggling to supply both its
domestic and export customers.[44]

Gazprom is one of the most inefficient energy companies in the
world, rivalled only by Pemex in Brazil. Its return on total assets –
at a time of sky-high energy prices – is a measly 8.9 per cent. In the
last year before it was attacked, Yukos, by contrast, returned 30 per
cent. Novatek, an independent gas producer now taken over by
Gazprom, returned 21.4 per cent. Hundreds of billions of dollars
flow into Gazprom's coffers, but they are plundered for other
purposes: colossal perks for the top management, overstaffing,
ludicrously grand buildings, holiday resorts, yachts and other
gimmicks. Although high energy prices have raised revenues, most
is frittered away in higher costs. Little is left for the important
business of finding new gas supplies. In the period 2000–6, it spent
only $12.5 billion on developing new fields, compared to $17.9
billion on buying companies outside the gas industry (such as a big
stake in Russia's coal and electric power industries). It spent a
staggering $30 billion on capital investments in non-gas areas.
Gazprom flatters its production figures by buying other gas companies – which are much more efficiently run, at least until they are
acquired. But it is unimpressive in the vital work of developing new
ones of its own. Indeed, Gazprom has not brought a big new gas
field onstream from scratch in its history. Its wealth rests on its
political connections, the export monopoly that they bring, and the
work of others: chiefly, long-forgotten Soviet-era engineers and
geologists.

Their legacy has been sadly neglected. Over 70 per cent of Russia's high-pressure gas pipelines were built before 1985; the average age of main pipelines is twenty-two years; 14 per cent are older than their design life. According to the IEA, at least 30 billion m^3 of natural gas, or a fifth of Russian exports to Europe, are wasted, mostly because of leaky pipes and worn-out compressors. Vast quantities of gas are 'flared' (simply burnt) because oil companies do not have access to the pipelines (thanks to Gazprom's ill-managed monopoly) needed to sell it. Flaring accounts supposedly for a 'mere' 15 billion m^3 but is estimated by other experts as being as much as 60 billion m^3. To deal with that, Gazprom needs not only to modernise, but also to develop new fields. The problem is that these are in some of the most inhospitable places on the planet: the far north and east of Russia. Getting the gas out is technically difficult and expensive; so is building thousands of miles of new pipelines to get it to new markets. Developing the supergiant new Yamal field in western Siberia, for example, will cost $70 billion. Gazprom itself, laden with costs and debts, cannot provide that money itself. Nor can the company raise it through Russia's underdeveloped financial system. After the way in which Western energy companies have been treated in Russia (described in Chapter Four), their shareholders may be unwilling to put up cash for an investment whose profits seem destined to be kept within Russia.

The problems are even greater in offshore development. Under the icy waters of the Barents Sea, some 550 kilometres (300 miles) from Russia's northern coastline, lies one of the world's largest gas fields, named after a Soviet-era geophysicist, Vladimir Shtokman. With up to 3.7 trillion m^3 of untouched gas, it could supply the EU's total needs for seven years. Discovered in 1988, it is one of the jewels in the crown of Russia's natural resource riches. The problem is turning the gas into cash. Norway's Statoil, one of the world's most technologically advanced companies in energy extraction, started development of its similarly challenging Snohvit field (which is less than a tenth the size of Shtokman) in 2002. It was due to ship the first cargo of LNG only on 1 December 2007. Gazprom insists that it is now getting ready to invest heavily in development and that it will raise its output to 570 billion m^3 in 2010 and 670 billion m^3 in 2020. Maybe it will. But the company is so secretive, and its history so poor, that outsiders have little basis to trust it. The lesson from Russia in the past fifteen years is that Kremlin interference plus corruption make a lethal mixture when long-term investment planning is concerned.

So the biggest question for Europe in the coming decade is likely to be how to deal with a Russia that is short of gas, and that has an increasing number of outside customers to sell it to. The effect of raising gas prices in Russia, and those paid by the ex-Soviet countries such as Ukraine and Belarus that have previously received it cheaply, is that Gazprom's loss-making sales in the home and ex-Soviet markets will shortly become profitable and therefore more attractive. Moreover, the closer to the source gas field a country is, the better a customer it becomes: the supplier does not need to worry about transit fees, or being held hostage to political rows. Furthermore, Gazprom is also hoping to sell gas from eastern Siberia to China, Japan and South Korea, and a big planned move into LNG will also allow it to sell to America.

That will change the balance of power in Europe. For now at least, the EU countries have a strong potential hold on Russia. They need it as a supplier, but it needs them as customers. The success of the Kremlin divide-and-rule policy has prevented the latter factor having much importance, but it is certainly there if the EU chooses to act on it. In future, though, that will change. Europe will still need gas, but Gazprom will have lots of places to sell it to. A sign of those coming times, and the likely profound political effects they will bring, comes from the behaviour of the companies that know Gazprom best: its German partners. Both E.ON and BASF have nailed down supply contracts with Gazprom up to 2036. Other European contracts run out much sooner – mostly in the course of the next ten years. That will give the Kremlin an unrivalled opportunity to drive a hard bargain, both commercially and politically, with those companies – and countries – that find themselves at the back of the queue.

Such worries still lie in the future. The immediate question is Gazprom's choice of partner in the development of Shtokman. The company initially shortlisted five Western partners: Total, Chevron, ConocoPhillips, Statoil and Norsk Hydro. All of these have the expertise in deep-water offshore gas development that Gazprom lacks. But in 2006 the Russian side announced that the foreign partners would not have equity stakes in the project, and could take part only as contractors. In July 2007 Gazprom announced that France's biggest oil and gas company, Total, would gain a 25 per cent share in a new company (51 per cent owned by Gazprom) to design, finance and build the first phase of the project. The remaining stake would go to other foreign partners. This was probably the worst deal a big Western energy company has ever had to accept from a resource-rich country. It separated for the first time access from ownership: Total has no rights to the gas itself, only a share in the company that extracts it. In effect, Gazprom auctioned the right to be involved in Shtokman among foreign oil companies desperate to be able to claim at least some share in Russia's hydrocarbons. Total expects to invest $15 billion in the field, in return for – supposedly – a 25 per cent share of the gas produced after it comes on stream in 2013.

The growing importance of offshore natural resources (and the scarcity of onshore ones) was highlighted by an audacious geopolitical adventure in and under the Arctic Sea in the summer of 2007, as popular inside Russia as it was troubling for outsiders. A Russian expedition made the first manned trip to the seabed at the North Pole, symbolically claiming it for Russia. The natural resources of the Arctic have been frozen both in law and in nature for decades. But global warming is making the Arctic look more accessible. Below the seabed lie not only perhaps 10 billion tonnes of oil and gas deposits, but also tin, manganese, gold, nickel, lead, platinum and diamonds. It may have some of the last untouched fish stocks in the northern hemisphere and − if the ice really thins or melts outright all year round − it could be an important route for maritime freight. The five countries around the Arctic Circle − America, Canada, Denmark (which looks after Greenland's interests) Norway and Russia − each have the 200 nautical mile (370 kilometres) 'economic zone' allowed by the United Nations Law of the Sea Convention. Russia argued in 2001 that its continental shelf stretched out into the Arctic, entitling it to a larger chunk. A UN tribunal said it needed to provide more evidence.

That is what the 2007 expedition, led by Russia's most glamorous explorer, Artur Chilingarov, aimed to supply. By taking samples from the seabed, it hopes to show that the Lomonosov Ridge, an underwater mountain chain, is indeed a continuation of Russia's landmass. If accepted, that would allow the Kremlin to annex a 460,000 square mile wedge of territory, roughly the size of Western Europe, between Russia's northern coastline and the North Pole. Such wrangles about international maritime borders normally go at snails' pace, and are stupefyingly boring. When Denmark allocated the equivalent of $25 million in 2004 to try to prove that the Lomonosov Ridge was connected to Greenland, few noticed or cared. The 2007 Russian expedition did not just collect symbolic rocks (real geological evidence would have come only from drilling deep below the seabed). It placed a titanium canister bearing the Russian flag on the yellow gravel 4,200 metres below the surface, at the site of the North Pole. That was the first manned mission to the polar seabed and one mounted by a flotilla that no other country could match. A mighty nuclear-powered icebreaker shepherded a research vessel that launched sophisticated submarines capable of pinpoint navigation under the Arctic ice. Adding an extra touch of technological wizardry, the submarines established a direct link from the seabed to the Mir space station. For outsiders used to stories of Russian bungling and backwardness, the stunt was a salutary reminder of the world-class technical clout and human talent the Kremlin can still command. Even more startling, though, was Russia's rhetoric. 'The Arctic is ours and we should manifest our presence,' said Mr Chilingarov, a charismatic figure whom Mr Putin has named as 'presidential envoy' to the Arctic. 'This is like placing a flag on the moon,' said a spokesman for Russia's Arctic and Antarctic Institute. Planting a Russian flag on the seabed has symbolic, not legal, force, but it still scandalised Canada's foreign minister Peter MacKay. 'This isn't the fifteenth century,' he complained. 'You can't go around the world and just plant flags and say "We're claiming this territory".' Russia's foreign minister, Sergei Lavrov, insisted that his country was doing nothing of the kind. But Andrei Kokoshin, chair of a Russian parliamentary committee dealing with the ex-Soviet region, said Russia 'will have to actively defend its interests in the Arctic', adding, 'There is something to think about on the military side as well. We need to reinforce our Northern Fleet and our border guards and build airfields so that we can ensure full control over the situation.'

The next day, Russia's top admiral said it was time to restore the navy's permanent presence in the Mediterranean. How seriously to take Russia's new military posture is the subject of the next chapter.

8

Sabre-rattling, or Selling Sabres?
Russia's Foreign Policy Unpicked

On the face of it, Russia is still an intimidating military power. It has one of the world's largest armies, excellent special forces and some remarkable modern weapons. The *Shkval* [Squall] torpedo, for example, is an underwater rocket that travels in a capsule of gas created by its specially designed cone; fired from a super-silent submarine, it is one of the few weapons that could endanger an American aircraft carrier. Another is the fearsome Moskit ship-launched supersonic missile. Russia's new S-400 air defence system has twice the range of American-made Patriot missiles. The Topol-M is an intercontinental ballistic missile (ICBM) with a multiple warhead. Unlike its liquid-fuelled counterparts that usually launch from vulnerable silos, it has a propulsion system based on much more stable solid fuel. It can be kept in constant readiness, and launched from anywhere. Russia has hugely increased its military procurement budget: the latest published figures are for nearly five trillion roubles (roughly $190 billion) to be spent in the period up to 2015.[1] The aim is to replace 45 per cent of Russia's arsenal with new equipment, with an emphasis on long-range nuclear weapons. Pride of place goes to a new submarine-launched ballistic missile, the Bulava, and to at least fifty new Topol-M land-based missiles.

Russia is certainly flexing its military muscles as never before: in the summer of 2007 it restarted the Cold War practice of regularly buzzing Western countries' airspace to test their reactions. Initially this was in the North Atlantic and North Sea, where British and Norwegian pilots used sometimes to fly so close to their Soviet adversaries that they could taunt them by waving *Playboy* centrefolds (even the softest porn was banned in the puritanical Soviet system). In August 2007, Russia made the practice explicit, flying two lumbering Tupolev-95 bombers from their base on the Russian–Chinese border to the American military base at Guam in the middle of the Pacific Ocean. That again was a familiar sight in the Cold War, when these bombers, the workhorse of the Soviet Union's airborne nuclear deterrent, would cruise down America's east coast. Mr Putin proudly announced that Russia could now afford to keep nuclear bombers in the air at all times.

But even thriller writers find it hard to imagine the Kremlin posing a direct military threat to NATO. In overall defence budgets, America outspends Russia by around twenty-five to one. Since the end of the old Cold War, Russia's nuclear arsenal has slipped far behind that of America, once its main strategic adversary. Most Russian nuclear weapons are old; many have exceeded their design life. Russia has the world's largest stockpile of nuclear weapons, with an estimated total of 16,000 warheads, half the Soviet Union's estimated total of 35,000 in the mid-1980s.[2] The Americans have a smaller stockpile, of 10,640. However, more of America's weapons – around 6,390 – are actually usable. As well as tactical nuclear weapons, Russia has 3,300–3,400 strategic nuclear warheads. But Russia also lacks modern means of delivering them from land, sea and air. Russia has built only one of a planned eight Borei submarines, the *Yuri Dolgoruky*, which after ten years of intermittent work was launched in 2007 and will be handed over to the Russian navy in 2008. But like Russia's remaining three huge Typhoon-class nuclear subs, the *Yuri Dolgoruky* has no ICBMs until the Bulava missile is working properly. So far it has failed four out of its five tests. And it is far from clear if Russia's run-down nuclear factories can manufacture it in the quantity or quality required.

The Topol-M launchers rarely venture out of their bases, just as the nuclear-armed submarines mostly stay in harbour. The early warning system is technologically backward and patchy. Conventional forces are in an even worse state. The Russian navy, for example, has barely twenty seaworthy surface ships, divided between the Black Sea, the Northern Fleet, the Baltic Sea and the Pacific. Russia has only a single aircraft carrier, the unreliable *Admiral Kuznetsov*; though it plans to build more, it lacks even a shipyard capable of such a task. Russia has found it hard to refurbish the Soviet-era carrier, the *Admiral Gorshkov*, which it sold to India in 2004, with a promised delivery date of 2008. It is now unlikely to be ready before 2011. If Russia does return to the Mediterranean, it will be with a token naval force that lacks air cover.

Once the fear was that Russia, with a surprise attack, could win a war against NATO. Now the question is whether America – at least in theory – could knock out Russia's entire nuclear arsenal in a first strike. Nobody in Washington is planning that, of course. But Russia's increasing nuclear weakness may make the Kremlin worryingly jittery. Russia's remaining military might does two things. It can tip the balance in other conflicts, hot or cold, either by projecting a mainly symbolic presence, or by selling weapons. Secondly, it allows the Kremlin to posture: in talks about arms control agreements already concluded, in agreements that NATO wants to update and in talks about weapons systems that have yet to be deployed.

The arms sales are growing fast. One of Mr Putin's first acts in power was to create a strong state arms export company, Rosoboronexport.[3] Since then, Russian arms sales have risen by more than 70 per cent, making the country the world's second largest arms exporter after America. The trend is accelerating: in 2006, the

order book more than doubled to $30 billion. The main bene-
ficiaries so far have been China, followed by India. In 2006, for
example, China received half of Russia's $6 billion arms sales. But
the new trend is sales to countries that detest the West. Oil-rich
Venezuela has bought $3 billion-worth of Russian weapons,
including fifty-three military helicopters and twenty-four advanced
Sukhoi SU-30 fighter jets. It is now planning to buy five Project
636 Kilo-class diesel submarines, with an option on four more
modern ones later. Russia has sold advanced anti-tank and anti-
aircraft missiles to Syria, matching its strong military intelligence
cooperation with the regime there. It has sold twenty-nine short-
range Tor missiles to Iran to protect the Russian-built Bushehr
nuclear reactor. It is discussing sales of the more advanced S-300 air
defence system and may have helped Iran develop its own version
of the *Shkval* – something that could be crucial in a naval confrontation with America in the Gulf. Russia has sold small arms and
other equipment to Sudan, some of which has been used in Darfur.
Before the war in Iraq it used Belarus as a backdoor means of selling
air defence systems to Saddam Hussein, and training Iraqi techni-
cians to operate them. Along with other Russian defence contractors, Rosoboronexport is as a result banned from doing business
in America.

The rhetoric that accompanies such sales seems straight out of
the Soviet playbook. Just days before he visited George W. Bush in
Maine in the summer of 2007, Mr Putin played host to Venezuela's
President Chávez, who called for a 'worldwide revolution' against
American 'tyranny'. His adoring remarks to Mr Putin were
redolent of the tributes paid by leaders of Soviet allies visiting
Moscow during the Cold War.[4] He then went on to visit Belarus
and Iran. Such moves are an irritant to NATO and its allies, and are
an ominous sign of the Kremlin's preferences. But they do not yet
come close to changing the strategic balance. America's military

planners worry about lots of things; Russian rockets are just one of them, and a long way from the top of the list. Even a huge increase in defence spending over many years would not restore Russia's military–industrial complex to the heights reached during the Soviet era. Brilliant design is one thing: turning it into mass production is another. Nearly two decades of neglect and mis-management mean that Russia's arms factories lack the people and tools necessary for a world-class weapons industry, either for export or for domestic use. The workforce is ageing, the necessary base of subcontractors is missing and the skills base has eroded sharply since the Soviet era. Russia's latest prototype fighter, the supposedly 'fifth generation' SU-47 *Berkut* (Golden Eagle), wows observers at foreign air shows – but it is just that: a single prototype. As with so many things, Russia is still living off the conscripted brilliance and perverse sacrifices of the past. Much of what counts as arms sales still involves flogging off mothballed Soviet-era equipment relabelled as new. Russia's main selling proposition is that its weapons are rugged, reliable and cheap, not that they are the height of technological sophistication. Customers for sophisticated weapons want reliable after-sales service, something that Russia has so far not been able to provide.

Sales of nuclear technology are another matter. Rumours persist that Russia not only supplied Iraq with weapons of mass destruc-tion but also moved them out via Syria before the American attack. Similar rumours now say that Russia is helping Iran not just with publicly acknowledged civilian nuclear technology, but also with enrichment and other capabilities necessary to build nuclear war-heads. But it is hard to see what Russia would gain from selling weapons of mass destruction to unpredictable dictators. It is more likely that the Kremlin enjoys hinting that it might sell terrifying weapons to America's adversaries, rather than that it actually does so. While not insisting that Iran gives up its plans to enrich uranium, Russia has stopped deliveries of nuclear fuel to Iran until that country makes peace with the International Atomic Energy Agency.

It is the same story – of sulks and threats and ominous trends, rather than immediate menace – with America's planned missile defence bases in Europe, and the Conventional Forces in Europe (CFE) treaty. Russia objects strongly to the first, saying that it will if necessary target its nuclear weapons on European countries involved in the project. And it has given notice that it wants to withdraw from the latter – a landmark agreement signed in November 1990, at a time when the Warsaw Pact was already disintegrating. Neither row is what it seems. As a glance at the globe shows, the American bases (interceptors in Poland and a radar base in the Czech Republic) are aimed at Iran's missiles, not Russia's. If Russia wanted to hit America with nuclear weapons, the least likely trajectory would be over Central Europe (a route over the Arctic and North Atlantic would be much more plausible). The ten interceptor rockets, once installed, might give an Iranian regime with only one or two missiles pause for thought. They would not affect the credibility of Russia's much larger nuclear deterrent.

American military scientists have explained this repeatedly to their Russian counterparts, with at least ten detailed technical presentations, including a full briefing at the NATO–Russian council, but have not succeeded in denting the Kremlin's furious opposition to the plan. As Stephen Blank, an American academic, notes,[5] 'abundant ironies exist in Russia's position'. For a start, the Kremlin does have a good case on other arms control issues that the American administration has refused to discuss seriously. In particular, it has rebuffed Kremlin proposals for a third Strategic Arms Reduction Treaty (START-3) to replace START-1, which expires in 2009. Strategic unilateralism in nuclear matters is not just unwise, it is dangerous. Simply trying to maximise the credibility of America's nuclear deterrence stimulates insecurity elsewhere, and encourages other countries to think nuclear weapons are the best means of fighting wars. But Russia's arguments on missile defence are much weaker. The Kremlin both complains that the new system threatens its security, while boasting that its missiles are so technologically advanced that it poses no threat. Secondly, the only powers that could actually hit Russia with intermediate range missiles are the Kremlin's so-called friends, Iran and China. Third, these countries have this capability thanks only to Russian technology and assistance. If Russia does take what it calls 'adequate' measures against America's new defensive installations, by targeting them with its own missiles, perhaps it will also do so against the far more dangerous potential threat from rogues and rivals in Iran, North Korea, Pakistan and China.

Even odder, Russians and others doubt very much whether this missile defence system, or indeed any foreseeable one, will work. The technical difficulty is akin to hitting a bullet with a bullet. It is conceptually flawed: would a rogue state mad enough to use nuclear weapons at all be deterred by the slight chance that they might be intercepted? Would not such a state try to smuggle a nuclear device into its target country, and detonate it terrorist-style, rather than go to all the trouble of delivering it via an ICBM? These are strong arguments. It may be that a future generation of missile defence systems will be cheap and effective. But for now, the only certain winners from the development of the planned system are the companies of America's own military–industrial complex. If the American politicians whose campaigns they finance are gullible, paranoid or corrupt enough to shower billions of tax dollars into these firms' pockets, why should Russia mind? Nor does the supposed Kremlin counter-measure, of retargeting missiles on European countries, make much sense. It is the number of missiles,

the size of their warheads, their range and their detectability that
affect the strategic balance, not their targets. To change the targets
is a matter of a few minutes' work on the computer. It has a
powerful symbolic effect, but almost no practical one. In fact, the
argument is heated because it has everything to do with politics,
and almost nothing to do with serious questions of nuclear strategy.

On the face of it, Russia is annoyed that America is basing
anything important in former Soviet satellite countries. That breaks
an undertaking, the Kremlin claims, made when the Russian forces
pulled out in the early 1990s. The Kremlin's real argument,
however, is a different and more subtle one, which becomes
alarmingly effective on issues such as this. The missile defence
plan is highly unpopular in Europe. West Europeans see it as a
characteristically ill-thought-out bit of hi-tech swaggering by the
global superpower. Even the Czechs and the Poles do not welcome
the new bases. The practical effect so far is that America's per-
emptory request, and lack of any obvious carrot to reward its allies
for the risk involved, has alienated public opinion in even these,
which are among the two most Atlanticist countries in the region.
By kicking up a fuss, even with empty threats based on the shakiest
logic, Russia moves closer to a strategic prize that has been the
Kremlin's aim ever since the start of the last Cold War: to split the
once formidable Atlantic alliance.

The means for that are now in place. The glue that held Europe
and American interests together for four decades was composed of
two ingredients: European fear of the Soviet Union and American
belief that Europe's fate mattered across the Atlantic, too. Twice in
the last century, America stood by at the start of a European fight,
only to have to intervene, belatedly and expensively, towards the
end. Post-war strategic thinking was based on the assumption that it
was better not to make the same mistake again. After the collapse of
communism both components weakened. European countries no

longer felt a military threat from Russia, while America saw more pressing threats elsewhere: chiefly China and – after 9/11 – the 'war on terror'. In neither regard did Europe look like a particularly useful ally. Indeed, it often looked like an ungrateful one. From this point of view, the main value of the missile defence system is symbolic: it shows that America's European allies are still valued and useful. But conversely, opposition to the plan has been a propaganda gift to anti-American politicians across the whole continent of Europe. 'Here are the Americans clumsily provoking Russia and endangering our security,' they argue. It isolates the pro-American politicians that agreed to host it.

America's allies are already exposed by the catastrophic failure of the Bush administration's war in Iraq. For reasons of both principle and pragmatism the ex-communist countries were among America's staunchest allies in Iraq. Toppling a brutal dictator and the one-party state he had imposed was a resonant cause. Joining the 'coalition of the willing' was not only a good way of showing gratitude to America for its support of NATO enlargement, but also of underlining that the ex-communist countries were not just consumers of security, but contributors to it. That goodwill and loyalty has been drained and strained, in most countries to the point of almost complete exhaustion, for lamentably little result. Politicians who backed the war now look stupid. Those who supported Russia's criticism of it have been vindicated. An extra, and especially damaging, issue is the alleged cooperation of Poland and Romania, and possibly others, in the CIA's 'rendition' of terrorist suspects for interrogation under torture. If the Kremlin had been writing the script itself it could hardly have found a better storyline: after fighting a greedy, brutal and incompetent war, America is now trying to put an unpopular, scary hi-tech defence system in Europe, despite the objections of almost all concerned. What better illustration could there be of the deep-seated

unfairness of the transatlantic relationship? When Mr Putin said in
September 2007 that Europe should drop its 'silly' Atlantic solidarity and concentrate on improving ties with Russia,[6] it was
striking that almost no voice was raised in criticism.

Russia's behaviour on arms control issues may lack military logic,
but it has profound if concealed political effects. The CFE treaty,
the cornerstone of conventional weapons reduction talks at the end
of the old Cold War, had a practical effect when both superpowers
had large, capable, conventional forces in Europe. Now it is of
mainly symbolic value; America's forces, once 600,000 strong, are
down to 60,000. The Kremlin has withdrawn completely from
European countries to its west and south. The treaty brings no
meaningful restriction on Russia's own military capabilities. Russia
is allowed to have 6,400 tanks, 11,480 armoured vehicles, 6,415
artillery pieces, 3,450 combat aircraft and 890 armed helicopters in
European Russia.[7] In every case, Russia has less than these ceilings
– usually by some way. When Russia did need more forces, during
its wars in Chechnya, it hugely breached its regional 'flank' ceilings,
prompting only murmurs of protest. In 1999, the flank ceilings
were revised, on condition (the West says) that Russia withdraw its
remaining forces from Moldova and Georgia. It didn't. Then in
2005, after years of prevarication, Russia suddenly agreed to
withdraw its forces from Georgia, except for the 'peacekeeping'
base in Abkhazia. It continues to keep a base in Transdniestria,
partly to protect the separatist regime there, and partly as a backstop
to ensure Russian influence over it.

For all its irrelevance, the CFE treaty has been the subject of
lengthy political wrangles. Because of Russian foot-dragging in
Georgia and Moldova, Western countries that had signed the CFE
treaty refused to ratify it. Russia claims to find that infuriating. Mr
Putin also complained, in an address to the Russian parliament in
2007, that the West is 'building up armed forces in direct proximity

to Russia's borders'.[8] It is true that under the treaty, armed forces of the new NATO members like Estonia count, oddly, as Russian, but these militaries are so small that they have no significant effect on the total numbers.

The only new factors are logistics and training bases America is developing in Bulgaria and Romania, plus the (planned) missile defence installations. Neither is directed against Russia: indeed, conventional capabilities in Europe are so rundown and over-stretched that it is doubtful if NATO could mount even a defensive operation in Eastern Europe, let alone an offensive one against Russia. In short, none of Russia's arguments stands scrutiny. The CFE's non-ratification remains a minor diplomatic inconvenience for the Kremlin, but only because it highlights the mildly embarras-sing fact that Russia props up two illegal regimes. Moreover, the practical steps Russia is threatening in response are as ill-grounded as the arguments. No provision for the planned 'moratorium' an-nounced by Mr Putin in April 2007 actually exists in the treaty.[9] It is, indeed, possible to withdraw from it, with a 150-day notice period. That notice should be based on a statement of 'extraordinary events' that have prompted the move; until the 150 days expire, the departing party must stick to the CFE.[10] It is questionable whether Mr Putin appreciated this, or whether he had the proper advice from international lawyers. At an emergency conference of the CFE members in Vienna in June 2007, Russia repeated its demand that all the parties to the treaty ratify it by 1 July 2008. As expected, the Western signatories simply repeated their demand that Russia first complete its withdrawal from Moldova and Georgia. The 'split in NATO' promised by the Kremlin-controlled press never materi-alised. Nor did the promised presidential decree on the moratorium. Military inspections by NATO countries within the CFE frame-work that had initially been denied, citing 'insurmountable circum-stances', were then granted.

So why is Mr Putin now making such a fuss? It is partly that the CFE was so unpopular with Soviet (and then Russian) generals, who saw it as codifying a retreat from their hard-won bridgehead in Central Europe. So talking about tearing it up is a symbolic gesture to them. More importantly, if Russia does eventually withdraw, it will no longer be bound by the treaty's notification, control and inspection regime. That will mean that, if it wants, it can concentrate forces on, for example, the border with Georgia or Estonia, without being obliged to explain what it is doing or why. In the worst case, that could be the first stage in a military intervention in either country. That is unlikely in the case of Estonia, a NATO member, but conceivable in an artificially stoked conflict between Georgia and South Ossetia, Abkhazia or both. As Pavel Felgenhauer, Russia's best-known independent military analyst, points out wryly, 'This will create less transparency and more mutual suspicion in Europe – much like the atmosphere inside Putin's Kremlin.'[11]

Withdrawal from the CFE also paves the way for a Russian pull-out from another cornerstone arms control agreement from the old Cold War, the Intermediate-range Nuclear Forces (INF) treaty. In February 2007 Mr Putin said that this 'no longer serves Russia's interests' and the chief of the Russian general staff, General Yuri Baluyevsky, said that if America pressed ahead with missile defence plans, Russia could pull out of the INF.[12] That would allow Russia to develop shorter-range nuclear missiles and target them on Europe. The scene would be set for another downward spiral in the transatlantic relationship. America could offer to put its own nuclear missiles in Europe, but as in the 1980s that would prompt frenzied protests from 'peace' campaigners. Yet without American nuclear protection, Europe's security would look even more precarious. Without nuclear forces based in Europe, a future American administration would find it hard to argue that it needed to keep any troops at all on the continent. That would suit the Kremlin just fine.

As well as missile defence and the CFE treaty, the third big European security issue for Russia is Kosovo, scene of the only military confrontation between NATO and Russian forces since the end of the Cold War. That was in 1999, after Serbian forces were retreating from Kosovo following the NATO bombing campaign to force Mr Milošević to stop persecuting the Albanian-speaking population of the province. Two hundred Russian soldiers from the international peacekeeping forces in neighbouring Bosnia rushed to seize the airport at the Kosovar capital Priština. The event is still shrouded in mystery. Russia was evidently planning to use the airfield to fly in more troops, but Ukraine and Hungary, reacting promptly to Western requests, denied overflight rights to Russian planes. It is still unclear whether the move was authorised by Yeltsin and his defence minister, or was an act of rebellion against them – and perhaps part of a broader plan.

At any rate, Russia since then has been content to let the West stew in a mess of its own making. Kosovo, nominally an international protectorate, is badly governed, a haven for organised crime and unable or unwilling to protect the rights of its remaining Serbian minority. Independence might be a way of forcing the Kosovar leaders to face up to their responsibilities. Serbia says it will not recognise or accept independence of a province which it regards as historically Serbian, and where the rights of Serbs are endangered. Partition might offer a solution, but this has been rejected by the international community as likely to spark even more fighting. America wants to hurry up. It fears that if the outside world does not recognise Kosovo, it will lose its remaining ability to influence events there. The EU broadly supports this, although some countries have broken ranks and taken a strongly pro-Serbian stance. The UN envoy, Martti Ahtisaari, has come up with an ingenious plan that offers Kosovo conditional statehood under international supervision. This has been modified to try to take account of Russian objections, by giving a longer period for Serbs and the Kosovar leadership to try to reach agreement. But what if they don't? Russia says blandly that it will only support an agreement acceptable to both sides.[13] That, in effect, gives the Serbs a veto. If the West ignores Russian objections, and tries to force the Ahtisaari plan through the UN Security Council, Russia will veto it. The result is a stalemate: damaging for Europe, but convenient for both the Kremlin and its Serbian allies. Attention inevitably turns to what Russia might want in return: perhaps that the West turns a blind eye to a one-off deal on Moldova? Or does Russia want Georgia's allies to tell it to forget about recovering South Ossetia and Abkhazia?

The main aim may be simply to look tough. In the Yeltsin years, Russia tried hard to persuade the Serbian strongman Slobodan Milošević to back down. Many Russians now regard that as a mistake. Nobody should any longer take Russia's goodwill for granted. Secondly, Russian intransigence usually has the paradox-ical result of making fair-minded Europeans cast around for a 'compromise'. That then puts pressure on those who still advocate the original policy of Kosovar independence – chiefly America and its closest allies. In short, the longer the impasse goes on, the better for the Kremlin. But the common factor in all three disputes, over missile defence, over the CFE treaty and over Kosovo, is that they give the Kremlin a pretext to sound cross, behave badly and to try to divide Europe and America. The most interesting question is why this policy is needed at all.

Russia has dropped three Soviet attributes from its foreign policy: a messianic ideology, raw military power and the imperative of territorial expansion. Instead comes the idea that, as Dmitri Trenin, a well-connected foreign-policy expert, puts it: 'Russia's business is business.'[14] That has special weight, he argues, because the people who rule Russia also own it. Stitching up world energy markets with other big producers, or finding customers for Russian weapons and raw materials, are much more interesting than the nuances of the Middle East peace process or the endless woes of the Balkans. In short, bad politics is bad for business. Capitalism is integrating Russia ever more deeply into the outside world, and surely making political conflicts less likely, not more. So what is going on? The Kremlin's explanation goes like this. The West takes Russia for granted, swallows concessions and offers only snubs in return. Russia abandoned the Soviet empire in Eastern Europe, on the strict understanding that NATO would not expand to the former Warsaw Pact countries. Yet that is exactly what happened. Far from winding up, or staying as a backstop security organisation, NATO started offensive operations for the first time in its history, intervening in ex-Yugoslavia to bomb Serbia, a traditional Russian ally. That cold shoulder during the 1990s demoralised the pro-Westerners in the Yeltsin Kremlin. Now, at least in some Russian eyes, the West has treated Mr Putin equally shabbily. In 2006, a former top Kremlin aide, Aleksandr Voloshin, went on a semi-official mission to explain Russia's frustration to American decision-makers, outlining what Mr Putin had done since 11 September 2001. This included offering unprecedented intelligence and security cooperation against militant Islamism, closing the two main overseas bases inherited from the Soviet Union[15] and allowing America to use air bases in Central Asia to support the attack on the Taliban in Afghanistan. All that, Mr Voloshin argued, had exposed Mr Putin to sharp criticism from hawks in the Kremlin. He had assured them that a bold gesture to America would pay dividends. But instead, America continued to interfere in Russia's backyard, stoking popular revolutions in Ukraine and Georgia, bringing the Baltic states into NATO and talking about new bases in Eastern Europe.

The arguments got nowhere. Though the Kremlin insists that NATO expansion is encirclement, a better way of looking at it is that Russia has wilfully cut itself off from the European mainstream. Switzerland and Austria are entirely surrounded by NATO members, but do not worry that they are encircled. NATO has in fact done rather little – too little in the view of some of its new members – to counter Russian muscle-flexing. Most of the new members are militarily weak, and struggle to meet their NATO commitments. The alliance's work in Eastern Europe is mainly based on strengthening its members' ability to work with each other in joint training and peacekeeping. The truth is that so long as the Kremlin insists on seeing NATO as an enemy, it strengthens the case for bringing vulnerable ex-communist countries into the alliance. In the early 1990s, that was off the agenda. Joining NATO was seen as too expensive by the potential applicants, and too destabilising by the alliance's policymakers. But Russia never seemed to understand why its former satellite countries might be worried about their security. By protesting loudly that NATO enlargement was provocative and 'impermissible'[16] (a favourite word in the Russian diplomatic lexicon), the Kremlin ensured that the applicants' desire grew stranger and more urgent; it also became morally all but impossible for existing NATO members to turn them away. The Kremlin may dislike this development. But it has only itself to blame for it.

Some Westerners may find it mildly offensive that their support for security, freedom and justice in ex-communist countries, and attempts to prevent genocide in Bosnia and Kosovo, are dismissed as nothing more than self-interested geopolitics. Such arguments seem to make no impact, however: in 2006 Mr Putin apparently decided that it was pointless trying to maintain a warm friendship with the West. Instead, Russia would have to gain respect by talking, and acting, toughly. That has some risks. Russia is now increasingly seen in the rich industrialised world as an authoritarian state that hangs out with international pariahs. Secondly, fear of Russia may make the Euroatlantic glue stickier. For the first time since the end of the old Cold War, it is now possible to argue that America and Europe need each other in the face of a Russian threat. But Kremlin cheerleaders do not see it that way. They argue that the world is changing: America and Europe may have put Russia in the deep freeze, but much larger countries such as India, Brazil, Mexico and Indonesia, all respectably free and law-governed, have not. America may be rich now, but developing countries, where Russia is much more popular, have brighter prospects. American hegemony, in short, is history.

Similarly, just because America is still the world's most powerful country does not make it synonymous with world opinion. The fire-breathing Mr Chávez[17] may be demonised in Washington, DC, but he is lionised elsewhere. As Aleksei Pushkov, a pro-Kremlin journalist, notes, there are no anti-Chávez demonstrations in Western capitals, and plenty of anti-Bush ones. 'Which is the pariah – Chávez or Bush?' he asks. Indeed, Russian anti-Americanism is mild compared to the depth of sentiment in supposed American allies such as Turkey, Pakistan, France, Germany or Britain. Not only that, a brusque approach to the self-appointed guardians of Euroatlantic virtue hardly seems to be hurting business. Since Mr Putin started criticising America publicly in 2003, foreign investment has soared. Mr Blair's warning to foreign businesses about political risks in Russia came just days before an investment summit in St Petersburg attended by a record number of corporate chiefs.

The tactics are increasingly clear and effective. But the goal is still puzzling. The short-term wish list is clear: recognition of Russia's

SABRE-RATTLING, OR SELLING SABRES?

primacy in the former Soviet empire; the energy 'Finlandisation' of Europe; and international parity of esteem, a seat, *de facto* or *de jure*, at the Western top tables. But these wishes are incompatible: bullying the Balts pretty much precludes a friendly reception in Brussels or Washington, DC. If anything, it guarantees a series of embarrassing public snubs. The Kremlin may be assuming that the West will eventually abandon its new allies, or that they will become indefensible by their own efforts. But pending a split in the West, or its surrender, Russia's choice is a stark one. It can drop its pretensions to empire and its peculiar version of history, in which case it can move sharply closer to the EU and NATO. Or it can go down the route of independent foreign policy, either in alliance with the Muslim world or with China.

The Kremlin is certainly making an effort to restore at least some of its Soviet-era clout in the Muslim world, to some extent on the basis of 'my enemy's enemy is my friend'. If America identifies Iran as part of the 'axis of evil' then that kick-starts Russian goodwill. Russia joined the Islamic Conference Organisation as an observer in 2005 and Mr Putin attended its 2003 conference in Kuala Lumpur, Malaysia, where, amid anti-Semitic tirades from some of the other participants, he described Russia as Islam's 'historical defender'.[18] Unlike almost all Western countries, Russia is prepared to talk to radical Islamist movements such as Hamas and Hezbollah. As Aleksei Malashenko of the Moscow Carnegie Center argues,[19] the Kremlin approach seems to be to draw a rather arbitrary (indeed, probably fictional) line between 'good' and 'bad' Islamic militants: the 'bad' are the Chechen separatists and their allies in the North Caucasus and Tatarstan. The 'good' are the ones who tweak America's nose. That echoes faintly the Soviet Union's attitude from twenty-five years earlier: 'good' Muslims attacked Israel and America. 'Bad' ones attacked the Soviet boys in Afghanistan.

Perhaps aware of the contradiction, the Kremlin tries to keep a little distance from Hamas and the like: they are welcomed warmly in Moscow by pro-Kremlin ideologues and propagandists, but not by senior Kremlin figures themselves. Aleksandr Prokhanov, editor of the 'red-brown'[20] *Zavtra* (Tomorrow), congratulated the Hamas leader Khaled Mashal 'with all his heart' on the movement's victory in the Palestinian territory elections.[21] Yet the same newspaper is an ardent supporter of the most ruthless tactics against Chechen rebels. Russia's engagement, such as it is, does not seem to have nudged either Hamas or Iran into a more moderate position. The latter's nuclear weapons ambitions are proceeding unchecked. Hamas shows no sign of wanting to recognise Israel, even tacitly. Russia seemed to have no leverage in the war in Lebanon in the summer of 2006, despite its supposedly close links to Syria and Hezbollah. Its influence in Iraq is close to zero – and when Russian embassy officials were seized, and eventually murdered, in Iraq in 2006, none of the Kremlin's Muslim allies seemed to do anything to help.

The main reason is simple: Russia's flirtation with the Muslim cause is seen, rightly, as opportunist. The Soviet invasion of Afghanistan (plus support for the American attack on the Taliban in 2001), two wars in Chechnya and strong support for the Milošević regime's harsh stance towards Muslim populations in Kosovo and Bosnia make it hard to regard Russia as a serious ally for the Islamic world. Muslims appreciate Russia as a counter-weight to American influence, and as a possible source of useful weapons (officially or unofficially). But it goes no further. Russia's relations with the Muslim world are complicated by another factor: Israel. During the old Cold War, relations were icy: the Soviet Union was profoundly anti-Semitic, and strongly supported Arab countries trying to destroy the Jewish state. Full diplomatic relations were restored only as the Soviet Union was already in its death throes. A million Russian-speaking immigrants in Israel makes the country now one of Russia's most important foreign cultural partners. More Russian books, newspapers and television programmes are produced in Israel than in any other country outside the former Soviet Union and Israel is a popular tourist destination (being one of the few places where monoglot Russians can feel at home in a 'real' foreign country). The majority of Russia's Jewish population has now emigrated; anti-Semitism has not disappeared,[22] but it is dormant – and eclipsed by prejudice against other minorities. Few Russians objected that the prime minister from 2004 to 2007, the low-key Mikhail Fradkov, is Jewish.[23] Many Russians feel instinctive sympathy for Israel's predicament: Russia has suffered ruthless Islamist terrorism, too, they feel. The presence (perhaps exaggerated) of 'Arab' fighters in Chechnya adds to the feeling of linkage. That is not enough to change Kremlin policy very much. Israel objects strenuously to Iran's nuclear ambitions, which depend almost wholly on Russian know-how and technology. Russian arms sales to Syria could shift the military balance significantly against Israel (though Russia did halt a planned sale of Iskander surface-to-surface missiles in 2005). After the Kremlin opened contacts with Hamas, Israel crisply snubbed the idea of a peace conference in Moscow

The Chinese option, at least in comparison, looks more attractive. The 'strategic partnership' between Russia and China is one of the big achievements of the Putin years in foreign policy. A long-standing squabble over the border has been settled. Worries about illegal migration (overblown in the Yeltsin years, but widely believed) have calmed down. Trade with China has more than tripled since Mr Putin came into the Kremlin. China has invested $500 million in Rosneft, the Kremlin's oil subsidiary, and Russia has agreed to build an ambitious gas pipeline to China.[24] Both countries share a strong dislike of Western universalist values and a belief that economic growth and stability are preferable to imported notions of freedom. The Kremlin's home-grown ideology of 'sovereign democracy' and China's nominal 'communism' have a lot in common: horror of instability, nationalism, and a belief that the proof of the authoritarian pudding is in the eating. The message, crudely, is 'who needs your kind of democracy when we have our kind of growth'.

Based on such similarities in worldview, it is possible to see Russia and China as two pillars of what some have called the 'World without the West', or WWW.[25] The WWW is strictly pragmatic, shuns idealistic political approaches (which it sees as hypocritical) and detests outside interference in other countries' affairs. It is the antithesis of the American idea of liberal internationalism: that intervening to prevent genocide, say, is not just the right but the duty of a civilised country. The WWW favours state-dominated market economies, where the heights of political and economic power converge. Yet it is not the embodiment of a comprehensive rejection of the West, so to speak an 'anti-West': it wants economic cooperation with the advanced industrialised world, particularly in order to catch it up in technology and education.

The most practical expression of the WWW is the Shanghai Cooperation Organisation (SCO), an outfit that creates a potentially formidable new security axis between Russia, China and Central Asia. In 2007 this started to develop a strong military component in the organisation: its summit in the Kyrgyz capital Bishkek in August 2007 was marked by ten days of joint military exercises[26] in Chelyabinsk in the Urals and Urumqi in Chinese Turkestan. These were the SCO's biggest military exercises; the first time that Chinese airborne forces have taken part in such military drills abroad; and the first time that Russian forces have exercised in China. The end was observed by the six defence ministers of the SCO core members: China, Russia, Kazakhstan,

Kyrgyzstan, Uzbekistan and Tajikistan. The SCO is linked to Russia's answer to NATO, the Collective Security Treaty Organisation (CSTO). This has the same five ex-Soviet members, plus Armenia and Belarus, creating an embryonic security sphere that stretches from the Arctic to the South China Sea, and from the Bering Strait to the Polish border. Mr Putin says any comparison between the SCO and the old Warsaw Pact is 'idle talk' and 'improper either in content or form'.[27] But the fact remains that a big anti-Western alliance, however loose, is taking shape.

The immediate aim is to force NATO to recognise the CSTO as a counterpart, chiefly on issues such as narcotics, Afghanistan and counter-terrorism (issues which often overlap widely). That is something that NATO has always resisted. It prefers to deal with CSTO members bilaterally – a policy that interestingly echoes Russia's attitude to Western collective security organisations. The SCO and CSTO have done well in signalling to America that no security vacuum exists in Central Asia. That kyboshes grand designs from previous years about bringing countries like Uzbekistan or Kazakhstan into close strategic relationships with the West. China strongly backs Russia's position in keeping NATO out of Central Asia, and in the row over missile defence (not least because its own smaller nuclear arsenal would be more directly affected if America's system ever became workable). The next big question will be whether to promote Iran from observer status to full membership of the SCO. The Iranian leadership has been strongly pushing for this, hoping that it will give it useful diplomatic support against America's increasingly alarming demands. China, which does not want to aggravate relations with America, has resisted so far. If the SCO agrees, it will crystallise the organisation's role as the core of a global anti-American alliance, however opportunistic.

It is one thing to agree on anti-American positions, another to agree who is the top dog in a shared backyard. Russia may have invented the SCO, but China clearly thinks of itself as the natural leader, by virtue of its size and economic weight. Russia and China may be partners in keeping America out of Central Asia, but they are also rivals there. Within the region, Kazakhstan and Uzbekistan each want to be the leader. China has been strenuously trying to do its own bilateral gas deals with Turkmenistan (not an SCO member) and with Kazakhstan (which is). That threatens Russian interests. The biggest problem is that Russians' old-fashioned zero-sum geopolitical thinking makes it hard to conceive of a deep strategic alliance with anyone. China's huge population and short-age of natural resources (coal aside) are a painful contrast to Russia's demographic collapse and mineral-rich eastern regions. As a result, the two countries may make common cause, but they are not natural allies. The sharp-witted Andrei Piontkovsky calls the notion 'an alliance between a rabbit and a boa constrictor'.[28]

That leaves Russia stuck. It is too weak to have a truly effective independent foreign policy, but it is too disgruntled and neurotic to have a sensible and constructive one. It wants to be respected, trusted and liked, but will not act in a way that gains respect, nurtures trust or wins affection. It settles for being noticed – even when that comes as a result of behaviour that alienates and intimidates other countries. It compensates for real weakness by showing pretend strength. Little of that – advanced weapons sales to rogue regimes aside – immediately threatens global peace and security. In that sense, the New Cold War is less scary than the old one. But Russia's behaviour is alarming, uncomfortable and damaging, both to its own interests and to those of other countries. And the trajectory is worrying. If Russia becomes still richer and still more authoritarian, all the problems described in previous chapters will be harder to deal with, not easier. Russia's influence in the West will be stronger; the willingness to confront it less. The

former satellite countries will be even more vulnerable; the
economic levers even better positioned. In other words, if the
West does not start winning the New Cold War while it can, it will
find it much harder in the future. The price of a confrontation now
may be economic pain and political uncertainty. But it still offers
the chance of a new relationship with Russia based on realism
rather than sentiment, and tough-mindedness rather than wishful
thinking. The price later will be higher – perhaps so high that the
West will no longer be able to pay it.

9

How to Win the New Cold War:
Why the West Must Believe in Itself

First a medieval fortress and then the citadel of Soviet totalitarianism, the Kremlin's rose-red walls have rarely made lovers of liberty
and justice feel at home. It is as if Britain's government were based
in the Tower of London, or France's in the Bastille. Certainly the
ideas now bubbling under its onion domes would have been all too
familiar to its past occupants: put bleakly, Russia is reverting to
behaviour last seen during the Soviet era. So the first step towards
winning the New Cold War is to accept what is happening.
History is not delivering the inexorable victory that it seemed
to promise in the 1980s. The collapse of communism has spread
freedom and justice only to a minority of the ex-captive nations. In
the rest, authoritarian bureaucratic capitalism, bolstered by natural
resources, effective secret police and stifled media, has taken root.
The dominant value is not freedom but economic stability,
protected not by the rule of law, but by strong government.
Consensus replaces the electoral mandate. The powers that be
are accountable to history, not to the citizenry. Opposition is
disloyalty at best, and outright treason if it is supported from
abroad. The individual is a means to an end, not a bearer of
inalienable rights; justice is a tool, not an ideal. The mass media are
an instrument of state, not a constraint on its power. Civil society is

an instrument for social consolidation, not diversity. Property rights and contracts are conditional; foreign policy is solely about the promotion of national interest. Intervention is hypocrisy. The *raison d'état* rules. 'Sovereign democracy' is just the latest label for this; anyone who has studied Russian history will see that many of these ideas go back centuries. Revisionist, nationalistic and jingoistic, Russia has hauled its old ideas out of the dustbin of history, burnished them and – for now – made them work.

Having accepted the magnitude of the problem, the next step is to give up the naive idea that the West can influence Russia's domestic politics. That was possible in the Yeltsin era, when the people running Russia – or at least some of them – truly wanted to join the West and were willing to take advice on how to achieve this goal. That era may have been illusory. It may have been wasted. It may not return for decades. At any rate, it is now futile to seek friends among the feuding clans of the Kremlin. Their hatred for each other may lead to change, but not necessarily change in the West's interests. Instead, we are back in an era of great-power politics. If we want to defend our interests, we will have to think clearly and pay dearly. The difficulties facing us are not mere bumps in the road. We are facing people who want to harm us, frustrate us and weaken us. Their main weapon is our greatest weakness: money. Just as we worried about the firepower of the Soviet war machine, now we should fear the tens of billions of dollars in its coffers, and the weakness of mind and morals on which it is applied. The 1990s are over: it is high time now to treat Russia as the authoritarian regime that it is: like China or Kazakhstan, rather than a member of the European family experiencing an unfortunate but temporary aberration.

A developed Western consensus on how to deal with Russia took shape only slowly in the last Cold War, and a new one will not be arrived at overnight now. But the elements are clear. First,

Europe and America must realise that the Kremlin's aim is to split them. America must not accept divisive deals from Russia on security (trading help in Iran for the abandonment of Georgia, for example). Similarly, the EU must drop its lingering disdain for America. Certainly this administration's foreign policy has been open to criticism. But the common transatlantic interests are far deeper and more important than the temporary disagreements over Iraq, the Middle East or climate change. Europeans may sometimes privately agree with Russian complaints about American arrogance or incompetence, but they should be careful about echoing them publicly. Faced with a resurgent Russia, Europe needs America more than America needs Europe. United, they are easily capable of standing up to a resurgent Russia. Divided, each is vulnerable, Europe most of all. The Atlantic alliance may never regain the unity and importance of the last Cold War, but it is still the basis for victory in this one.

Secondly, it would be neither possible nor desirable to block trade with Russia or investment there outright. The lesson of sanctions is that they create wonderful opportunities for corruption, stoke the paranoia and isolation of the targeted regime and do little or nothing to dislodge it. But Russia cannot expect to take advantage of the liberal and open economic system of Europe and America if it does not play by the same rules at home. The EU is already rightly alarmed by the investments made and planned by state-run 'wealth funds' from Russia and China. That alarm needs urgently to turn into firmly enforced rules. Countries that do not respect outsiders' property rights cannot expect to buy whatever assets they like in countries that do: those who defraud shareholders in Yukos should not then be able to use that loot to buy up more companies abroad. It is time to stop the Kremlin having the best of both worlds. Most of the time it claims its companies are normal economic actors maximising profits like everyone else – until suddenly it claims national interest and, for example, cuts off oil deliveries to Lithuania and Latvia, or electricity to Georgia, because of pressing political reasons. That is entirely rational in current conditions from a Russian point of view, but intolerable from a European one. In future, the Kremlin cannot have it both ways. If it depoliticised and demonopolised its own energy industry – chiefly by allowing third-party access to its gas pipeline monopoly – it could defuse the controversy over energy security. Until that happens, the outside world must regard every investment Russia makes abroad as a politically loaded expression of foreign policy, and not a neutral business transaction. In other words, energy security is national security, and cheap energy from ill-wishers is a bad bargain.

The EU must focus sharply on gas, which is now the continent's greatest vulnerability. Securing supplies and breaking Russia's growing monopoly may be painful and costly. The Kremlin has already said that if America or the EU start blocking its investments on national-security grounds, it will retaliate against Western companies in Russia. That may be bluff: Russia needs Western technology and would be foolish to scare such companies away. If it is not bluff: too bad. The price is worth paying. It is better to shave pennies off these companies' dividends than to let the Kremlin into the heart of our economic and political system. Putting security of supply above cost means both bargaining collectively with Russia, and making Europe's own energy infrastructure more robust and therefore less vulnerable to outside pressure. That means, for example, enforcing competition laws so that Nord Stream is not built, while providing taxpayers' money and political backing to make sure that Nabucco is. Similarly, LNG terminals are expensive and no cure-all, but still worth the money because of the diversification that they allow. Europe needs better strategic gas storage and to link its national 'energy islands' with interconnecting pipelines and electricity lines. The result will be a gas supply system that is both physically and economically robust, and therefore much harder for an outside supplier to dominate. Once supply shocks are less painful, it is less likely that anyone will bother to inflict them. Such a policy will mean a change of course: liberalisation and competition, the great goals of the past decade, are desirable for many other reasons, but they have not brought these changes about so far and are unlikely to do so now: national security is a job for politicians, not businessmen.

Similarly, the regulators of the world's financial centres must rethink how they deal with Russian (and, for that matter, Chinese) companies wanting to use them. The free market cannot be decoupled from the free society. The industrialised world has shown its capacity for collective action in dealing with money-laundering. It could do the same for corporate governance and property rights. That would mean, for example, that any company wanting to list its shares or sell its bonds in London, New York or Frankfurt had to make it clear that it was engaged in a real business, not the collection of artificial rents;[1] that its property was not stolen and that its ownership was clear and truly private. Gazprom and Rosneft, along with most big Russian companies, would be immediately disqualified. Only those blinded by greed can overlook Gazprom's legally entrenched export monopoly; the majority shareholding held by the state, the management's fondness for related-party transactions and relationships with dodgy intermediary companies. Similarly, Rosneft's participation in the rigged auctions and forced dismemberment of Yukos should disqualify it permanently from any access to international capital markets.[2] Just as NATO would not have arranged its defence spending solely to suit arms manufacturers during the old Cold War, the West now must make its banks' and energy companies' commercial interests

take second place to the question of national defence. Capitalism
thrives under freedom, security and justice, but a good business
climate is a symptom, not a goal, of a well-governed country.

Winning the New Cold War means not just rewriting the rules
for business, finance and the energy market; it means rediscovering
the virtues of collective action and solidarity in traditional politics
and diplomacy. The West should bargain where it needs to,
cooperate where it can – but not assume that there is much in
the way of common ground. Such wishful thinking is most
tempting when reality is truly ghastly. The idea of building a
'strategic partnership' with Russia is deeply rooted, even though
the 'shared values' that are meant to be the foundation for this are
now almost nowhere to be seen. As Katinka Barysch of the Centre
for European Reform, a think tank, puts it:[3]

> Many Europeans are still struggling to come to terms with the fact
> that their initial blueprint for EU–Russia relations has not materi-
> alised. The EU had hoped that by working closely with Russia, and
> by offering aid, advice and its own best practice, it could help the
> country become more open and democratic. During the decade or
> so that the EU has followed this approach, Russia has moved in the
> opposite direction. Yet many Europeans have been reluctant to
> question the underlying assumption of the EU's original Russia
> policy, namely that Russia wants to be 'like us'. Rather than
> conducting a cool-headed re-assessment, the EU has sometimes
> behaved like a sulking lover whose well-meaning advances have
> been rejected. For the EU, what happens inside Russia is of great
> importance. But it needs to stop pretending that it can somehow
> convert Russia to pluralism and liberalism.

A powerful and immediate weapon may be simply to do nothing.
The West, particularly the EU, must stop dangling carrots, in-
dividually or jointly, in front of Russia in the vain hope that

concessions will build confidence, weaning Russia from bad habits and promoting good ones. Those carrots have been munched, but the habits have changed for the worse, not for the better. Russia systematically breaks the promises it makes; far from provoking outrage, the response is mere disappointment, followed by a scramble to find yet more inducements for good behaviour. A simple decision by the West to sit quietly, or, in the jargon of the foreign policy world, to take a 'strategic pause', sends a powerful signal. When Russia is ready to cooperate, the West is ready. So long as it is not, we have plenty of other problems to worry about.

Nor should it accept the carrots dangled by the Kremlin. Bilateral bargains are not only immoral, but fruitless, meaning that we penalise our friends while supporting our enemies. Outrageously, it is easier for Russians to get visas to visit the EU than it is for the citizens of countries that are on the verge of starting membership talks.[4] The main aim now must be that Russian neo-imperialism gains not an inch more territory. The threats, interference and mischief directed against the ex-Soviet republics need to meet a consistent, firm response, not shilly-shallying and equivocation. When Russia bombs Georgia it should prompt the same storm of protest as would be raised if it fired a missile at Finland.

Georgia is on the brink of being offered a Membership Action Plan that will bring it into NATO once its military modernisation and other reforms are complete. The single most important thing the West can do now to protect both itself and its protégés is to make that offer to Georgia and stick to it. Secondly, both Ukraine and Georgia need as much help from the EU as possible: the more they experience the free movement of goods, capital, services and people, the more closely integrated they are into our world, and the less leverage the Kremlin has on them. The more Russians live in freedom and prosperity outside Russia, the harder it is for the

Kremlin to maintain its posture of exceptionalism. Countries like Estonia, Georgia and Moldova may seem too obscure, faraway or unimportant to care about, but now they are the crux of our own security. It is all too easy for Russia to think that when it bullies Estonia, it is treading only on the tiny toes of a flyweight ex-colony. A central message of this book is that the world's richest and strongest free countries must stand behind these small states now under threat from Russia. It may be inconvenient, costly or even painful to do so, but if we do not win the New Cold War on terms of our choosing, we will fight at a time and place chosen by our adversary, and the odds will be tilted against us.

The West must also hold Russia to the commitments it made when it joined international clubs based on freedom and justice, and downgrade the importance of bodies that now seem con-signed to paralysis by the Kremlin. The UN Security Council was useless for much of the Cold War because of Soviet vetoes. If the Kremlin tries the same tactics now, it will guarantee that the council – the only international decision-making body to which it belongs by right – becomes useless again. The same applies to the OSCE. Russia cannot be expelled, but if it continues to hamper the organisation's work, then it will end up with a mere talking shop. In bodies where Russia's membership is conditional, the conditions should be applied strictly. The time for wishful thinking is over. Agreeing to Russia's membership of the Council of Europe in 1996, for example, now looks a catastrophic mistake. Belarus was suspended from that body's Parliamentary Assembly in 1997, at a time when repression there was mild compared with Russia now; the Kremlin must realise that its policies at home and abroad will inevitably and speedily bring the same penalty, and one that would be much more effective than the perennial complaints that Russia's elections are not free. It is hard to see why Russia should belong to the G8. Either it should become a big-economies club (in which case China, India and Brazil should join), or it is a body for rich countries that respect the rule of law and political freedom. In that case Russia does not even belong in the waiting room.

Exclusion from Western clubs will bring tantrums, but it will also bring clarity. As with the old Cold War, the New Cold War was not started by the West and we are fighting it reluctantly. But like last time, it is up to us to limit the damage. Where we can cooperate on nuclear power, on preventing the proliferation of weapons of mass destruction, and on seeking peace in the Middle East we should. It may be possible to do more: new talks on strategic nuclear issues are urgently needed, to keep reducing stockpiles, reduce the risks of accidental launches and mispercep-tions of each side's posture. Another urgent issue is Afghanistan, one of the few places where NATO–Russian cooperation had a real effect. It is hard to think of another issue where Iran, Russia and NATO all share at least some common interest. If Russia sincerely wants to contribute to global security, and to be treated as a great power, Afghanistan is a good place to test its willingness for serious cooperation – though only an arch-optimist would believe that the Kremlin fully shares our long-term aim of a stable, prosperous and pro-Western Afghanistan. In all dealings with Russia, we should jettison the last vestiges of wishful thinking: if we allow ourselves to hope for the best, that must not distract us from preparing for the worst.

The biggest question is how to fight the war of values. It is tempting to argue that we should save our breath. If the Kremlin spin doctors try to provoke us, we should ignore them, just as we do the bilious outpourings of North Korea or Osama bin Laden. That would be a mistake: despite the hostile propaganda of the state-run media, millions of Russians and others in the ex-Soviet countries still look up to the open societies of the West. It is important to show them that our dislike of the Kremlin is not motivated by Russophobia. Anti-Westernism in Russia may be bad now among the country's rulers, but it is not yet either deep or solid. It is in our interest to prevent it spreading from the ex-KGB people in the Kremlin deep into the public's worldview. As in the last Cold War, soft power is still our greatest asset.[5] It is worth recalling the effect of the ideological challenge in the past: the differences between a free society and a closed one were central themes of international and domestic political discussion. The desire to outperform the Soviet Union on what it said it did best was a useful stimulus to good government, thus increasing further the West's competitive advantage. If the Soviet Union proclaimed a triumph, the West looked closely, and tried to see how it could be copied, on everything from the space race to the treatment of chess prodigies. A renewal of both that moral competition and moral distance is needed now. In the old Cold War mainstream Western politicians might differ on the details of defence spending, *Ostpolitik* or the emphasis to give human rights issues in the Soviet bloc. But everyone outside the political fringes agreed that the essence of the Soviet system was alien, repulsive and dangerous. Moral equivalence, which matched every Soviet misdeed with a real or imagined example of a Western one[6] was a minority pursuit. Yet one of the most peculiar features of the Putin years has been the number of Western commentators who are so keen to protest about the 'demonisation' of Russia and so unwilling to criticise what is happening there.

Tempting though it may be to ignore it, the best course is to take anti-Westernism seriously. It may well be that individualism and materialism are an inadequate basis for a happy life; that corruption and influence-peddling in Western political systems may be an indefensible distortion of the principles on which they are founded; freedom may conflict with justice or stability. If Russia's caustic criticism makes those in positions of power in the West think more clearly and govern more cleanly and fairly, that is all to the good. But that is not the same as taking the Kremlin's claims about its own system at face value. Such a balanced approach would be absurd. Our system is not perfect, but it is better: cleaner, fairer, kinder and more tolerant than Russia's authoritarian crony capitalism. It is self-critical: where it falls short of our ideals, we have to burnish it. But it must not be self-hating. The West preaches, and tries to practise, different forms of what it loosely calls 'democracy': i.e. open, law-governed political pluralism. The details may vary, but the central principles are the same: the rule of law, the separation of powers, the accountability of the executive and the core principles of due process and the presumption of innocence in the legal system; plus the freedoms of speech and association, crowned by freely contested and fairly counted elections. Western governments feel at least loosely obliged to offer high-quality public services, to uphold honesty in public life and provide social protection for the weak. The West believes in international law, and the duty of free countries to promote universal human rights everywhere. These ideas are chipped and faded now and tainted by compromises, short cuts and hypocrisies, particularly those stemming from the disastrous 'war on terror'. But they are real. Until we make it clear that we believe in our own values, we cannot defend ourselves against the subversion and corruption that are leaking into our citadels of economic and political power. And we stand not the slightest chance of persuading Russians themselves that the authoritarian, xenophobic and distorted version of capitalism peddled by their rulers is not a new civilisation but a dead end.

Notes

INTRODUCTION

1. www.russianwill.org. Although 'enemies of the nation' is no longer on the site, it can be viewed using an internet archive tool on http://web.archive.org/web/20061121213231/http://www.russianwill.org/material/vragi.html

2. I use the 'Kremlin' in this book as a shorthand term for the extraordinary concentration of political, bureaucratic, legal and economic power, mainly among KGB veterans, over which Mr Putin presides. The Kremlin is not monolithic. It includes clans whose rivalry is based on competing commercial interests (for example, between the gas giant Gazprom and its oil counterpart Rossneft) and on their personal allegiances, for example to the (supposedly) more liberal-minded ideology chief Vladislav Surkov, and the ex-military spy Igor Sechin. Though these conflicts are fluid and fast-changing, the central features of Kremlin power remain constant: opacity, wealth and ruthlessness.

3. I use the 'Mr/Ms' title only for people who are still alive. No disrespect is intended to the dead.

4. Her books included *A Small Corner of Hell: Dispatches from Chechnya* (2003), *Putin's Russia* (2004) and *A Russian Diary: A Journalist's Final Account of Life, Corruption, and Death in Putin's Russia* (2007)

5. In an interview with Germany's *Süddeutsche Zeitung* Mr Putin said, 'A murder is a very serious crime both with respect to society and with respect to God. The criminals must be found out and correspondingly punished. Unfortunately, this is not the only such crime in Russia. And we will do everything we can to bring the criminals to justice.

'And now, with respect to the political aspect of this affair. The investigation is looking at all possible variants. And of course, one of them, one of the most probable, is related to her work as a journalist. She really was a critic of the present authorities – something that is common to all media representatives – but she often adopted radical positions. And recently she mainly concentrated her attention on criticising the authorities in the Chechen Republic. I must say – and I think that experts would agree with me – that her political influence inside of Russia was negligible and that she was probably better known among human rights organisations and in the Western media. In connection with this I think that one of our newspapers was correct when it stated today that Anna Politkovskaya's murder has caused much more damage to the current authorities in general, and to the Chechen authorities in particular, than her reporting did. In any case, I repeat that what has happened is absolutely inadmissible. This horrendous crime is damaging for Russia and must be solved. It causes both moral and political damage and is damaging for the political system that we are building, a system which must have places for all people, independently of their points of view. On the contrary, we must ensure that people receive the possibility to expose their points of view, including in the media.'

http://kremlin.ru/eng/speeches/2006/10/10/1519_type82916_112362.shtml

In a speech at a meeting in Munich, Mr Putin expressed himself in similar vein:

'Perhaps because Ms Politkovskaya held very radical views she did not have a serious influence on the political mood in our country. But she was very well known in journalistic circles and in human rights circles. And in my opinion murdering such a person certainly does much greater damage from the authorities' point of view, authorities that she strongly criticised, than her publications ever did. Moreover, we have reliable, consistent information that many people who are hiding from Russian justice have been harbouring the idea that they will use somebody as a victim to create a wave of anti-Russian sentiment in the world. I do not know who has carried out this crime. But whoever they were and whatever their motives, they are criminals. They must be found, brought to justice and punished. The Russian authorities will do everything they can to ensure that this takes place.'

http://www.kremlin.ru/eng/speeches/2006/10/10/2138_type82914type84779_112411.shtml

6. I use 'Western' and the 'West' as shorthand for the advanced industrialised countries of the world, chiefly in Europe, America, east Asia and Australasia. A common feature is membership of the Paris-based OECD.

7. *Federalnaya Sluzhba Bezopasnosti* (Federal Security Service).

8. The full statement is on http://news.bbc.co.uk/1/hi/uk/6180262.stm

9. At the price charged by a Western commercial supplier for the tiny quantities used in industry, the large dose used against Litvinenko would have cost $10m (£5m).

10. Extradition is illegal under the Russian constitution. But what really riled British officials was the attitude on the Russian side that they were fussing about nothing. Other countries such as Israel also do not extradite their citizens – but close cooperation with foreign criminal justice systems mean that wrongdoers rarely go unpunished.

11. The manufacturing process of Polonium-210 leaves a 'fingerprint', a residue of other isotopes that can identify the precise date of manufacture and even the reactor used.

12. After its unsuccessful intervention in the Russian civil war from 1917 to 1920, nearly three decades of communist rule in Russia proved little worry for the West, which largely ignored the terror imposed by Lenin and Stalin. Under Herbert Hoover, the American taxpayer even helped Soviet Russia fend off starvation. Outside investment poured in. Many believed that Stalin stood for tough modernisation of a backward country, not mass murder and enslavement fuelled by his personal paranoia. Not until 1946, nearly three decades after the Bolshevik revolution, did Winston Churchill coin his fateful phrase the 'Iron Curtain'. The Cold War lasted for the next thirty years, until the Helsinki agreement of 1975, at the then Conference on Security and Cooperation in Europe (CSCE), which marked the beginning of the Soviet Union's ideological surrender. The West accepted the division of Europe on its current frontiers (with some countries slightly reserving their position on the Baltic states). In return, the Soviet bloc signed up for universal human rights. The Soviet leadership mistakenly thought this would be merely a paper concession. In fact, it allowed dissidents behind the Iron Curtain to complain that their governments were violating their international commitments, something that became a potent propaganda weapon.

13. I use 'Communist' when referring to a specific party, and 'communist' for the general ideology and sentiment.

14. From *Nomenclatura*, a Latin word meaning literally a list of names. In the Soviet Union it meant the upper reaches of the Communist Party who were entitled to an array of personal and professional privileges.

15. However, the authorities have tightened control over the internet (see Chapter Two). Even before Mr Putin took power, service providers had to

install a device that allows the authorities to track all incoming and outgoing information. During his first week as president, Mr Putin gave seven other federal agencies access to the intelligence gathered.

16. Such measures of public opinion are inherently suspect in a country with state-controlled mass media, and a long tradition of producing bogus statistics.

17. http://www.lewrockwell.com/blog/lewrw/archives/006682.html is one of many such examples. Members of the ill-named British Helsinki Human Rights Group and the *Guardian* journalist Jonathan Steele have also made similar arguments, along with many Russian commentators. However, arguing foreign policy by analogy is usually mistaken: New England was not forcibly incorporated into the United States by a totalitarian regime that imposed an alien language and culture and deported the brightest and best to slave labour camps in Alaska.

18. On 11 March 1990, the Lithuanian parliament declared independence. The West was alarmed, and painfully timid. Few countries had formally recognised the Soviet annexation of the Baltic states. A handful of elderly exiled diplomats still staffed dusty embassies in America, Britain and Italy, but the idea that these historical curios might suddenly mean something practical was deeply unsettling to a generation of Western diplomats and policy-makers who were still whistling with relief that the Soviet leadership had suddenly become so amenable. I was a correspondent for the *Independent* at the time and decided, with the help of my London-based colleague Steve Crawshaw, to offer some symbolic support. I took the only direct route to Lithuania (a weekly Aeroflot flight from east Berlin), managing to check in and board the plane without a Soviet visa. British citizens had required no visa before 1940, we reasoned, so why should I need one now?

At the airport in the Lithuanian capital Vilnius a grim-faced Soviet border guard confiscated my passport. But minutes later I was met by a delegation led by the new Lithuanian foreign minister, Algirdas Saudargas. 'What if I don't get my passport back?' I asked, as we sat nervously on the red velvet sofas of the VIP lounge. 'Then we climb out of that window. You can get another passport. But we cannot get another you,' said the biochemist-turned-politician, in stilted but heartfelt English. For a brief moment, I was a symbol of the Lithuania's perilously fragile status. If they could get at least one foreigner into their country across a Soviet-controlled border, then it was a sign to the rest of the world that their independence was more than a brave declaration. When the border guard returned, Mr Saudargas produced a stamp from his pocket and gave me Lithuanian visa 0001.

19. From the Greek word meaning rule by a few. David Hoffman's *The Oligarchs: Wealth and Power in the New Russia* explores their origins as power, as does Chrystia Freeland's *Sale of the Century: Russia's Wild Ride from Communism to Capitalism*.

20. See Peter Duncan, 'Contemporary Russian identity between East and West', *Historical Journal*, 48, pp. 277–94, Cambridge University Press, 2005.

21. After the financial crash of August 1998, when Russia seemed mired in chaos and incompetence, I wrote an article in *The Economist* entitled 'The Western Man's Burden', in ironic reference to Kipling's famous (or notorious) poem 'The White Man's Burden'.

> When a country habitually lacks people or governments capable of keeping essential services going, outsiders sooner or later begin to fill the gap. One word for this is colonisation. It is early days, but something of the kind may be starting to happen in Russia.

I could hardly have been more wrong.

22. Literally so, given the way in which senior spooks began gaining lucrative positions in industry.

23. Lithuania's Mažeikiai refinery and Latvia's Ventspils oil terminal are both prime takeover targets for Russia's energy giants. The sale of Mažeikiai to a Polish energy company, PKN Orlen, in 2006 infuriated Russia's energy companies. Shortly afterwards Russia cut off supplies from the pipeline feeding the refinery, saying that it needed to be repaired. The issue has been extensively discussed in the Jamestown Foundation Eurasia Daily Monitor http://www.jamestown.org/edm/article.php?article_id=2372212

24. Covered by many Western media including *The Economist*.
    http://www.economist.com/opinion/displaystory.cfm?story_id=9116990
    and
    http://www.economist.com/world/europe/displaystory.cfm?story_id=9122766

25. Their combined population of around 7m is slightly smaller than Austria or New Jersey; Estonia has 1.3m people, Latvia 2.4m and Lithuania 3.6m.

I PUTIN'S RISE TO POWER:

HOW THE KGB SEIZED POWER IN RUSSIA

1. The weak but reform-friendly Sergei Kiriyenko left after the August financial crash. The Duma rejected the man Yeltsin tried for two weeks to reinstall as his successor, Viktor Chernomyrdin, who had been prime minister for much of the 1990s. Russia then had eight months under Yevgeny Primakov, a steely career spy-turned-foreign minister. But his

growing alliances with powerful regional chiefs made him too powerful in Kremlin eyes, and he allowed the prosecutor-general's investigations into the Yeltsin family's financial dealings to reach a dangerous pitch. He was replaced from 12 May to 9 August 1999 by Sergei Stepashin, a former interior minister, who then gave way to Mr Putin.

2. Often described as 'fluent' and 'native-level', Mr Putin's German is grammatically correct but heavily accented and would be better described as 'passable' or 'comprehensible'. See http://www.youtube.com/watch?v=yMifzZehatE for an edited sequence in which he clumsily berates a protester at a press conference. It may have been better in his days as a spy.

3. Then still known by its Soviet-era name, Leningrad.

4. 'He [Putin] is credited by his successors with having brought Coca-Cola, Dresdner Bank, and Crédit Lyonnais to St. Petersburg. He was also responsible for creating two economic-development zones on the outskirts of the city that ended up attracting firms such as Gillette and Wrigley.' *The Petersburg Experience: Putin's Political Career and Russian Foreign Policy*, Samuel Charap, *Problems of Post-Communism*, vol. 51, no. 1 (January–February 2004).

5. The KGB was supposedly dissolved after the failed hard-line coup of August 1991. In fact, it was relabelled. The notorious Fifth Directorate, responsible for persecuting dissidents, became the core of the new tax police. Many other functions transferred to the Federal Counter-Intelligence Service, known by its Russian initials FSK; a law passed in April 1995 renamed this body the FSB.

6. The *Ministerium für Staatssicherheit* (MfS / Ministry for State Security).

7. http://www.economist.com/world/displaystory.cfm?story_id=9682621

8. Olga Kryshtanovskaya and Stephen White, 'Putin's Militocracy', *Post-Soviet Affairs*, vol. 19, no. 4, pp. 289–306 (October–December 2003).

9. Another handy term for them was 'securocrat', first coined by the South African liberal politician Frederik van Zyl Slabbert to describe apartheid-era security and military chiefs.

10. He repeated this in a speech on Chekists' Day in 2005.

11. *Komsomolskaya Pravda*, 29 December 2004, '*Moda na KGB? Nevedomstvennye razmyshlenia o professii*' (The KGB in fashion? Unconscious thoughts about the profession).

12. *Judo: History, Theory, Practice* (North Atlantic Books, 2004). The co-authors were Vasily Shestakov and Alexandr Levitzky.

13. The Chechens had been deported en masse to Central Asia by Stalin in 1944, as a punishment for their presumed Nazi sympathies. Tsarist imperial expeditions had found them the hardest nut to crack in the nineteenth

century, and many Chechens hoped that the collapse of the Soviet Union would mean independence for them, just as it had for the Baltic states. But an accident of history meant that Chechnya's status was not a Soviet Socialist Republic (SSR), like its neighbour Georgia, but an 'Autonomous Soviet Socialist Republic', a lesser status and one that was within the Russian federation. When the Soviet Union collapsed the fifteen SSRs regained statehood whether they wanted it or not. For Chechnya to leave Russia was going to be much harder. For three years, the republic enjoyed (or, rather, suffered) an uneasy semi-independence. The clan-based Chechen society was even less suitable for building the institutions of good government than that of Russia. Banditry flourished, and Russians came to loathe the Chechen 'mafia', whose ruthlessness and impenetrable mutual loyalties fitted them ideally for running protection rackets. In 1994, in an effort to distract attention from his political problems, Yeltsin had been persuaded to mount what was supposed to be a 'short victorious war' against the pint-sized autonomous republic, in which around half of Russia's 1.36m Chechen population lived. The war was neither short nor victorious and turned a mess into a disaster. The Russian army's lumbering tanks and raw conscripts were beaten back by the well-led, lightly armed separatists. In 1996 Russia signed a ceasefire with Chechnya, offering roughly a return to the status quo: independence, but not quite. That was a chance for stability and freedom, but it was woefully mismanaged. Part of the blame rests with Russia, which continued to destabilise the republic, but much of it lay with the Chechens themselves. Inside Chechnya, alarming banditry turned into atrocious warlordism. Their leaders, such as Shamil Basayev, were ruthless warriors but hopeless politicians. Kidnappings were rife, sometimes ending in gruesome beheadings. Foreigners, including those linked to Al-Qaeda, used Chechnya as a base for training camps – and, some said, as a toehold for Islamic rule in the whole of Russia's impoverished and ill-governed south-ern fringe. That theory was supported by the raid on Dagestan, one of many such provocations, and led by Basayev, a Kremlin ally-turned-foe whom most Russians regarded as the country's top terrorist. Russia responded by bombing some villages in Dagestan occupied by Islamist radicals. Few took notice: low-intensity warfare in the northern Caucasus, sadly, was nothing new.

14. Another example of Mr Putin's foul-mouthed turn of phrase came in a meeting with prime minister Ehud Olmert of Israel in October 2006, when he praised the Israeli president Moshe Katsav, who was facing accusations of multiple sexual assaults against employees. 'Say hello to your president . . .

he really surprised us,' said Mr Putin approvingly. 'We did not know he could deal with ten women.'

15. And no bombings of such scale and sophistication have been organised since.

16. http://www.economist.com/business/displaystory.cfm?story_id=E1_PNQRSS

17. http://news.bbc.co.uk/1/hi/business/the_economy/441916.stm gives a contemporary account of the credit card affair.

    http://query.nytimes.com/gst/fullpage.html?res=9C01E4DE143D-F93AA3575AC0A96F958260&sec=&spon=&pagewanted=print is a longer and more sceptical *New York Times* story.

18. The street name can also be transcribed Novosyelov.

19. He cast doubt on the nature of the 'bomb', saying only that FSB laboratories in Moscow would have to investigate further.

20. Broadcast on the *Vesti* evening news. Translation from Yuri Felshtinsky and Alexander Litvinenko, *Blowing Up Russia: Terror from Within*, Gibson Square Books, London, 2007.

21. Felshtinsky and Litvinenko, *Blowing Up Russia*.

22. A detailed investigation of the Ryazan 'bombing' can be found in David Satter's *Darkness at Dawn: The Rise of the Russian Criminal State*, Yale University Press, New Haven, Conn., and London, 2003.

23. Furthermore, if Ryazan was truly a dummy run, it broke all the rules. In bureaucracy-bound Russia, such exercises involve extensive planning and paperwork. Official observers must be nominated, every detail of the 'plot' written down and the whole thing approved by senior officers. The start and finish are minuted and the conduct of all participants assessed. In particular, the head of the local FSB must be informed.

    The Ryazan exercise breached all these. Most signally, in Russia as in most other countries with serious armed forces, conducting exercises that involve 'active duty' armed personnel is strictly forbidden: in other words, a military base cannot test its readiness by having one lot of soldiers 'attack' somewhere guarded by real sentries armed with live ammunition. The reason is simple: those taking part in the exercise risk being maimed or killed. The sentries might end up shooting fellow soldiers. So such an exercise could not have been planned for Ryazan, which was already on high alert because of the previous bombings in Moscow: the FSB officers planting the 'sugar' risked being shot if caught by a trigger-happy policeman. If it was truly an exercise, it was an almost insane risk for its planners.

24. Even odder was a story that emerged from a special-forces base near Ryazan. *Novaya Gazeta* reported that a paratrooper called Alexei Pinyaev, while guarding a warehouse, noticed some sacks labelled 'sugar' and had opened

one with a bayonet in the hope of using some of the contents to sweeten his tea. The result had tasted nasty. He informed his commanding officer who, remembering news reports of the sacks found in the basement of Novo-syolov Street, informed the local FSB. Experts identified the contents as hexogen.

The authorities reacted sharply. First they claimed that *Novaya Gazeta* had invented the story. Mysteriously, the paper's next issue failed to come out, after someone hacked into its computer network and deleted the files that were due to be sent to the printer. Then Pinyaev's unit commander and fellow soldiers were dispatched to Chechnya, while he made a public retraction, and was then disciplined for breaching state secrets and stealing state property – in the form of sugar.

That might have seemed absurd enough, but in March 2000 his regiment sued *Novaya Gazeta*. Its commander, Colonel Oleg Churilov, said Pinyaev did not exist and no one with his supposed duties would have had access to an ammunition warehouse anyway. If that was supposed to squash the story, it certainly failed.

25. In March 2000, for example, a motion to ask the prosecutor-general to answer to outstanding questions about the incident passed by 197 to 137, but failed to reach the absolute majority needed in the 450-strong body because the pro-Kremlin party (which at the time was called 'Unity') voted unanimously against it.

26. Shchekochikhin died suddenly on 3 July 2003 after a sudden illness. The authorities refused to release his medical records to his relatives or to supply tissue specimens for independent analysis. They did manage to send a skin sample to a London toxicologist, who made a tentative diagnosis of poisoning by radioactive thallium, a toxin used by the KGB during the Cold War. They and his colleagues believe his investigative work brought him a death sentence.

Yushenkov was shot dead by an unknown assassin near his Moscow home in April 2003. Four people were convicted of his murder in a controversial verdict denounced by friends and relatives. Those convicted include a colleague from his opposition Liberal Russia party who strenu-ously protests his innocence.

27. Sometimes known as Latsis, which is how the Russian spelling of his (Latvian) surname would be rendered in English.

28. http://www.yavlinsky.ru/news/index.phtml?id=357

29. The fifteen Soviet Socialist Republics were the constituent parts of the Soviet Union (though some outsiders regarded the three Baltic states as

being occupied terrritories because of their contested legal status). Russia was by far the largest of the fifteen, and itself a federation, hence its full name, the Russian Soviet Federative Socialist Republic. Its constituent parts included ethnic Autonomous Soviet Socialist Republics (ASSRs) such as Chechnya and Tatarstan, which are now, along with cities such as Moscow and regions such as Novgorod, among the eighty-nine 'federal subjects' of the post-communist Russian Federation.

30. From the West's point of view, Mr Gorbachev had been an improvement on any of his predecessors. He saw that the Soviet system was not only unworkable but abhorrent. Whereas Andropov had tried to fix it by toughening up, he decided to try liberalisation. That meant freedom of speech, contested elections, modest decentralisation and some limited economic reforms. In 1987 he allowed state enterprises to trade their surplus production freely. In 1988 he permitted the establishment of cooperatives, outside the planned economy. He allowed some foreign investment. Censorship slackened and disappeared. In May 1989 the first partially free election in Soviet history produced a lively legislature: the Congress of People's Deputies. In the space of a few months, the Communist Party of the Soviet Union gave up its 'leading role' (i.e. monopoly of power); the media began exposing the lies and crimes of the past. Outside Europe Mr Gorbachev briskly closed down a series of Soviet-stoked conflicts in Southern Africa, Afghanistan and Latin America. It was welcome, but doomed. The Soviet system was so ramshackle and unstable that once the binding threads of command and control were loosened, the economy, and the whole Kremlin empire, started a rapid collapse. The satellite countries of Central Europe, and the peoples of the Soviet Union, realised that the Kremlin would no longer kill to keep control. They took their chance. In quick succession Hungary, Poland, East Germany and Czechoslovakia ripped up the Warsaw Pact rulebook and regained their sovereignty. The Baltic states of Estonia, Latvia and Lithuania did the same, making modest suggestions for autonomy that soon catalysed into forthright demands for restoration of independence.

   The gratitude in the West was immense. For all Mr Gorbachev's muddle and wobbles he had done the world a great service. He had allowed communism to collapse with astonishingly little blood being shed. By the standards of other European empires, that was a praiseworthy feat.

31. Interview with the author, 1994.

32. Yeltsin's second volume of memoirs brought him $3 million, largely thanks to the intervention of Mr Berezovsky and others. The monthly interest on

this was deposited in cash in Yeltsin's office safe. He apparently regarded this as a solid nest egg. By the standards of the provincial Soviet Union it was indeed a fortune. But by the standards of those around him, it was chicken feed.

33. Mr Putin also benefited from the economy's recovery from the 1998 crash. Though the boom in oil and gas prices was yet to come, a cheap rouble stoked demand for Russian-made goods. Imports had suddenly become four times more expensive and Russian manufacturers seized their chance, producing properly packaged food and consumer goods at competitive prices. Russian-made beer, soap, juice and detergent, once shunned by all but the poor, began appearing on the shelves of the smartest supermarkets.

34. It is interesting to speculate what hold they had on him, in order to be so sure that he would honour his side of the bargain.

2 PUTIN IN POWER:
THE WINNERS AND LOSERS OF THE NEW REGIME

1. One featured the 'Napoleon' cake, which contains a large dose of egg custard. A man goes into a shop and asks for a 'Putin' cake. 'What's that?' asks the sales assistant. 'It's like a Napoleon, but without eggs' comes the reply. (*Yaitse*, literally 'eggs' in Russian, is also the common slang term for 'balls'.)

2. http://www.youtube.com/watch?v=vLWscHHG8_8

3. Since Estonia introduced a 'flat' (non-progressive) tax on incomes in 1994, this has become a popular and successful policy across much of the ex-communist world. Although it involves a large tax cut for high earners, it has so far always resulted in higher tax revenues, because it becomes attractive to repatriate earnings and end tax-dodging scams. It is particularly well suited to countries with large black economies where tax might otherwise go uncollected, and where administrative weaknesses put a premium on simplicity and transparency. As well as Russia, flat-tax countries include Albania, Bosnia, Bulgaria, the three Baltic states, Georgia, Macedonia, Montenegro, Romania, Serbia Slovakia and Ukraine. No ex-communist country that has introduced a flat tax has yet reversed it.

4. Mr Naryshkin's rapid ascent to power suggests he may be a contender for the presidency or other high office. He is deputy prime minister for foreign economic relations, and has been an adviser at Gazprom, head of investment at Promstroibank and on the board at several military shipbuilding companies. Although he has worked with all the important factions and clans in

the Kremlin, he has so far remained neutral between them; if he maintains that, it may be a powerful recommendation in the president's eyes.

5. Some of the connections are almost comically nepotistic. Andrei Patrushev, the 26-year-old son of the FSB chief, was seconded from the FSB to Rosneft, where he is now advising Mr Sechin. The lucky Mr Patrushev Jr received a Kremlin medal from Mr Putin after only a few months, citing his 'many years of conscientious work'.

    Even those officials without a visible KGB background enjoy close ties to the business world. Dmitri Medvedev, a first deputy prime minister, is the chairman of the board of directors of Gazprom; Victor Khristenko, the minister of industry and energy, is the chairman of the board of directors of Transneft; the science and education minister, Andrei Fursenko, has been appointed to head a new state nanotechnology corporation; Alexei Gordeev, the minister of agriculture, is the chairman of the board of directors of Rosagroleasing; Anatoly Serdukov, the defence minister, is the chairman of the board of directors of Chimprom, a chemicals giant. German Gref, the minister of economic development and trade, is the chairman of the board of the Russia Venture Company; Igor Levitin, the transport minister, is the chairman of the board of directors of the company running Moscow's Sheremetyevo airport; Igor Shuvalov, a foreign-policy adviser to the president, is the chairman of the board of directors of Russian Railways; his colleague Sergei Prichodko is the chairman of the board of directors of Tactical Missile Weapons. The issue is discussed in a Hudson Institute colloquium, 'US–Russian Relations: Is Conflict Inevitable?', available at http://hudson.org/files/publications/HudsonRussianGroup-Jun26_2007.pdf

6. *The Captive Mind*, 1953, is a classic account of the intellectual compromises forced by communist rule.

7. The most dedicated blackmarketeers were from a distinct criminal caste, known as *Vory v zakone* (Thieves-in-Law). Set up for mutual support among criminals in the prison camps of the Stalin era, the 'Law' was a mixture of rituals, solidarity and hierarchy enforced by death or mutilation. It forbade any cooperation with the Soviet system in any way, whether in prison or outside it. Members were allowed to live solely by criminal activity, and had to cut ties with existing friends and family. Marriage was forbidden. Rank was indicated by a graduated system of tattoos; communication was in *Fenya*, an impenetrable argot originally developed by pre-revolutionary pedlars.

8. In a hotel lobby in 1991 I encountered a professor carrying a metal container filled with three kilos of bee venom; he hoped to sell it to a Western

pharmaceutical company for 'some thousands of dollars'. My fax machine, in an office previously occupied by a fly-by-night metals trader, used to spit out offers of kilos of rare metals such as osmium and scandium. A suitcase full of that would go for many thousands of dollars in Europe.

9. Websites run by opposition groups and Chechen separatists are sometimes blocked; how far this is on explicit official instructions is unclear. Bloggers have been running foul of extremism and other laws, too. In August 2007 a 21-year-old blogger called Savva Terentyev from Syktyvkar was charged with inciting hatred towards the police after a post appeared on his blog saying that corrupt policemen should be publicly incinerated.

10. The BBC has lost its FM frequencies, apparently for political reasons.

11. The OECD says of Russia's goal of reaching a standard of public administration similar to the G-7: 'Russia will find it extremely difficult to reach that goal, even over the very long term, if the reform of public administration is approached in a narrow, technocratic fashion rather than proceeding in tandem with improvements in the institutional environment within which the state bureaucracy operates. In this respect, the greatest dangers may arise from the apparent disjuncture between, on the one hand, a reform approach that aims to empower citizens vis-à-vis the bureaucracy and to make public bodies more transparent, responsive and accountable to them, and, on the other hand, a political system that appears to be moving in the direction of less transparency and accountability.' From *'Clientelism' to a 'Client-centred Orientation'? The Challenge of Public Administration Reform in Russia*, OECD 2007.

12. In the form of the British 1980s TV series *Spitting Image*, the show used grotesque but highly recognisable puppets. In the early weeks of his presidency it portrayed Mr Putin variously as an impotent young king on his wedding night, a monarch dithering over his coronation robes, and as an ignorant literary censor. By 2003, when it was finally taken off air, Mr Putin was appearing as a hideous and malevolent dwarf.

13. On almost my last day in Moscow in 2002, I reluctantly apologised to Mr Khodorkovsky for the negative coverage of the past years, which included an article in 1998 called 'Oily Charm', mocking his clean-up efforts. That had prompted an angry and rather scary threat of a lawsuit for defamation. But the Yukos share price had risen tenfold since my article. At least in *The Economist*'s moral universe, in which market capitalisation is the purest representation of outsiders' trust, Mr Khodorkovsky had been vindicated. I had therefore been mistaken. He accepted my rather qualified apology with surprised graciousness.

14. The demand had first been made on 30 December the previous year, and was still being challenged by Yukos.

15. Cut to eight years on appeal.

16. A breach, incidentally, of a Russian law that says prisoners should serve their sentence close to home.

17. At the time of the Soviet Union's break-up, these numbered 89. After some mergers, there are now 85, comprising 47 oblasts (provinces), 21 republics, 8 krais (broadly the same as oblasts), 6 okrugs (autonomous districts with slightly lesser status), two federal cities (Moscow and St Petersburg) and the Jewish Autonomous Oblast.

18. http://www.kremlin.ru/eng/speeches/2004/09/04/ 1958_type82912_76332.shtml

19. Though ethnic Russians make up 75 per cent of the population in the country as a whole, in some parts they are barely a plurality, and the birthrate among the Muslim minorities is much higher than among ethnic Russians.

20. It is interesting to imagine the furious way Russia would have reacted, by contrast, if one of the Baltic states had suggested writing Russian in the Roman alphabet.

3 SINISTER PRETENCE:
THE KREMLIN'S USE OF STATE POWER AGAINST DISSENT

1. Although not fully teetotal, his abstemious habits certainly make him a 'non-drinker' in a country where drinking half a litre of vodka in an evening is considered unremarkable.

2. When the Russian leader caught a 20-inch sea bass from President George Bush's boat during a fishing trip in 2007, two of the three main television news channels in fishing-mad Russia referred to it sardonically as 'not too big' – though the third, NTV, inflated the modest catch to 'many' fish.

3. Though plenty of jokes suggest that this will eventually change: that the first town on the moon will be called Putinsk, for example.

4. Among those who spent years wrongly incarcerated in psychiatric hospitals was Vladimir Bukovsky, who now lives in the British university city of Cambridge; at the time of writing he was planning to stand in the presidential election due on 2 March 2008.

5. *Yezhednevniy Zhurnal* (Daily Journal) reported this case in detail on 22 June 2007. The article, in Russian, is on http://ej.ru/?a=note&id=7182 (accessed 9 September 2007).

6. He is held in harsh conditions and recently wrote me an anguished personal letter, saying that his eyesight was failing and that he feared he would die in prison, forgotten by the outside world.

7. Certainly his trial was a sham; the looting of Yukos by the Kremlin's business cronies counts as one of the most scandalous abuses of property rights Russia has seen since the Bolsheviks expropriated industrialists after the Russian Revolution. The truth is that almost all Russian businesses break the law, because the laws are so vague and contradictory. Khodorkovsky's early business career makes it hard to count him as saintly or blameless, but he was clearly singled out for prosecution because of the political challenge that he presented to the Kremlin. His lawyer Yuri Schmidt says: 'When Khodor-kovsky was arrested, I determined at once that this is my case – a political case, a case related to the advocacy of human rights, a law-forming case. This is a case concerning the crucial challenges of our society and our common survival – not physical, but human and intellectual. [. . .] The issue of the Khodorkovsky case will determine a further development of Russia.' On http://www.sovest.org/gb/

8. Known as Gorky in the Soviet era. Andrei Sakharov, Russia's greatest dissident, was exiled there under Brezhnev in 1981 and triumphantly returned at the personal invitation of Mikhail Gorbachev in December 1986. Nizhny Novgorod became known as a cradle of economic and political reforms. A full account of the demonstration can be found at www.opendemocracy.net/ globalization-institutions_government/iceberg_report_4558.jsp and (in Russian) www.newizv.ru/news/2007-03-26/66305/

9. Some of the harassment was more bizarre than thuggish: according to Tatyana Lokshina of the Moscow Helsinki Group, one organiser found his front door glued shut from the outside. He climbed out of his window and joined the march anyway.

10. The extremism law can cut both ways, squashing not opposition causes but discussion that the Kremlin finds too inflammatory. In September the newspaper *Izvestia* received an official warning from *Rossvyazokhrankultury* (whose full name is the Orwellian 'Federal Service for Supervision in Mass Communications, Communications and Preservation of Cultural Heritage') for an article it published in May about discrimination against ethnic Russians in Sakha, a vast, thinly populated territory in the east of the country. In a classic example of bureaucratic intimidation, *Rossvyazokhran-kultury* said it had discovered 'signs of extremism' in the article after a 'commission of linguistics specialists' (unnamed) had examined the article. In a protest against the move, *Izvestiya* wrote: 'The "signs of extremism", in

our opinion, are contained not in the words in which we described what we saw [. . .] The "signs of extremism" are contained in what actually happened there.' www.izvestia.ru/opinion/article3107705/

11. In November 2005 the management dismissed Olga Romanova, presenter of its flagship programme, after she told Radio Liberty that the channel had declined to report some important stories for political reasons. One concerned an accident involving a car driven by the son of the then defence minister, Sergei Ivanov, in which a woman died. Several fellow journalists resigned soon thereafter.

12. *Novaya Gazeta*'s independence is thanks to its proprietor, a KGB officer-turned-banker, Aleksander Lebedev. Originally a supporter of Mr Putin, he has become an increasingly outspoken critic of the Kremlin, saying that the current lack of press freedom is 'completely unacceptable' and comparing it to the Brezhnev era.
www.spiegel.de/international/world/0,1518,503609,00.html

13. The magazine appears under the English version of its title, though the publishing house uses the Russian equivalent, *Novoye Vremya*. Its website is www.newtimes.ru

14. Hoping to help, I featured *New Times* in a column. I urged everyone interested in the future of Russian press freedom to subscribe. Mischievously, I also suggested that businesses in countries that suffer Kremlin-imposed economic sanctions, such as Georgia and Estonia, should take out advertisements to fill the gap left by the browbeaten Russian businesses. The result, Yevgenia Albats told me sadly, was to scare potential advertisers even more.

15. http://www.cpj.org/news/2007/europe/russia28jun07na.html

16. Published in *Novaya Gazeta*, 2 June 2003, available on www.novayagazeta. ru/data/2003/39/00.html

17. The murder of journalists is nothing new in Russia. Even in the Yeltsin era, when the media was considerably more pluralistic, brave reporters risked being killed. Dmitry Kholodov, a young reporter investigating corruption in the military, died after picking up a booby-trapped briefcase at a Moscow railway station in October 1994. His newspaper accused the military leadership of ordering the contract killing. Six men were acquitted after an investigation denounced by his parents. The difference is that Kholodov's murder caused a national outcry – albeit not one fully shared in the Kremlin.

18. In September 2007 Russian prosecutors arrested eleven people, including figures with alleged connections to the Chechen criminal underworld and an FSB colonel. Senior Russian figures said that those arrested had been working on behalf of a foreign enemy of the Kremlin's – taken as a reference

to Mr Berezovsky, who has always denied all involvement in the case. Politkovskaya's family and colleagues said they feared that political interference would derail the investigation, and criticised the authorities for sidelining Pyotr Gabriyan, one of Moscow's most competent prosecutors, who had previously had charge of the case.

19. The public is unconvinced. An FOM poll conducted in June 2006 showed that 31 per cent of respondents thought television was objective. http://bd.english.fom.ru/report/map/az/0-9/edomto625_1/edo62521. A Levada Centre poll on Chechnya in March 2007 showed 49 per cent saying that coverage is superficial; 28 per cent said it concealed problems; only 11 per cent pronounced themselves satisfied.

20. A further amendment in December 2006 enlarged the list of citizens ineligible to participate in elections to include those convicted of 'extremism'.

21. http://www.osce.org/documents/odihr/2004/06/3033_en.pdf

22. By one account, it started with a hotel in Turku, Finland, acquired when he was in charge of the city of St Petersburg's foreign economic ties. Certainly St Petersburg companies with shadowy ownership structures have flourished under his rule. A mobile phone company founded by his friend Leonid Reiman (now communications minister) and in whose parent company his wife Ludmila worked in 1998–9, has acquired coveted licences with remarkable ease. Western intelligence services say his personal fortune is $11 billion; a well-informed Swedish source puts it at several times that. A colossal yacht has supposedly been ordered in Finland for an unknown Russian customer; other shipyards have been told that no Russian now wants anything over 180 metres in order not to give offence to Mr Putin. And what of Mr Putin's relationship with Mr Abramovich? The multi-billionaire tycoon used to be the Yeltsin family's closest financial confidant, and now divides his time between London (where he owns Chelsea Football Club) and Moscow. See 'Mr Putin becomes the richest candidate', *Kommersant*, 4 February 2004, http://www.kommersant.ru/doc.aspx?docsid=446423

23. Dirty tricks are not always so spectacular, but they are endemic in Russian politics. *Kompromat* (compromising material) is the main political currency. It can be real, or invented. During an election in the Siberian town of Tomsk in 2007, opponents of the small liberal-conservative Union of Right Forces (SPS in its Russian acronym) produced a leaflet purporting to offer AIDS patients lucrative work on the campaign, plus the chance to shake hands with voters: an effective smear in a country deeply prejudiced against both homosexuals and those infected with HIV. In Krasnoyarsk, slogans on SPS placards reading *Za Dostroyku* (To complete construction) were neatly

replaced with ones reading *Za Dovoruyku* (To complete the looting), an effective jibe at the party's unpopular business backers.

24. *Rossiiskaya Gazeta*, 13 July 2007, 'The Other Russia and The Others' by Valery Zyzhutovich. http://www.rg.ru/2007/07/13/vyzhutovitch.html. However, foreign scholars have come to different conclusions.

25. According to Transparency International, a lobby group, in 2006 Russia came 121st out of 163 countries surveyed, jointly with Benin, Gambia, Guyana, Honduras, Nepal, the Philippines, Rwanda and Swaziland. In 2007 it was in 143rd place out of 179, jointly with Gambia, Indonesia and Togo.
    http://www.transparency.org/policy_research/surveys_indices/cpi/2007
    http://www.iht.com/articles/ap/2006/11/07/business/EU_FIN_Russia_Corruption.php and http://www.rg.ru/2006/11/07/buksman.html

26. Though 'democracy' is usually treated as being synonymous with political freedom and pluralism, representative government, the rule of law and other good things, I have tried to avoid using the word in this book. It is worth remembering that 'democracy' came into common usage during the 1930s as a way of highlighting the weakness of the authoritarian regimes in Germany, Italy and elsewhere. Before that it was more often regarded as having connotations of 'mob rule'. Since then it has been so debased by its use as a fig leaf for dictators who claim popular backing that it has become almost useless, as in the 'German Democratic Republic' (as the Soviet zone of Germany became called) or the grotesquely authoritarian Democratic People's Republic of Korea.

27. Even using the English word 'judiciary' to describe it is misleading. It would be better termed the 'Office of Penal Affairs', or perhaps simply the 'Inquisition'. The International Bar Association's 2005 report, *Striving for Judicial Independence: A Report into Proposed Changes to the Judiciary in Russia*, provides a detailed account of shortcomings in the Russian system. It is available at
    http://www.ibanet.org/images/downloads/2005_06_June_Report_Russia_Striving%20for%20Judicial%20Independence_Final_English.pdf

28. Reuters Russia Investment Summit, 10 September 2007.

29. It is overly romantic to see Russian criminal justice as portrayed by Martin Cruz Smith, author of *Gorky Park* (1983) and its sequels: as the same world-weary but ultimately well-meaning affair as its counterparts in Western countries.

30. Yuri Kostanov, a member of the Independent Council of Legal Experts in Moscow and vice-chairman of the Moscow bar, commented to the *Washington Post* on 3 June 2007: 'She's a brilliant and professional lawyer, and everyone understands very well that if they can disbar her, they can

disbar anyone.' He added, 'I believe this is all the work of the special services. They are doing it to make everyone dance to their music and tell everyone: "We are the power".'

  www.washingtonpost.com/wp-dyn/content/article/2007/06/02/ AR2007060201135.html

31. With only 18 per cent of the population covered by the court, Russia makes up 23 per cent of the cases heard.

32. In 2007, Russia's top judge went further, saying that citizens should be allowed to turn to the court only after they had exhausted every legal avenue inside the country, rather than after simply losing an appeal as at present.

33. 'Public-spirited' is what people call activists they approve of. Self-appointed do-gooders and busybodies are harsher but sometimes more accurate descriptions.

34. Two well-worn Soviet-era sayings are telling. 'Initiative is punishable' and 'If I'm the boss, you're an idiot. And if you're the boss, I'm an idiot'.

35. Though in remarks to editors in August 2007 he seemed to signal that Ms Aslamazyan should not be prosecuted. 'Yes, I am well familiar with this case. But it is not worth a pin. She can return to her home country without any worry. Of course, no one will release her from administrative responsibility for her mistake, but one should not confuse a mistake with a crime.' He also added: 'While I am president, she absolutely does not need to worry.'

36. Still known in some international English media by its Russian name, Kiev.

37. Though Ukraine has become a much freer country, it is not a better-governed one. Mr Yushchenko proved a chronically indecisive president, and Ukraine's politics have remained in acrimonious and bewildering stalemate.

38. The British government, spinelessly, chose not to make a big fuss about this for fear of jeopardising British investments in Russia.

39. One of the charms of life in Moscow is that you can find a 'Gypsy taxi' simply by standing on the street. The resulting ride may well be without insurance, brakes or road sense, but the conversation is fascinating and the price – negotiated on the spot – almost invariably low. The drivers come from all ethnic backgrounds, in nondescript cars that escape the notice of the ubiquitous and predatory traffic police. This utterly deregulated market is one of the last relics of the anarchic life of the Russian capital in the 1990s. It is also a way in which ordinary people of all backgrounds can earn extra roubles.

40. http://www.newizv.ru/news/2007-07-17/72924/ estimates that these number over 140.

41. Sarah Mendelson and Ted Gerber, *The Putin Generation: The Political Views of Russian Youth*, 2007. Available on http://www.csis.org/images/stories/mendelson_carnegie_moscow_corrected.pdf

42. So far, the Kremlin's own phoney mass movements have been remarkably docile and have stayed focused on the intended targets. Anti-Semitism, for example, which is ingrained in Russian nationalist circles, is surprisingly absent in the rhetoric of all the Kremlin-sponsored youth groups. (Mr Putin has excellent relations with the hand-picked leaders of Russia's surviving Jewish community.) But what happens, for example, if the generals try to switch off some campaign they have launched, but the troops disagree? The danger of teaching people to organise demonstrations, print leaflets and raise public awareness is that they may decide to do it on their own.

43. The two families became neighbours in north London.

44. This allegation, vehemently denied by Russian officials on Mr Putin's behalf, was based on the flimsiest of evidence: an occasion during a walkabout in the grounds of the Kremlin, when the Russian president was chatting to a family and kissed their small boy on the stomach.

45. Yuri Felshtinsky, Alexander Litvinenko and Geoffrey Andrews, *Blowing up Russia: Terror from Within*, Gibson Square Books, London, 2007.

46. Like many such operations, it was botched. The Qatari authorities arrested three men, who turned out to be GRU agents. After intense diplomatic pressure they were released, and returned home to a hero's welcome. Russia argues that it is just eliminating terrorists and that there is no difference between their attempts to destroy the leadership of the Chechen separatists, who have wrought mayhem in Russia for years, and the American hunt for Osama bin Laden. One difference is that most of the Chechen leadership – at least in the early years of the war – consistently denounced the killing of civilians and repeatedly called for talks with Russia on a peaceful resolution to the conflict. By killing the only Chechen leaders willing to talk peace, the Kremlin has also killed the best chance of ending the war.

47. The latter did not help his public profile with an ill-advised media interview in which he said he supported the overthrow of the Russian regime 'by force'. British officials let it be known that they would be delighted if their unwelcome guest would move elsewhere.

48. *Guardian*, 18 July 2007, http://www.guardian.co.uk/russia/article/0,,2128844,00.html

49. *Daily Telegraph*, 19 July 2007, http://www.telegraph.co.uk/money/main.jhtml?xml=/money/2007/07/18/cnrussia118.xml&DCMP=ILC traffdrv07053100

50. Julie Anderson, 'The HUMINT Offensive from Putin's Chekist State', *International Journal of Intelligence and Counter-Intelligence*, vol. 20, issue 2, June 2007.

4 WHY MONEY IS RUSSIA'S GREATEST STRENGTH AND OUR GREATEST WEAKNESS

1. Such averages can be misleading; they are flattered by some very rich Russians declaring their income.
2. http://www.russiaprofile.org/page.php?pageid=Business&articleid=a 1187177738
3. The Kremlin wants to revive Russia's hi-tech fortunes. In April 2007 Mr Putin announced a $7 billion programme to promote nanotechnology; another $1.2 billion is going into a state-backed technology fund. But past experience suggests that this will be at best stolen, or else wasted. The Russian state has proved an extremely poor steward of the national wealth. The chief recipient of the largesse is the Kurchatov Institute in Moscow, which just happens to be run by a close colleague of Mr Putin's, Mikhail Kovalchuk. If the Kremlin really wanted to improve the fortunes of the IT sector, it could try modernising the rudimentary levels of computerisation in the Russian public sector, and introducing and enforcing strong intellectual property laws.
4. http://news.bbc.co.uk/1/hi/world/europe/4562718.stm
5. http://www.cato.org/realaudio/illarionov-2006-03-07.ppt and www.iea.ru/article/present/pres060307.ppt
6. It is easy to see the attractions. In 2006 a Swiss court ruled that the then communications minister, Leonid Reiman, a close personal friend of Mr Putin's, owned telecommunications assets in Russia worth more than a billion dollars. This caused no difficulty for Mr Reiman, who simply issued a denial and continued in his post.
7. http://www.finiz.ru/articles/article1243452/?print
8. http://ej.ru/?a=note&id=7187
9. Such as 3,500 research institutes, and universities that turn out 200,000 science and engineering graduates every year.
10. Galina Stolyarova in *Transitions Online*, 12 July 2007 - http://www.ceeol.com/aspx/issuedetails.aspx?issueid=a791f8d8-778c-40aa-8907-024c97095276&articleId=474a662c-7893-4d2f-8eb3-8142ccb7aa23
11. The Russian population has been falling by 0.5 per cent annually since the end of the Soviet Union, from nearly 149m in 1992 to 142m now. Some of that was masked by migration of ethnic Russians from other parts of the

former Soviet Union, a reservoir that has largely been exhausted. Now the decline is accelerating.

There are some slightly encouraging signs. Infant mortality has fallen by a fifth in the past two years, and maternal mortality by 8 per cent. The birthrate has risen from 8.27 per 1,000 in 1999 to 9.95 per 1,000 in 2006. (By comparison the American birth rate in that year was 14.14 and the UK's was 10.71.) Some of this may be to do with Mr Putin's exhortations, falling poverty and better state benefits for mothers. But mostly it is a statistical fluke: the birth rate in the Soviet Union in the early 1980s was high, and that cohort of women are now at prime child-bearing age.

12. Abortions number at least 1.5 million annually. Surveys suggest 10–15 per cent of all abortions are not recorded. Mr Putin defined the population crisis as Russia's biggest problem; and has asked parliament to increase to $166 per month the stipend given to families that adopt children.

13. http://www.pwc.com/extweb/ncpressrelease.nsf/docid/ FB66FD4D8CBB5640802573050019EB74

14. http://www.pwc.com/extweb/ncpressrelease.nsf/docid/ 7CB1C559F9811342802572660030A670

15. http://www.pwc.com/extweb/ncpressrelease.nsf/docid/ CE48734DA6D884778025729C0031D354

16. http://www.pwc.com/extweb/ncpressrelease.nsf/docid/ 7CB1C559F9811342802572660030A670

17. Its real value, bankers estimate, could be several times that.

18. http://www.kommersant.ru/doc.aspx?DocsID=633868

5 THE NEW TSARISM: WHAT MAKES RUSSIA'S LEADERS TICK

1. However much they hated Western materialism and hypocrisy, even the most naive and idealistic foreigners soon found Soviet communism boring. If they stayed interested in left-wing ideas at all, they drifted off to Trotskyism or even mainstream socialist parties. Only in trades unions in a handful of West European countries did orthodox communism retain a foothold. And that owed as much to secret Kremlin subsidies as to any usefulness of communist ideology.

2. This was set up by the then prime minister, Mr Chernomyrdin, in 1995; it described itself as 'liberal' and 'centrist'. When he left power it morphed into the equally blandly named Unity, set up by Mr Putin's supporters, to fend off the Fatherland party of Yeltsin's main regional challengers in the run-up to Duma elections in December 1999.

3. The definition was a loose one. Dark-skinned people from the Caucasus and

Central Asia had until recently been Soviet citizens; many of them now had Russian citizenship. They were 'foreign' only in the narrowest racial sense.

4. 'Vladimir Zhirinovsky on the sexual problems of Condoleeza Rice' (in Russian), by Yaroslava Krestovskaya, *Pravda*, 9 January 2006. http://www.pravda.ru/world/09-01-2006/73182-zhirinovsky-0

5. Andrei Sakharov, a Soviet physicist and human rights campaigner, was the best-known champion of freedom in the Soviet Union. He won the Nobel Peace Prize in 1975, though the Soviet authorities refused to let him travel to Stockholm to accept it. After protesting against the invasion of Afghanistan, he was exiled in Gorky (now once again known by its pre-revolutionary name of Nizhny Novgorod). He died on 14 December 1989, aged sixty-eight.

6. A Soviet icon, he was the first man in space on 12 April 1961.

7. Including the right to use the more suitable Latin alphabet rather than the Cyrillic one.

8. Yeltsin replaced that with the (wordless) Patriotic Song by the Russian composer Glinka. Mr Putin wanted the old anthem restored, but settled for the old tune and new words. These drop any Soviet allusions but keep the notion of ancient Russian 'brotherhood' (which in the eyes of the non-Russian peoples of the country may sound pretty much like imperialism).

> Russia – our sacred state,
> Russia – our beloved country.
> A mighty will, a great glory
> Are yours forever for all time!
> Chorus:
> Be glorious, our free Fatherland,
> Ancient union of brotherly peoples,
> Ancestor-given wisdom of the people!
> Be glorious, country! We are proud of you!

9. Historians' estimates differ. Robert Service thinks it was around 300,000; Robert Conquest reckons about 500,000; Norman Lowe says 50–200,000 were executed, 400,000 died in prison or were killed in revolts.

10. Penguin Classics edition, 1977, p. 260.

11. The money was stolen or misappropriated by the communist rulers and mostly never reached the intended beneficiaries.

12. That would be as if Russia would elect as its leader a veteran Cold War critic of the Soviet Union such as the British-based Vladimir Bukovsky.

13. Japan, of course, is another story altogether.

14. Vladimir Putin, Annual Address to the Federal Assembly, 25 April 2005.

http://kremlin.ru/eng/speeches/2005/04/25/2031_type70029type
82912_87086.shtml (in English, slightly misleadingly translated). The phrase
used in Russian was '*Prezhde vsego sleduyet priznat, chto krusheniye Sovetskogo
Soyuza bylo krupneishei geopoliticheskoi katasrophoi veka*' (Above all it must be
ackowledged that the collapse of the Soviet Union was the goepolitical
catastrophe of the century). The speech is avaiable in Russian on http://
kremlin.ru/eng/speeches/2005/04/25/2031_type70029type
82912_87086.shtml

15. 'Butterfly-Polka' (Polka-Babochka) is, incidentally, an unusual choice of
phrase straight from the Stalinist propaganda lexicon, when it was used to
indicate something utterly alien. See the explanation by Pavel Felgenhauer,
a hard-hitting journalistic critic of the Kremlin ('Kremlin Rejects "Foreign"
Approach to Russian History', *Eurasia Daily Monitor*, The Jamestown
Foundation, 27 June 2007), available at http://www.jamestown.org/
edm/article.php?article_id=2372256

16. Meeting with participants in the National Russian Conference of Human-
ities and Social Sciences Teachers, 21 June 2007, Novo-Ogaryovo. Excerpts
in English at http://www.kremlin.ru/2007/06/21/1702_ type63376
type63381type82634_135323.shtml and in Russian in full at
http://www.kremlin.ru/appears/2007/06/21/1702_type63376type63381
type82634_135323.shtml

17. Prosveshcheniye, Moscow, 2007.
Two interesting articles (in Russian) give some background to the issue:
http://www.ng.ru/ng_politics/2007-07-03/10_uchebniki.html;
http://www.ng.ru/politics/2007-07-05/3_pozor.html

18. http://www.kremlin.ru/eng/text/speeches/2005/05/07/
0852_type82916_87605.shtml

19. The accusation '*u vas negrov linchuyut*' (and you are lynching negroes) became
a catchphrase epitomising Soviet propaganda based on this principle.

20. On 25 August 1968 Tatyana Baeva, Konstantin Babtsky, Larisa Bogoraz,
Vadim Delaunay, Vladimir Dremluga, Viktor Fainberg, Natalya Gorbanevskaya and Pavel Litvinov assembled in Red Square with a Czechoslovak
flag and banners bearing slogans including 'For your freedom and ours' and
'Glory to free and independent Czechoslovakia'. They were almost instantly
arrested. Encouraged by the others, Ms Baeva claimed to have been there by
accident and was released. Bogoraz was sentenced to four years in Siberia
and became Chairman of the Moscow Helsinki Group in 1989. She died in
2004. Delaunay was sentenced to two years in a labour camp. He emigrated
to France in 1975 and died in 1983. Mr Litvinov was sentenced to five years'

exile in Chita. He emigrated to America in 1973 and still lives there. Ms Gorbanevskaya was not tried, as she had recently given birth. Viktor Fainberg was pronounced insane and spent five years in psychiatric hospital. The Tom Stoppard play *Every Good Boy Deserves Favour* is dedicated to him.

21. *Rossiiskaya Gazeta*, 8 September 2007, commentary by Aleksandr Sabov. This is not available on the newspaper's website but can be accessed at http://community.livejournal.com/ru_katyn/12893.html

22. Little mention is made of British and American help to the Soviet war effort.

23. Each side thought they were getting the better deal. Germany could mop up the countries of Central Europe and then concentrate on crushing France and forcing Britain to sue for peace. The Soviet Union, in chaos after Stalin's purges, hoped to stand back while the 'imperialist powers' fought and weakened each other. http://www.fordham.edu/halsall/mod/1939pact.html has the text of the pact, and the secret protocol. http://www.regnum.ru/news/411620.html (in Russian) gives a good account of Kremlin thinking about it now.

24. Estonia is almost the only country to have made inroads into the post-communist world's biggest outstanding problem: reforming public admin-istration. Unlike almost any other country, Estonia built its most important institutions from scratch, shunning the temptation to use 'experienced' communist-era leftovers. The result is that the country has by some way the region's most modern and effective organs of state, ranging from a highly effective foreign ministry to security and intelligence services deeply trusted by their Western counterparts. Its heavyweight president increasingly speaks for the whole post-communist region.

25. To be fair, some Americans thought the same of Nicaragua under the Sandinistas, and still do about communist Cuba.

26. The journal in question was described, quite wrongly, in the Soviet ultimatum as an 'Organ of the Baltic Military Entente'. Fired by this historical example, I set up an English-language weekly in Tallinn in 1992. Intentionally provocative, it carried a column called 'Troopwatch' that monitored the occupation forces' misbehaviour.

27. Born in 1920, his best-known work in English is probably *The Czar's Madman* (Harvill, London, 1992, English translation).

28. Quoted in www.jamestown.org/edm/article.php?article_id=2369743 (in English) and http://www.rian.ru/world/foreign_russia/20050510/39960964-print.html and http://www.lenta.ru/news/2005/05/10/putin (in Russian).

29. Romualdas Misiunas and Rein Taagepera, *The Baltic States: The Years of*

Dependence, 1940–90, Berkeley, 1993, gives the full story. I have focused on Estonia here because this country is at the time of writing the main target of Kremlin displeasure.

30. I am indebted to Robert Gellately's *Lenin, Hitler, Stalin*, Cape, London, 2007, p. 389, for this remarkable fact.

31. In Putin's words in October 2007: 'As a result of a shock therapy of the 1990s, the 1998 financial crisis, and the tragic events in the Caucasus the country's economy and social sphere were in depression. The same can be said about the public's morale at the time. The country's territorial integrity was under threat.' Opening remarks at VIIIth United Russia Party Congress, 1 October 2007, Gostiny Dvor, Moscow. In English at http://www.kremlin.ru/eng/speeches/2007/10/01/1418_type82912type82913type84779_80868.shtml and in Russian at http://www.kremlin.ru/appears/2007/10/01/1900_type63374type63376type63378type82634_146479.shtml

32. 'Hang the Kaiser' was a popular post-war slogan in Britain.

33. It also stresses that Russia should not be dictated to from outside, celebrates the campaign to bankrupt Yukos, justifies Russia's disastrous intervention in the Ukrainian 'Orange Revolution' and says that the exigencies of the war on terror have forced both Russia and America to limit civil liberties in a similar way.

34. Lilia Shevtsova, *Anti-Westernism is the New National Idea* www.carnegieendowment.org/publications/index.cfm?fa=view&id=19480

35. Responses to questions from Russian journalists, 6 December 2004, Ankara, Turkey. In English at http://www.kremlin.ru/eng/speeches/2004/12/06/1232_type82915-80868.shtml and in Russian at http://www.kremlin.ru/appears/2004/12/06/1409_type6380_80827.shtml

36. Annual Address to Federal Assembly, Moscow, 2006. In English at http://www.kremlin.ru/eng/speeches/2006/05/10/1823_type20029type82912_105566.shtml and (with ' "comrade" wolf') in Russian at http://www.kremlin.ru/appears/2006/05/10/1357_type63372type63374type82634_105546.shtml

37. Thomas E. Ricks and Craig Whitlock, 'Putin Hits U.S. Over Unilateral Approach: Rebuke Is Called Unusually Hostile', *Washington Post*, 11 February 2007, sec. A01: http://www.washingtonpost.com/wpdyn/content/article/2007/0210/AR2007021000524.html (in English). For text (in English): Speech and the Following Discussion at the Munich Conference on Security Policy, 10 February 2007: http://www.kremlin.ru/eng/speeches/2007/02/10/0138_type82912type82914tuype82917type84779_118123.shtml. In Russian: http://www.kremlin.ru/appears/200702/

10/1737_type63374type63376type63377type63381type82634_
118097.shtml. And for a video of the event: http://media.kremlin.ru/
2007_02_10_01.wmv

38. Such snide and sometimes strident commentary is still mixed with an almost fawning official desire on occasion to talk up the relationship with America. Mr Putin has invited Mr Bush to his dacha and let him drive his prized 1956 Volga; at the Victory Day parade in Red Square marking fifty years since the end of the Second World War, Mr Putin ostentatiously put his American counterpart in the best seat, and described him as a guest of 'special importance'. http://www.gazeta.ru/2007/05/11/oa_238815.shtml

39. Much as the international legal and bureaucratic order chafes, the Kremlin is determined to join every club it can, and fiercely resists any suggestion that it does not belong in the G8 or the Council of Europe. None of the so-called patriots in the Kremlin has explained how Russia can be an equal partner with the West while also repeatedly denouncing the principles of interdependence, multilateralism, human rights and openness on which the civilised world operates.

40. http://www.carnegie.ru/en/pubs/media/76677.htm

41. Lilia Shevtsova, *Anti-Westernism is the New National Idea.*

42. By contrast, 21 per cent said they were superstitious, 9 per cent admitted to believing in horoscopes, 8 per cent in magic and 6 per cent in UFOs. http://bd.english.fom.ru/report/cat/man/valuable/ed072321 gives another view with interesting insights.

43. http://www.newyorker.com/archive/2002/04/01/020401ta_talk_lipman

44. See article by Igor Torbakov on http://www.jamestown.org/publica tions_details.php?volume_id=414&issue_id=3681&article_id=2370960

45. Quoted in the *Los Angeles Times*, 11 April 2005.
http://www.otechestvo.org.ua/main/20068/1708.htm and
http://www.evrazia.org/modules.php?name=News&file=article&sid=2625 (both in Russian) are also interesting. Coupled with the authorities' own suspicion of both foreign organisations and minority rights, the ROC's stance has led to a sad decline in religious freedom. Non-Orthodox churches find it hard to register; their foreign clergy find it hard to get visas and residence permits.

46. The idea that Russia, like every country, is nothing more than a historical accident is not considered.

47. http://www.viperson.ru/wind.php?ID=322805&soch=1

48. http://www.viperson.ru/wind.php?ID=322805&soch=1

49. Had he wanted to give a more conventional spin to his ideas about legality, Mr Putin could have spoken of *vlast* (rule) or *verkhovenstvo* (supremacy) *zakona*. But he didn't.

50. This centralising approach is questionable. Common sense suggests tightly controlled rule from the centre may pose problems in the world's largest country by land area. Even China finds it expedient to give local rulers some flexibility. America and Brazil flourish as federations.

51. https://www.oecd.org/dataoecd/58/49/37656835.pdf

52. As much as Mr Putin preaches the virtues of tight control, he and other senior figures are only too willing to shirk responsibility when they need to. In the case of the Litvinenko poisoning, for example, the Russian line was that the state could not possibly be held accountable for the theft of a large quantity of a lethal radioactive substance from a supposedly tightly guarded nuclear research institute, or for the way in which a security service veteran left trails of it on his journey to London and back. The line was, in effect: 'It's Russia. These things happen. Get used to it.'

53. What Russia really needs is a *vlastnaya gorizontal* (literally, a power horizontal) in which the state is accountable both to its own institutions and to society. But Mr Putin's solution, supposedly fitting Russian political culture, is not joined-up government and public accountability, but stern top-down pressure. What makes the state work is fear, not conscience.

54. *Komsomolskaya Pravda*, 6 November 2004 and http://www.press-attache.ru/ArticlePrint.aspx/news/321

55. *Tretiya Imperiya. Rossiya, kotoraya dolzhna byt*, Limbus Press, Moscow, 2006 (in Russian only).

56. http://www.frontpagemag.com/Articles/Printable.aspx?GUID=3E0AF111-0918-4A94-947F-E1E6D2E1E5D4

57. http://www.mediacratia.ru/owa/mc/mc_project_news.html?a_id=17121

58. Interviewed in *Vedomosti*, 5 July 2007.

59. http://www.russiaprofile.org/page.php?pageid=Experts%27+Panel&articleid=a1183125261

6 HOW EASTERN EUROPE SITS ON THE FRONT LINE
OF THE NEW COLD WAR

1. The German-speaking border regions of Czechoslovakia, claimed by Hitler.

2. The Slovak foreign-policy expert Mário Nicolini's definition is a good one: 'Euroatlanticism represents a policy that seeks a strong Europe and strengthens the multilateral reflexes of America.'

http://www.ceeol.com/aspx/getdocument.aspx?logid=5&id=b6a97a38
0a1c-4df9-849d-9d1e608287af

3. The Czech Republic, Estonia, Hungary Latvia, Lithuania, Poland, Slovakia and Slovenia joined in 2004; Romania and Bulgaria joined in 2007. The next candidates for membership are Macedonia and Croatia.

4. The Czech Republic, Hungary and Poland joined in 1999; Bulgaria, Estonia, Latvia, Lithuania, Romania, Slovakia and Slovenia joined in 2004. The next wave of enlargement is likely to include Albania, Croatia, Macedonia and, with luck, Georgia.

5. Igor Rodionov, 'Approaches to Russian Military Doctrine', speech given at General Staff Academy conference 27–30 May 1992, reprinted in *Voyennaya mysl* (Military Thinking), July 1992.

6. The Baltic states and their more pedantic friends insist that they were not 'Soviet Republics' but occupied territories. Most Western countries never recognised their annexation by the Soviet Union, and refused to have formal or high-level contact with the officials of the local administrations in the 'Soviet Baltic Republics'.

7. A somewhat chastened Mr Mečiar has now returned as junior partner in the coalition government formed after the June 2006 elections.

8. He died in a jail cell in the Netherlands in 2006, while on trial for war crimes.

9. In 2007 Mr Karimov ranked eighth in the 'world's worst dictators' hit parade, down from fifth place the previous year. http://www.parade.com/export/sites/default/articles/web_exclusives/2007/02-11-2007/dictators08.html

10. http://www.ferghana.ru/article.php?id=521&print=1&PHPSES-SID=2d1d1ca13806e42db563aa39ccb889f8

11. Strongly supported by Turkey, Azerbaijan believes that Armenia is illegally occupying its territory of Nagorno-Karabakh (or Karabagh). Armenia says that history, demography and conquest give it the strongest title. Peace negotiations have got nowhere, and Armenia is the grateful host to a Russian military base, while also quietly improving ties with Iran. In the event of a peace deal with Azerbaijan and rapprochement with Turkey, few doubt that Armenia would soon be an enthusiastic member of the Euroatlantic camp.

12. As his name would be transcribed from the Belarusan language; in Russian it would be Aleksandr Lukashenko.

13. Dmitry Zavadsky, a journalist; Yury Zakharenko and Viktor Gonchar, politicians, and Anatoly Krasovsky, a businessman. From Belarusan their names would be transliterated as Zmitser Zavadsky, Viktar Hanchar, Yuri Zakharanka and Anatol Krasousky.

14. It is run by Mr Borodin, formerly of the Kremlin's property department, where Mr Putin worked after his move from St Petersburg.

15. This grew out of the original 'Shanghai Five', of Russia, China, Kazakhstan, Kyrgyzstan and Tajikistan that was set up in the mid-1990s.

16. This started when Armenia, Kazakhstan, Kyrgyzstan, Russia, Tajikistan and Uzbekistan signed a collective security treaty in May 1992, which came into force in April 1994, by which time Azerbaijan, Georgia and Belarus had signed, too. In April 1999 Armenia, Belarus, Kazakhstan, Kyrgyzstan, Russia and Tajikistan agreed to extend the treaty for a further five years, upon which Azerbaijan, Georgia and Uzbekistan withdrew. In October 2002, the six remaining members renamed it the Collective Security Treaty Organisation. In June 2006, Uzbekistan joined.

17. When I was trying to get a residence permit to live in Czechoslovakia in 1998, I timed my application to coincide with a CSCE session on media accreditation. If the Czechoslovak authorities adopted their usual stone-walling tactics in my case, a friendly British diplomat explained, they would immediately present an 'open goal' to their Western critics. I got the necessary papers within a couple of weeks.

18. Though some Western countries, notably America, insisted that this did not affect their non-recognition policy towards the occupation of the Baltic states.

19. Even Belarus enjoyed a few months of independence in 1918. A government-in-exile descended from those few months of statehood maintains an exiguous presence to this day. See 'Home thoughts from abroad', *The Economist*, 20 December 2001, http://www.economist.com/world/africa/displayStory.cfm?Story_ID=883955, And 'The sorrows of Belarus' (online only), Europe View, 16 November 2006, http://www.economist.com/agenda/displayStory.cfm?story_id=8171305&fsrc=RSS

20. This would mean not only free elections, but the lifting of restrictions on independent organisations, the media and opposition political parties, the withdrawal of Russian troops, military intelligence and weapons, and the end of illegal economic activities such as counterfeiting, trafficking and smuggling. It is worth noting that Moldova is no paragon in these respects either.

21. By mid-2007, the outlines of that seemed to be taking shape. However, at the time of writing, outside pressure seemed to have derailed, or at least stalled, this deal.

22. Who made up barely a fifth of the population in their nominal homeland.

23. I went to visit a new finance minister once, who was being energetically promoted by the ever-optimistic American Embassy. His office was bright,

modern and computerised. We had an enjoyable chat about e-government and zero-based budgeting. It was pretty clear that his talents were not matched by political clout. As I left, I used an old journalist's trick and asked to use the restroom, saying that I would find my own way out. Not only was the toilet worse than a midden, but my detour to some of the other offices produced a much more convincing picture: a warren of ill-lit and dingy offices, each filled with rickety wooden furniture. Dumpy little men in ill-fitting brown suits were engaged in chain-smoking conversation with thickset men in leather jackets. Not a computer was in sight, and bare light bulbs dangled from the ceilings.

24. The use of the Georgian currency, the lari, in South Ossetia is growing, displacing both the rouble and the coupons issued by the local authorities.

25. Known as Borjomi, Georgia's pungent sulphurated mineral water is an acquired taste. It was one of the best-selling bottled drinks in the Soviet Union.

26. See, for example, http://www.washingtonpost.com/wp-dyn/content/article/2006/10/01/AR2006100100898_pf.html; or in Russian: http://www.rg.ru/2006/10/02/prezident.html; http://www.vsesmi.ru/news/134556/; http://www.annews.ru/news/detail.php?ID=32208&print=Y

27. http://hrw.org/reports/2007/russia1007/russia1007web.pdf

28. HRW, ibid.

29. The same happened with the Baltic states in the early 1990s. Russian economic sanctions and energy blockages simply accelerated the reorientation towards other markets.

30. http://www.robertamsterdam.com/2007/01/druzhba_shut_down_europe_cut_o.htm ;
http://www.spiegel.de/international/0,1518,458401,00.html and http://www.spiegel.de/international/0,1518,458573,00.html and in Russian: http://portnews.ru/digest/2637/

31. http://www.balticbusinessnews.com/newsletter/070724_bbn_newsletter.pdf

32. Robert L. Larsson, *Russia's Energy Policy: Security Dimensions and Russia's Reliability as an Energy Supplier*, FOI, Stockholm, 2006), www.foi.se

33. The same twisted logic was used in the aftermath of the Litvinenko poisoning, when the Russian Embassy in London blamed Mr Berezovsky.

34. http://online.wsj.com/article/SB118350332439357187.html?mod=googlenews_wsj and in Russian: http://www.inosmi.ru/translation/235319.html

35. http://www.kommersant.ru/doc.aspx?DocsID=793939

36. The CIS election monitors found no evidence of the massive fraud reported

by outsiders from the OSCE; Mr Putin hurried to congratulate Viktor Yanukovych as the 'winner' even before the official result had been declared.

37. 'Neftegazovaia Diplomatia kak Ugroza Marginalizatsii', *Nezavisimaya Gazeta*, 28 December 2004.

38. http://www.iss.niiit.ru/doktrins/doktr02.htm

39. Their most powerful weapon was defending the status of the Russian language, which under Soviet rule had driven Ukrainian out of public life, to the point that even speaking it in Kyiv was a strong political statement. Since independence, Ukrainian has made a strong comeback in central Ukraine, but remains a minority language in the Russified east of the country. Although the two languages are closely related (more so than Spanish and Portuguese, for example) older and less-educated Russian-speakers fear that a 'nationalist' government may somehow penalise them for a failure to speak Ukrainian. After all, say pro-Russian propagandists, that is exactly what happened in the Baltic states.

40. http://www.novopol.ru/print2355.html

41. Ibid.

42. *Adolf* by Pip Utton, www.pip-utton.com/putton/adolf.htm

43. http://www.kp.ru/daily/23929.4/69696/
Mr Lang responded here: http://www.rosbalt.ru/2007/7/27/400684.html

44. Although the entry has now been moved to one on Astroturfing, some traces on Wikipedia survived as of late 2007, such as this: http://en.wikipedia.org/wiki/Media_in_Transnistria#International_Council_for_Democratic_Institutions_and_State_Sovereignty

45. See 'An old friend comes back' and 'Covering tracks' (online only), *The Economist*, 3 August 2006.

46. Under international law, it is prohibited for the occupying power to settle its population in the territories concerned. The Soviet Union, of course, did not regard the Baltic republics as occupied.

47. In the borders of the current Estonia the figure was still higher, around 96 per cent. The 8 per cent pre-war Russian minority lived largely in the areas transferred to the Russian Federation in 1945.

48. Trying to buy some stamps in the main post office in Tallinn in early 1990, a clerk told me to 'talk like a human being' when I spoke Estonian – in theory an official language.

49. Certainly more could be done to speed integration. The big efforts made in the 1990s have tailed off. The current Estonian government is so focused on economic growth that it tends to ignore social issues. But Russia is not

interested in the practicalities of integration. It does nothing to encourage non-citizens in Estonia to learn the language. In fact it barely supports them at all. What the Kremlin does do is stoke ethnic disharmony, in the hope of undermining the Estonian government.

50. http://www.rg.ru/2007/05/03/nashi.html

51. http://www.gazeta.ru/2007/04/28/oa_237922.shtml and http://www.newsru.com/russia/03may2007/marina.html

52. Author's translation: The full version in Russian is at http://www.kp.ru/daily/23896.3/66766

53. The *Sluzhba Vneshnei Razvedky* is the renamed First Chief Directorate of the KGB, Mr Putin's old employer.

54. http://www.tldm.org/News11/RussiaMoreMilitary.htm

55. Such influence is not confined to the ex-Soviet region, however. Russia also hopes to use its former satellites' membership of Euroatlantic institutions to plant its agents there, too. Even if they are then exposed, it serves another Kremlin aim: to discredit these countries in the eyes of their Western allies.

56. http://www.wired.com/politics/security/magazine/15-09/ff_estonia has an extensive account of the incident.

57. Another possible flashpoint is eastern Ukraine. Russian-speakers there have so far proved hard to ignite. But with a really serious political crisis in Kyiv, that might change: for example, Russia might covertly back an ultra-nationalist party in order to stoke separatist sentiment in the eastern part of the country.

58. '*Aus dem Osten setzt ein neuer Massenansturm ein: Der Wettlauf nach Westen*' (A mass onslaught brews up in the East: the race to get to the West); October 1991 http://service.spiegel.de/digas/find?DID=13492070

59. Or more fairly, less used to the rules.

60. http://www.nytimes.com/2007/05/22/world/europe/22europe.html?_r=1&n=Top/News/World/Countries%20and%20Territories/Russia&oref=slogin

7 PIPELINE POLITICS: THE THREAT AND THE REALITY

1. Vladimir Putin, *Strategicheskoye planirovaniye vosproizvodstva mineralno-syryevoy bazy regiona v usloviyakh formirovaniya rynochnykh otnosheniy*, State Mining Institute, St Petersburg, 1997. The American scholar Clifford Gaddy has produced interesting evidence that suggests the book is in fact heavily plagiarised. http://www.cdi.org/russia/johnson/2006-78-3a.cfm

2. http://www.heritage.org/Research/RussiaandEurasia/bg2048.cfm

3. Quoted in Michael Fredholm, *Gazprom in Crisis*, CSRC, Swindon, October 2006.

4. LNG is compressed gas that can be carried by tanker. Though the compression and decompression are expensive, it can be traded freely, unlike pipeline gas which is almost always delivered under a long-term contract.

5. http://www.eni.it/wogr_2006/gas-international_trade-81.htm

6. See, for example http://ec.europa.eu/energy/russia/overview/index_en.htm and http://ec.europa.eu/energy/russia/presentations/doc/2004_berlin_en.pdf

7. 7 June 2007: http://www.rian.ru/world/world_community/20070607/66873834.html;

   7 December 2006: http://www.prime-tass.ru/news/show.asp?id=646546&ct=news;

   19 October 2006: http://www.lenta.ru/news/2006/10/19/charter/

   20 June 2006: http://www.vedomosti.ru/newsline/index.shtml?2006/06/20/279956

8. See Agata Loskot-Strachota, *Russian Gas for Europe*, Centre for Eastern Studies Warsaw, October 2006, and Katinka Barysch's 2007 pamphlet http://www.cer.org.uk/pdf/policybrief_russia_FINAL_20july07.pdf

9. See Barysch, 2007, and also Paul Belkin, *The European Union's Energy Security Challenges*, http://fas.org/sgp/crs/row/RL33636.pdf

10. Quoted in Barysch, 2007. The American software giant has been engaged in a lengthy wrangle with the EU over allegedly monopolistic features of its Windows software. See http://www.cer.org.uk/pdf/policybrief_russia_FINAL_20july07.pdf

11. http://www.nord-stream.com is the home page. For information on the project's impact on gas distribution to Europe see *From Russia with Gas: An Analysis of the Nord Stream Pipeline's Impact on the European Gas Transmission System with the Tiger-Model* on http://www.ewi.uni-koeln.de/ewi/content/e266/e283/e5011/ewiwp0702_ger.pdf

12. http://www.nabucco-pipeline.com/

13. http://www.youtube.com/watch?v=2EZ4QMjh2zo&eurl=http%3A%2F%2Fmedienkritik%2Etypepad%2Ecom%2Fblog%2Fschroeder%2Findex%2Ehtml

14. http://www.heritage.org/Research/Europe/upload/bg_1980.pdf , p. 4.

15. Though Russia's embassy in the heart of Stockholm is probably a more effective listening station than anything that could be built at sea.

16. http://www.rferl.org/featuresarticle/2006/04/04805ae4-dc2a-401c-83e2-d85524b4d90d.html, and (in Russian) http://www.newsru.com/finance/08dec2005/putingas.html

17. http://www.rferl.org/featuresarticle/2006/04/eb61f3cc-87b2-4bf2-a572-

4175d1663f7e.html, and the EU's response, http://www.rferl.org/features article/2006/05/6eca53e0-0e24-48bc-9a90-afdc96a6e870.html

18. http://www.ffa.se/upload/english/reports/foir2251.pdf , p. 27.

19. http://www.ce-review.org/01/2/germanypress2.html And http://fazar chiv.faz.net/webcgi?WID=59433-2780937-22101_1

20. http://www.kommersant.ru/doc.aspx?DocsID=633868

21. http://jamestown.org/edm/article.php?article_id=2368342 and http://for eignaffairs.house.gov/110/bar072507.pdf , p. 5. give more details.

22. http://www.fbi.gov/wanted/alert/mogilevich_s.htm

23. http://www.total.com/energies/N11/en/comprendre/details/dossier03.htm, and http://www.ffa.se/upload/english/reports/foir2251.pdf , p. 33.

24. See, for example, Carl Mortished's article in *The Times* on 5 July 2007, http://business.timesonline.co.uk/tol/business/industry_sectors/natural_ resources/article2029023.ece and (in Russian) http://www.annews.ru/ news/detail.php?ID=108478&print=Y

25. Germany lobbied hard to ensure that Poland, despite its evident unreadiness in some respects, was included in the first wave of EU enlargement in 2004.

26. At the request of the previous German chancellor, Helmut Schmidt, America was planning to base Cruise and Pershing nuclear missiles in Europe. By putting part of America's nuclear arsenal in Europe, the idea was to make the NATO nuclear deterrent more credible, and the Warsaw Pact's overwhelming superiority in conventional forces less threatening. But by the time the missiles were actually deployed, in the early 1980s, German public opinion was far more worried about the dangers of nuclear weapons than the threat from the east.

27. http://en.internationalepolitik.de/archiv/200/fall2000/russia-and-german —investors.html

28. Known as the 'Weimar Triangle'. See http://www.diplomatie.gouv.fr/en/ country-files_156/germany_335/the-weimar-triangle_3451/the-weimar- meetings_4339.html

29. http://palm.newsru.com/finance/25apr2007/strabag.html. In May 2007, Mr Deripaska acquired a US $1.5 billion stake in Magna, a Canadian car parts manufacturer, and is reported to have a 5 per cent stake in America's General Motors. http://auto.lenta.ru/news/2007/08/07/deripaska/

30. http://www.aktuell.ru/russland/wirtschaft/putin_schroeder_und_russland _auf_der_hannover_messe_1096.html

31. See Ariel Cohen at http://www.heritage.org/Research/Europe/bg1980.cfm

32. See, for example, http://www.jamestown.org/edm/article.php?article_ id=2372380 and http://www.wintershall.com/pi-07-04.98.html

33. http://www.iht.com/articles/2006/04/27/business/rusgas.php
34. Weeks later Rosneft tried a similar deal, offering Royal Dutch Shell access to the Severo-Komsomolsk onshore oil field in return for the Western company's stake in Germany's largest oil-industry complex, MIRO, going to Russia's Rosneft. If that goes ahead, it will mark the first big investment by a Kremlin firm in Europe's private-sector oil industry.
35. http://europe.eu.int/comm/energy/electricity/publications/doc/ten_e_en.pdf Energising Europe's Infrastructure
36. http://www.rian.ru/economy/20070624/67725613.html (in Russian).
37. http://interfax.ru/r/B/politics/2.html?menu=21&id_issue=11774951
38. http://budapest.cafebabel.com/en/post/2007/09/17/Hungary-fully-behind-Nabucco-pipeline.
    In Russian: http://www.uk2watch.com/energy/article.jsp?14066
39. http://www.rian.ru/analytics/20070524/66054411.html
40. The move was little surprise to those who remember Austria's chummy relations with the Soviet Union during the Cold War, when Vienna was a playground for Eastern bloc intelligence agents. After the collapse of communism, the Austrian capital offered a warm welcome to Russians wanting to polish their legitimate credentials – Austria, almost alone in Europe, offered anonymous bank accounts. The Austrian state, which still owns a 31 per cent stake in ÖMV, was the first capitalist country to buy gas from the Soviet Union.
41. http://www.iht.com/articles/2007/08/09/bloomberg/energy.php
42. Some senior foreign business executives' behaviour towards Russia is barely explicable except in terms of the expectation of future rewards. For a Western oil company boss, a decision has only to be defensible, rather than correct, in order to get past shareholders' scrutiny now, and open the way to a lucrative consulting contract with a Russian company once the brief stint at the top is over.
43. www.energypolicy.ru/files/milov%20June26-2007.ppt
44. http://www.city.ac.uk/law/dps/Dept_dps/riley_papers/CEPSGasDeficitPaperFinal.pdf

8 SABRE-RATTLING, OR SELLING SABRES?
RUSSIA'S FOREIGN POLICY UNPICKED

1. http://www.warfare.ru/?lang=&catid=239&linkid=227
2. http://www.cdi.org/friendlyversion/printversion.cfm?documentID=2967 gives an up-to-date summary.

3. http://www.roe.ru/ is the home page.

4. http://www.prime-tass.ru/news/show.asp?id=611581&ct=news

5. *Perspective*, vol. XVII, no. 4, Institute for the Study of Conflict, Ideology and Policy, Boston University, July–August 2007.

6. http://www.lenta.ru/news/2007/09/15/west/

7. http://www.pircenter.org/data/news/fedorov_u200804.pdf

8. http://www.gazeta.ru/2007/04/26/oa_237723.shtml

9. http://www.rferl.org/featuresarticle/2007/4/F33954AF-D1B2-491E-823E-40D8197C7E22.html

10. The treaty text is on http://www.fas.org/nuke/control/cfe/text/cfe_t.htm

11. http://www.jamestown.org/edm/article.php?article_id=2372138

12. http://www.ng.ru/courier/2007-03-05/13_munhen.html

13. http://www.rferl.org/featuresarticle/2007/07/27947831-dfcd-4d49-afec 77455719385e.html. In Russian on http://www.polit.ru/news/2007/07/ 12/kosovoresolution_print.html and http://www.rian.ru/world/world_ community/20070712/68862719.html

14. Trenin's arguments are well expressed in his book *Getting Russia Right*, Carnegie Endowment for International Peace, 2007.

15. The Lourdes eavesdropping post in Cuba and the Cam Ranh naval base in Vietnam. Russia retains bases in the CIS, including two in Belarus (a radio station for communicating with its submarine fleet and an anti-missile radar). It is now restoring a semi-derelict naval base in Syria.

16. http://www.rv.ru/content.php3?id=806 and http://www.rus-imperia. com/2_2002/politic3.htm

17. See, for example, http://www.izvestia.ru/world/article3096827/

18. http://www.carnegie.ru/en/pubs/media/76545.htm

19. http://www.carnegie.ru/en/pubs/media/76059.htm

20. Red for Soviet nostalgia, brown for ultra-nationalism.

21. http://www.zavtra.ru/cgi/veil/data/zavtra/07/694/11.html

22. It has probably declined since the Yeltsin years, when it was stoked by the Jewish family history of most of the oligarchs.

23. He now heads the SVR.

24. http://en.rian.ru/russia/20061025/55110192.html

25. http://www.nationalinterest.org/General.aspx?id=92&id2=14798

26. http://www.pinr.com/report.php?ac=view_report&report_id=672&lan guage_id=1

27. http://www.rian.ru/world/20060616/49576897.html

28. http://www.moscowtimes.ru/stories/2005/08/15/007.html

9 HOW TO WIN THE NEW COLD WAR:
WHY THE WEST MUST BELIEVE IN ITSELF

1. That would automatically exclude companies such as Itera and Rosukrenergo.
2. The natural organisation to deal with this is the Paris-based Organisation for
   Economic Co-operation and Development (OECD). This has already
   developed from being a think tank that mainly produces statistics to become
   a global guardian of good economic policy in the widest sense. It includes all
   the world's advanced economies and, crucially, Russia is not a member. The
   OECD is therefore in a perfect position to set new tough rules on corporate
   governance and access to global financial markets, and then monitor their
   observance. Just as gangsters cannot expect to use the global financial system
   to launder cash, the kleptocrats of the Kremlin should not be able to use it to
   launder assets.
3. www.cer.org.uk/pdf/briefing_russia_16may07_kb.pdf
4. That does not mean making visa applications harder for ordinary Russians,
   but it should be harder for those connected with the Kremlin and other
   branches of lawbreaking Russian officialdom and business. Gazprom and
   Rosneft would find their access to international capital markets much less
   easy if their senior executives were unable to visit America, Britain or
   Germany.
5. It is important not to be too sentimental. The Cold War may have been the
   struggle of good against evil at a global level, but the West had plenty to be
   ashamed of in the details: the support for corrupt and authoritarian dictators
   in the Third World, bully-boy tactics against leftwingers in Europe and
   America and the cynical conflation of Western economic interests with the
   wider cause of freedom were among the most salient shortcomings.
6. Leftwingers protesting against martial law in Poland in 1981 used the slogan
   'Russian tanks, Western banks, Hands off Poland!' which equated the
   Western bankers, admittedly greedy and naive, who were trying to recover
   the $20 billion they had ill-advisedly lent the regime with a communist
   dictatorship responsible for the deaths of many tens of thousands of people.
   A more recent example is the way that such commentators treat Mr Putin's
   career in the KGB. It would be unthinkable for a post-war German
   politician, let alone a head of state, to have had a career in the SS or
   the Gestapo. Instead, Mr Putin's career is commonly equated with George
   Bush Sr's stint as head of the CIA in 1976–7. One of many such
   commentators is Eric Margolis http://www.ericmargolis.com/archives/

2001/06/son_of_cia_meet.php. Yet the two are not comparable. Mr Bush was a political appointment, just as he was in his previous job as America's top diplomat to China. A possible comparison might be Mr Putin's year as head of the FSB in 1998–9. But even that is stretching the facts. The FSB is an unreformed part of the old KGB, which was the terrifying and bloody weapon of a totalitarian secret-police state. For all its faults and blunders, than cannot be said of the CIA.

Acknowledgements

My thanks go first to my editors at the *Economist*, for giving me a sabbatical to write the book. But its arguments are mine alone, and do not necessarily represent the newspaper's editorial line on Russia or anything else.

I am particularly grateful to my friends who commented on, and vastly improved, the manuscript. They include Martin Dewhirst, Jeff Myhre, Greg Pytel, James Sherr and Zinovy Zinik. During my time in Moscow, Yevgenia Albats, Konstantin Eggert and three Mashas – Gessen, Lipman and especially Slonim – helped me greatly. Foreign correspondents' best sources, and best friends, are often colleagues: Kadri Liik and Christian Caryl as well as Isabel Gorst and Ana Uzelac all offered unstinting helpings of both friendship and their far greater knowledge of Russia; so did Marc and Rachel Polonsky. Without Claudia Sinnig I would have never done more than scratch the region's surface.

Two decades' worth of friends in what is now the ex-communist world have my deepest gratitude and affection: Tarmu Tammerk and my other colleagues at the former *Baltic Independent*, plus Kersti Kajulaid, David Mardiste, Eve and Mihkel Tarm and Tiia Raudma in Estonia; Baiba Braže, Nils Mužnieks and Pauls Raudseps in Latvia; Daiva Vilkelytė, Virgis Valentinavičius, Mirga Šaltmiras and the Dvarionis family in Lithuania; Pawel Dobrowolski, Marek Matraszek, Pawel Žak and most of all the Jablońska family in Poland; in the Czech Republic Alena Doležalová, Andrei and Marta Ernyei and Jan Urban; Ingrid Bakše in Slovenia and Edward Serotta in Vienna; as well as Bill Hough throughout the Baltic independence struggle. In Britain, Chris Cviić and Timothy Garton Ash first encouraged me to head east in 1988; the late Kari Blackburn, Steve Crawshaw, Daniel Franklin and Ed Steen gave me my first big breaks in journalism. Michael Bordeaux, Paul Goble, Vladimir Socor, Peter Reddaway and David Satter have provided historical, moral and strategic perspective over many years.

Government officials have been staunch allies, too. Tomas Bertelman, Dag Hartelius and Lars Freden from Sweden; Laura Kakko, Markus Lyra, and Rene Nyberg from Finland; Emma Baines, Janet Gunn, Richard Samuel, John and Judith Macgregor and Elizabeth Teague from Britain; and John Kunstadter have all shared their thoughts generously and warmly, as did those whose talents are cloaked in anonymity, protocol or shadow.

Ruthlessly though I have taken advantage of the help of these and many others, the mistakes of fact and interpretation in this book are mine alone.

This book was written at breakneck speed, requiring exceptional efforts from my literary agents, Zoe Waldie in London and Melanie Jackson in New York, who grasped the urgency of the project and found publishers willing to bring it out quickly. Stephen Edwards and Laurence Laluyaux sold the foreign language rights with exemplary efficiency. Bill Swainson and Emily Sweet at Bloomsbury, and Luba Ostashevsky and Yasmin Mathew at Palgrave, tolerated the questions and blunders of a first-time author with endless patience, while meeting a schedule that left little room for such pedagogy.

My parents, siblings and children have tolerated the absences,

arrests and assaults of a foreign correspondent's life with extraordinary stoicism and given me unquestioning love at all times. My
brother Richard and sister Helen have been founts of sanity and
support; furthermore, his wisdom and humour over more than
twenty years on the subjects of planned economies and post-
communist business have been invaluable.

Without the Odone family, the book would not have been
written; Francesco lent his house. Most of all, Cristina gave her love
and inspiration. The book is dedicated to her.

Index

11 September 2001 attacks, 3, 38, 253, 259

Abashidze, Aslan, 184
Abkhazia, 110, 146, 182–3, 189–90, 254
abortions, 122, 302
Abramovich, Roman, 87, 297
Abros bank, 81
Abu Ghraib, 3
Adenauer, Konrad, 222
adoption, 92, 219
advertising, 82, 114
Aeroflot, 31, 50, 61
Afghanistan, 14, 166, 259, 266, 277, 290;
    Soviet invasion, 138, 144–5, 262–3
Africa, 49, 290
Afrikanisatsiya, 9
Ahtisaari, Martti, 257–8
aircraft carriers, 245, 247
airspace violations, 13, 189–90, 246
Ajaria, 183–4
Akayev, Askar, 174
Akunin, Boris (Grigory Chkhartishvili),
    186
Albania, 231, 291
Albats, Yevgenia, 1, 80–2, 296
alcohol, 42, 51, 121–2, 156; *see also* vodka
Aleksei, Patriarch, 157
Algeria, 236
Almaz-Antei, 50

alphabets, 69–70, 151, 180, 303
Al-Qaeda, 287
Amnesty International, 37, 77–8, 96
anarchy, rise of, 45
Anderson, Julie, 111
Andropov, Yuri, 20–1, 27–8, 290
Angarsk, 105
anti-monopoly laws, 171
anti-Semitism, 156, 262–4, 300
apparatchiks, 49–50
Arabian Gulf, 129, 248
Arabs, 263–4
Arap, Larisa, 76, 91
Arctic and Antarctic Institute, 243
Arctic region, 16, 250, 266
Arctic Sea, 241–3
Argentina, 117
Armenia, 137, 175, 229, 266, 309
arms control, 13, 81, 247, 250, 254–6, 277
arms sales, 23, 83, 119, 247, 264, 267
army, Russian, 97, 245
Aslamazyan, Manana, 100, 299
Associated Press, 84
atom bomb, dropping of, 144
Australia, 139, 202, 235
Austria, 19, 139, 204, 210, 260, 316; and
    gas supplies, 213, 230, 232–3
aviation, 119, 121
Avtovaz, 115

Azerbaijan, 137, 175, 188, 309; and energy
    supplies, 228–30, 234

Bagrov, Yuri, 84
Baikalfinansgrup, 64
Bakhmina, Svetlana, 78
Baku–Tbilisi–Ceyhan oil pipeline, 234
Balkans, 15–16, 209, 228, 230–1, 234,
    259
Baltic Fleet, 221, 247
Baltic Sea, 98, 169; seaports, 171–2; and gas
    pipeline, 130, 215–16, 221
Baltic states, 7, 15–16, 20, 40, 135, 262;
    Germany and, 20, 225; nationalism, 69;
    and history, 145, 150, 152, 196; and
    NATO, 171–2, 185, 259; Soviet
    annexation, 152, 284, 289–90, 309–10,
    312; citizenship and language rights,
    178, 196, 312; period of independence,
    179; Stalinist terror, 182; oil supplies,
    187–8; and military incursions, 189–90;
    and Russian foreign policy, 196–203;
    and 'two-speed' Europe, 209
Baluyevsky, General Yuri, 256
banking, 9, 14, 40–1, 43–4, 52–4, 119, 123,
    273
Barclays, 233
Barents Sea, 239
Barysch, Katinka, 274
Basayev, Shamil, 287
Basescu, Traian, 231
BASF, 215–16, 226, 241
Basic Element, 224
Bavaria, 67
BBC, 7
Belarus, 15, 248, 266, 317; closeness to
    Russia, 175–6; and gas supplies, 217–18,
    240; suspended from Council of
    Europe, 276; period of independence,
    310
Belgium, 227
Beltransgas, 176
Benefit, 65
Berdimuhammedov, Gurbanguly, 175
Berezovsky, Boris, 31, 37, 52, 61–2, 81,

290, 297; and presidential election, 87–
    8; and Litvinenko affair, 106–7, 311
Beria, Lavrenti, 185
Bering Strait, 266
Berlin, 7, 16
Berlin Wall, fall of, 204
Berlusconi, Silvio, 19, 210
Beslan school siege, 68, 82
bin Laden, Osama, 277, 300
Bishkek, 265
Bismarck, Otto von, 142
Black Sea, 43, 169, 184, 228
Black Sea Fleet, 203, 247
Blair, Tony, 123, 261
Blank, Stephen, 250
Blok, Aleksandr, 155
Blue Stream gas pipeline, 228–30
Bolivia, 235
Bolshevik Revolution, see October
    Revolution
Bolsheviks, 90, 135, 137
books, 55–6
Borodin, Pavel, 31
Bosnia, 172, 231, 257, 260, 263, 291
'botnets', 202
Bourgas, 230
BP, 17, 109, 126–8
Brandt, Willy, 139
Bratislava, 233
Brazil, 113–14, 121, 238, 261, 277, 308
Brenton, Sir Anthony, 103
Brezhnev, Leonid, 20, 27, 42, 165
Britain, 13–14, 58, 61, 269; and Litvinenko
    affair, 2, 106–8; money-laundering, 109;
    demographics, 121; Russian influence
    in, 128–9; and history, 139–40, 146–7,
    149, 169; and former Soviet states, 173,
    194; and migration, 206–7; and 'two-
    speed' Europe, 209; and gas supplies,
    212–14, 221, 226; and electricity
    generation, 227; anti-Americanism, 261
British Council, 99–100
British Helsinki Human Rights Group,
    284
Browder, William, 127–8

Brussels, 82, 89, 173, 191, 208, 210, 232, 262

Budapest, 232

Buinaksk, 30

Bukovsky, Vladimir, 294, 303

Bulgaria, 19, 43, 202, 291; demographics, 121; and history, 151; NATO membership, 172; and gas supplies, 213, 230–1; American bases in, 255

Bush, George, Sr, 318–19

Bush, George W., 3, 16, 81, 154, 253, 261; supports Estonia, 16; meets Putin, 248, 294, 307

business interests, pro-Russian, 13–14, 16–17, 19, 58, 108–10, 122–9, 188–9, 226; and foreign policy, 258–9; and New Cold War, 273–4

businesses, Russian, 48, 115–17, 119, 160; small, 51, 57–8, 152, 160; IT sector, 115–16, 301

Butingë oil terminal, 188

cab drivers, 103–4, 299

Canada, 67, 235, 237, 242–3

capitalism, in Russia, 6, 15, 28, 57, 66, 120, 136, 259, 279; welfare, 17, 133; memories of, 40; under Yeltsin, 42–3, 52; municipal, 59; ethical basis, 130, 274; state, 165; and Cold War victory, 170; in Georgia, 183

car plants, 119

career choices, 117

cars, 49, 51–2, 54, 109, 115, 156

Carter, Jimmy, 20

Caspian Sea, 215, 229–30, 234

Catherine II (the Great), Empress, 142, 222

Cato Institute, 116

Caucasus, 15–16, 84, 137, 140, 182, 184–5, 194; people from, 105, 302

censorship, 167, 290

Central Asia, 69, 140, 173–4, 177, 303; and gas supplies, 215, 228, 232, 237; air bases, 259; and SCO and CSTO, 265–7

Central Europe, 15–16, 40, 114, 169, 233, 250, 256

Centre for European Reform, 274

Centre for International Legal Defence, 97

Centrica, 128

Chamberlain, Neville, 169

Chaplin, Vsevolod, 158

Charter 77, 178

Chávez, Hugo, 117, 248, 261

Cheboksary, 74–5

Chechenpress website, 106

Chechens, 137, 183, 286–7; separatists, 1, 6, 29–31, 68, 84, 88, 98, 162, 262–3, 300; exiled leader, 106–7

Chechnya, 61, 65, 68, 97, 162, 192, 287; Russian wars in, 1, 6, 10, 32–3, 48, 59, 69, 87–8, 254, 263; human rights cases, 95; American policy on, 154; 'Arab' fighters in, 264

Cheka, 27

Chelyabinsk, 265

Cheney, Dick, 38

Cherepovets, 95

Cherkesov, Viktor, 28

Chernenko, Konstantin, 28

Chernomyrdin, Viktor, 61, 285, 302

chess, 278

Chevron, 241

children, 121–2

children's homes, 206

Chilingarov, Artur, 242–3

China, 122, 174, 253, 270–1, 273, 277, 319; relations with Russia, 15, 23, 251, 262, 264–7; and SCO, 15, 177, 265–7; and world economy, 113–14, 121, 129, 166; and gas sales, 126, 240; arms purchases, 248; military, 265–6; demographics, 267; federalism, 308

Chirac, Jacques, 210

church and state, 156–7

Churchill, Winston, 283

Churilov, Colonel Oleg, 289

CIA, 194, 318–19; 'rendition', 3, 253

City of London, 14, 16, 129

civil service, 161, 164

civil society, 95–6, 269–70

Cohen, Ariel, 211

Cold War, 3–5, 7, 13–16, 19–20, 270–1, 273, 277–8; bases closed, 58, 259; and blackmail, 88; and human rights, 97; harassment of cultural organisations, 100; and Litvinenko affair, 107; and business interests, 130; and history, 147; negotiations, 167; victory in, 169–70; role of CSCE, 178; Germany and, 222–3; airspace violations, 246; allies visit Moscow, 248; arms control agreements, 250, 254, 256; and Israel, 263; vetoes, 276; Western shortcomings, 318

Collective Security Treaty Organisation (CSTO), 266, 310

collectivisation, 137, 144

Committee to Protect Journalists, 83

Common Economic Space, 177

Commonwealth of Independent States (CIS), establishment of, 176–7

Communist Party, 4, 8, 21, 25, 27–8, 53, 165; under Zyuganov, 38, 45; dissolved under Yeltsin, 39; and United Russia, 85; and Just Russia, 89; mass membership, 89; under Stalin, 141–2

computers, 55, 301

Conan Doyle, Arthur, 51

Conference on Security and Cooperation in Europe (CSCE), 178, 283

Congress of Estonia, 197

Congress of People's Deputies, 91, 290

ConocoPhillips, 241

Conquest, Robert, 303

conscription, 88, 95

Constantinople, 158

constitution, Russian, 5, 8, 71, 74, 163, 283

Constitutional Court, 93–4

construction, 52, 207

Conventional Forces in Europe (CFE) treaty, 250, 254–8

corruption, 8, 18, 22, 55–6, 77, 83, 92–3, 160; under Yeltsin, 31–2, 44; in Western countries, 18, 278; in Eastern Europe, 205, 207

Council of Europe, 5, 179, 276, 307

Crawshaw, Steve, 284

Crimea, 137, 146, 203; Ukraine and, 146, 192–3

Croatia, 172, 231

Cuba, 305; Russian bases in, 58, 317

customs agency, 110

cyberwarfare, 22, 202

Cyprus, 19, 109, 223

Czech Republic, 172, 213; and gas supplies, 217; and missile defence, 226, 250, 252

Czechoslovakia, 7, 290, 310; and history, 138, 144, 147, 169–70, 304; protests against Soviet invasion, 144, 304–5

Dagestan, 29–31, 287

Daiwa, 165

Danilov, Valentin, 77–8

Darfur, 248

democracy, 39, 44–5, 93, 154, 163, 265, 279, 298

demographics, 121, 267, 301–2

Denmark, 216, 221, 242

Der Spiegel, 204

Deripaska, Oleg, 59, 66, 223

derzhavnichestva, 159

dezinformatsiya, 22

Dickens, Charles, 51

dictatorship, 45, 61

diet, 51

diktatura zakona, 159

disinformation, 194–6, 201

Dmitriyeva, Tatyana, 75–6

Dmitriyevsky, Stanislav, 97

Dniestr, River, 180

Doha, 235

Dostoyevsky, Fyodor, 167

Dresden, 26, 219

Dresdner Bank, 219

drug abuse, 122

Duma, 9, 32, 80, 87, 91–3; deputies, 36, 75, 91–2; elections, 85, 92–3, 108, 134, 302; foreign affairs committee, 191

E.ON Ruhrgas, 128, 216, 224, 227, 241
East Germany, 25–6, 138, 140, 147, 223–4, 290; *Stasi*, 26, 219
East Prussia, 140
Eastern Europe, 23, 114, 223; and history, 137–8, 145, 148; and Euroatlanticism, 170–2, 194; English-language newspapers in, 194–5; integration into EU, 203–10; and NATO, 255, 259–60
Economist Intelligence Unit, 114
economy, Russian, 11–12, 20–1, 23, 48, 71, 90, 113–31, 171, 269; Soviet, 5, 21, 28, 39–43; domestic investment, 14, 17, 110–11, 160; foreign investment, 16, 66, 109–10, 114–15, 120, 122, 127–9, 160, 225, 261; under Yeltsin, 40–3; public preference for state planning, 45; black market, 52, 292; and WTO membership, 110; GDP, 113–14, 116–17, 122; foreign exchange reserves, 114; public-sector debt, 114; contrasted with Estonia, 148
Educated Media Foundation, 100
education, 43, 52, 54–5, 95; in Mari, 98; and religion, 156; in EU countries, 170; in Eastern Europe, 207
Eesti Gas, 189
efesbefikatsiya, 10
Egypt, 54
Ekho Moskvy, 56, 80, 82
election monitoring, 177–8
elections, 21, 23, 85–6, 95, 152, 279; parliamentary elections, 12, 85, 92–3, 108; presidential election (2008), 71, 103; presidential election (2004), 86; regional elections, 88; *Nashi* involvement in, 103; and centralisation, 161, 163, 166
Energy Charter, 213
energy industry, 12, 16, 20, 63, 110, 117, 120, 130, 272–4; control of energy supplies, 14–15, 21, 23, 176, 187–9; foreign investment in, 126–7; inefficiency and conservation, 217, 221, 237

energy policy, 209, 211–43, 262
English language, 51, 62, 106, 109, 158, 181, 194
ENI, 215, 230, 236
Enlightenment, 90
Enron, 124
entertainment, 54, 84
environmental standards, 171
espionage, 13–14, 26, 78, 99, 202, 206, 216
Estonia, 13, 15, 58, 80, 169, 172, 276, 290; cyberwarfare attack, 22, 202; Russians' hostility to, 69, 92; Mari links with, 98–9; defamation of, 102; economy, 120, 182, 188; Soviet annexation, 145, 149–50, 179; war memorial row, 148, 188, 198–201, 227; and history, 148–51; borders, 179, 256; modernisation, 182–3, 305, 312–13; and gas supplies, 189, 213, 216, 221, 227; and military threat, 189; Russian separatists in, 192; citizenship and language policies, 196–8, 200, 203, 312–13; and Finland, 204; intelligence services, 206; armed forces, 255; introduces flat tax, 291
ethnic minorities, 69–70, 90, 97–8, 137, 312
ethnic Russians, 178, 189, 192, 196–9, 294
Eton College, 53
EuralTransGas (ETG), 219–20
Eurasian Economic Community, 177
euro, 171, 205, 208–9
Euroatlanticism, 170–5, 181–2, 185, 192, 308
Europe, 15, 54, 198; gas supplies, 14, 211–41; Russian visitors, 54; think tanks, 101, 172; and history, 140, 146, 151; frontiers, 178; migration, 206; 'two-speed', 208–9; energy security, 235–6, 272–3; alliance with America, 252–4, 256, 261, 271; energy 'Finlandisation', 262
European Bank for Reconstruction and Development, 14, 117, 126, 179
European Court of Human Rights, 94, 179

European Union, 16, 18–19, 81, 151, 181, 223; expansion, 5, 170–1, 173, 204–5, 208; Samara summit, 79, 209–10; and Litvinenko affair, 108; energy liberalisation, 130–1; and Russian opinion, 155; rivals to, 177; and Georgia, 182, 185, 275–6; and Estonia, 201; energy policies, 212–15, 218, 221, 225, 230, 233–4, 272–3; and Turkey, 228–9; and former Yugoslavia, 231, 257; potential for relations with Russia, 262, 274–5; disdain for America, 271; foreign investment, 271–2; visas, 275, 318; and Ukraine, 275
evolution, 156
extremism law, 80–1, 295–6
Exxon, 126

Fainberg, Viktor, 304–5
famines, 137, 143–4
Fatherland-All Russia party, 45, 302
FBI, 220
federalism, 67–8, 308
Federation Council, 86, 192
Felgenhauer, Pavel, 256
Fenya, 292
feudalism, 90, 122, 135, 158
Finland, 69, 98, 149, 275; and Estonia, 204; and gas supplies, 213, 216, 221
Finno-Ugric languages, 69, 98–9
First World War, 153, 155
Firtash, Dmitriy, 220
flag, Russian, 242–3
Fluxys, 227
Forbes magazine, 83
Ford, Henry, 145
Ford, 115
foreign policy, Russian, 58, 63, 71, 172–210, 258–68, 270, 272; and Baltic states, 15, 196–203; and Eastern Europe, 172–3; and Central Asia, 173–5; and Belarus, 175–6; and CIS, 176–7; and Moldova, 179–82; and Georgia, 182–7; and military incursions, 189–91; and NGOs, 193–4; and disinformation, 194–6

Fradkov, Mikhail, 264
France, 19, 223, 269; and history, 139, 147, 149; and former Soviet states, 169; and 'two-speed' Europe, 209–10; and gas supplies, 213–15; anti-Americanism, 261
Frankfurt, 123, 273
FSB, 27, 135, 193; and Litvinenko, 2, 77, 105–7; formation of, 10, 286; Putin heads, 25, 28, 319; and Ryazan bomb incident, 33–5, 288–9; arrests Khodorkovsky, 64; interrogations, 76; and Moscow apartment bombings, 77; and opposition, 80, 84; illegal bugging operations, 94; museum, 136; and Orthodox Church, 156; and NGOs, 194; licensed to operate abroad, 201
Fursenko, Andrei, 292
Fursin, Ivan, 220

G8, 5, 276–7, 307
Gabriyan, Pyotr, 297
Gaddy, Clifford, 313
Gagarin, Yuri, 136
Gamsakhurdia, Zviad, 182–3
Gandhi, Mahatma, 73
gas, 12, 14, 20, 109–10, 169, 211–42, 272, 316; pipelines, 20–1, 23, 126–8, 130, 188, 209, 212–35, 238–9, 264, 272–3; revenues, 114, 117; state ownership, 118; foreign investment in, 126–7, 214; in Central Asia, 174; and Belarus, 175–6; and Transdniestria 181–2; and Georgia, 186; LNG, 212, 221, 235–6, 240, 272, 314; shortages, 221, 236–8, 240; inefficiency and conservation, 237–8; domestic price rises, 237–8, 240; gasification, 238
Gas-Exporting Countries' Forum (GECF), 235–6
Gasunie, 226
Gaz de France, 215
Gazprom, 14, 50, 80, 273, 318; buys media outlets, 60, 214; and Yukos affair, 64–6; sponsorship of *Nashi*, 102; acquisitions,

118–19, 238; accounting, 124; and BP and Shell, 126–7; and Belarus, 176; and Georgia, 186; and Estonia, 189; and control of pipelines, 212, 214–21, 224, 226–9, 232–3; military forces, 221; and Algeria, 236; shortages, 236–8; inefficiency, 237–9; developments and contracts, 240–1
General Motors, 115
Georgia, 20, 58, 98, 137, 179, 182–7, 271; Rose Revolution, 102, 173, 259; and Abkhazia, 110, 145–6, 182–3, 189–91, 256, 258; economy, 120, 183; demographics, 121; and NATO membership, 172, 185, 275; withdrawal from CIS, 177; and Ajaria, 183–4; and South Ossetia, 184–5, 256, 258, 311; and energy supplies, 188, 229, 272; and military incursions, 189–91; Russian withdrawal, 254–5; EU and, 275–6; introduces flat tax, 291
Gerashchenko, Viktor, 43
Gerasimenko, Yevgeny, 83
Germany, 7, 16, 19–20, 58, 67, 166; Nazi (Third Reich), 102, 138–41, 143, 146, 154, 169, 206; and Litvinenko affair, 108; Russian influence in, 128, 130, 218–19, 222–6; and history, 138–40, 150, 153, 155; and former Soviet states, 169; and Polish exports, 204; and 'two-speed' Europe, 209–10; and gas supplies, 213–18, 221–2, 224, 226–7, 234, 237; reunification, 223; anti-Americanism, 261
Geroi Dnya, 33
glasnost, 7
Glazyev, Sergei, 86
global warming, 242
globalisation, 211
Goethe Institute, 99
Gogol, Nikolai, 160
Gonchar, Viktor, 309
GONGOs, 100
Google, 116
Gorbachev, Mikhail, 3, 7–8, 13, 28, 48,

133, 290; putsch against, 39, 50; and economy, 41; era of, 48, 57, 145, 290; frees political prisoners, 77, 295; criticised, 135; and Russian history, 137; and Germany, 222–3
Gordeev, Alexei, 292
Gordievsky, Oleg, 106
gosudarstvennik, 158
Gotland, 216
Grant, Des, 195
Great Patriotic War, *see* Second World War
Great Terror, 144
Greece, 19, 204, 210; and gas supplies, 213, 230–1, 234
Greenland, 242
Gref, German, 292
Gromov, Aleksei, 50
Grozny, 33
GRU, 27, 49, 165, 185, 193, 201
Grushko, Aleksander, 108
Guam, 246
Guantánamo Bay, 3
Gulag system, 74, 136–7, 145
Gusinsky, Vladimir, 52, 59–60
Gutseriyev, Mikhail, 65–6
Gyurcsány, Ferenc, 232

Hamas, 262–4
healthcare, 43, 49, 122, 162; in Eastern Europe, 206–7
Helsinki Agreement, 283
Helsinki Final Act, 178
Heritage Foundation, 211
Hermitage Capital, 127
Hezbollah, 262–3
Hiroshima, 144
history, 90, 133–67, 262, 269–70; Putin and, 141, 143–4, 150, 153; Estonian and Russian views of, 149–50; revisionism, 152–3, 158, 270
Hitler, Adolf, 3–4, 137, 140–1, 143, 147, 149, 154, 194, 199
Hitlerjugend, 102
HIV/AIDS, 297

Hochtief, 224
homosexuality, 4, 54, 96, 206, 297
Hoover, Herbert, 283
housing, 43, 57, 121–2, 162
human rights, 28, 90–1, 94–7, 157;
    agreements, 5, 18, 178–9; promotion of,
    14, 278–9; in Uzbekistan, 173; German
    criticisms, 223, 225; Soviet bloc signs up
    to, 283
Human Rights Watch, 96, 186–7
Hungary, 19, 69, 290; and history, 138,
    144, 151; NATO membership, 172; and
    gas supplies, 213, 227, 230, 232–4; and
    Bosnia crisis, 257
Hussein, Saddam, 248

ideology, 50, 131, 133–67, 258; 'sovereign
    democracy', 6, 23, 163–7, 191–2, 265,
    270; 'ideological vacuum', 153–4;
    ideological vocabulary, 158–9; of
    centralisation, 159–63; and 'New Age'
    thinking, 164
Ifanov, Vyacheslav, 83
Illarionov, Andrei, 116–17, 129
Ilves, Toomas Hendrik, 80, 148, 200
Imendayev, Albert, 74
immigrants, illegal, 103–4
imperialism, 136, 139, 275
India, 74, 113–14, 121, 140, 247–8, 261,
    277
Indonesia, 261
Instituto Cervantes, 99
Institut Français, 99
intellectual property laws, 301
interior ministry troops, 67, 79
Intermediate-range Nuclear Forces (INF)
    treaty, 256
International Atomic Energy Agency, 250
International Bar Association, 93
International Commission of Jurists, 93
International Council for Democratic
    Institutions and State Sovereignty
    (ICDISS), 195–6
International Energy Agency, 221, 237,
    239

international law, 279, 312
International Monetary Fund, 109, 113
internet, 55, 194–5, 202
Iran, 83, 251, 271, 277; and nuclear
    proliferation, 5, 229, 248–50, 263–4;
    relations with Russia, 15, 262–3; and gas
    supplies, 228, 234–5; and SCO, 266
Iraq, 228–9, 248, 263; war in, 3, 63, 166,
    253
Ireland, 116
Islamic Conference Organisation, 262
Islamic extremism, 71, 97, 203, 259, 262,
    264
Israel, 60, 138, 141, 262–4, 283
IT sector, 115–16, 301
Italy, 11, 19, 206, 209–10; and gas supplies,
    213–15, 230, 233–4, 236
Itera, 219, 318
Itogi, 60
Ivan the Terrible, 27
Ivanov, Sergei, 49, 103
Ivanov, Viktor, 50
Izvestia, 4, 82, 295

Jabelia, Manana, 187
Japan, 114, 119, 144, 147, 153, 240
Jews, 140, 144, 149, 151, 264, 300, 317
Jordan, Boris, 93
journalism, 51, 59–60, 62
journalists, 78–84, 100, 155, 296; Eastern
    European, 194–5
JP Morgan Chase, 233
judiciary, 13, 74, 83, 93–4, 159, 164, 170
judo, 25, 29
Just Russia party, 88–9

Kaczynski, Lech, 205
Kadyrov, Akhmed, 162
Kaliningrad, 203
Kaljurand, Marina, 200
Karachinsky, Anatoly, 115
Karelia, 69
Karimov, Islam, 173
Kartofelnikov, Aleksei, 32–3
Kasparov, Garry, 76, 78–80, 210

Kaspersky, Yevgeny and Natalya, 115–16
Kasyanov, Mikhail, 81
Katowice, 148
Katsav, Moshe, 287
Katyń massacre, 137, 145
Kazakhstan, 173–4, 177, 228–31, 265–7, 270
KazMunayGaz, 231
Kent State University, 144
Kerensky, Aleksandr, 40, 90
KGB, 4, 8, 10, 22, 52, 75, 105–6, 115; Putin's career with, 25–6, 219, 318; increasing power, 27–8, 44, 49–50; placed under civilian control, 39; 'active reserve', 49; and blackmail, 88; and Orthodox Church, 157; Fifth Directorate, 286
Khakamada, Irina, 86–7
Khodorkovsky, Mikhail, 62–6, 78, 94, 97, 124, 293, 295
Kholodov, Dmitry, 296
Khristenko, Victor, 292
Khrushchev, Nikita, 133
Kipling, Rudyard, 285
Kiriyenko, Sergei, 285
Klebnikov, Paul, 83
Kodori gorge, 189
Kohl, Helmut, 223
Kokoshin, Andrei, 243
Kolerov, Modest, 194, 201
Komi, 69, 136
Komsomol, 102
Komsomolskaya Pravda, 200
Kondopoga, 105
Kosachev, Konstantin, 191
Kosovo, 172, 257–8, 260, 263
Kostanov, Yuri, 298
Kouchner, Bernard, 210
Kovalchuk, Mikhail, 301
Kovalev, Sergei, 77
Kovykta gas field, 126
Kozlov, Vladimir, 98
Kozluduy nuclear power station, 231
Krasnodar, 81
Krasnoyarsk, 297

Krasovsky, Anatloy, 309
Kross, Jaan, 150
Kryshtanovskaya, Olga, 27
Kuala Lumpur, 262
Kukly, 60, 81
Kurchatov Institute, 301
Kurdish separatism, 228–9
Kursk submarine, 47–8, 60, 94
Kuznetsov, Boris, 94
Kyiv, 88, 101, 193, 312–13
Kyrgyzstan, 173–4, 177, 265–6

Laar, Mart, 179
Lacis, Otto, 36
Lake Seliger, 102
Lang, Rein, 194
languages, 69–70, 98, 196–8, 312
Lantos, Tom, 216
Larsson, Robert, 188
Latin America, 144, 290; see also South America
Latvia, 15, 19, 172, 210, 290; money-laundering, 109; and history, 149–50; borders, 179; oil supplies, 188, 272; and military threat, 189; citizenship and language policies, 196–8, 203; and gay rights, 206; and gas supplies, 213, 221, 227; introduces flat tax, 291
Latynina, Yulia, 80–1
Lavrov, Sergei, 243
law, rule of, 17–18, 21, 40, 43–4, 57, 84, 93–7, 159, 166, 269, 277, 279; see also judiciary
Lebanon, 229, 263
Lebedev, Aleksander, 296
Lenin, Vladimir Ilyich, 21, 38, 42, 133, 136
Lesnevskaya, Irena, 82
Levitin, Igor, 188, 292
Liberal Democrat party, 108, 134–5
Liberal Russia party, 289
Libya, 121, 226
Lipman, Masha, 163
Lithuania, 7, 15, 98, 175, 290; and history, 149, 151–2; relations with Poland, 151–2; politicians' links with Russia, 172–3;

oil supplies, 187–8, 272; citizenship and
language policies, 196–7; and
Kaliningrad, 203; and gas supplies, 213;
introduces flat tax, 291
Litvinenko, Aleksander, 2, 77, 105–8, 308,
311
Lokshina, Tatyana, 295
Lomonosov Ridge, 242
London, 2, 51, 53, 61, 77, 82, 88, 106, 123,
273; see also City of London
London Stock Exchange, 110, 129–30
Lowe, Norman, 303
Lubyanka, 28, 156
Lugovoi, Andrei, 2, 107–8
Lukashenka, Alyaksandr, 175–6
Lukin, Vladimir, 90
Luzhkov, Yuri, 32, 38, 59, 192

Mabetex, 31
Macedonia, 151, 231, 291
MacKay, Peter, 243
mafia, Russian, 30, 52–3, 58
Malashenko, Aleksei, 262
Malaysia, 262
mammoths, 102
Mangold, Klaus, 224
manufacturing industry, 119, 121
Mari-El, 69, 98, 136
Markelov, Leonid, 98
Markov, Sergei, 153
Marxism-Leninism, 6, 17, 133, 165
Mashal, Khaled, 263
Maskhadov, Aslan, 68
Mažeikiai oil terminal, 187–8, 285
Mečiar, Vladimír, 172, 309
media, 12, 23, 27, 95, 100; under Yeltsin,
9, 52; and Ryazan bomb incident, 36;
under Putin, 55–6, 59–61, 67; and
opposition, 74, 80–2; and elections, 85–
7; and rewriting of history, 152; and
centralisation, 161, 163, 166; and war
memorial row, 199; see also newspapers;
radio stations; television
Mediterranean, 13, 243, 247
Medvedev, Dmitri, 103, 165, 292

Merkel, Angela, 210, 215, 224, 226, 229
Mestnye, 103
Mexico, 261
MI6, 194
Microsoft, 215
middle class, 9, 50–1, 54–6, 70, 121
migration, 121, 192–3, 197, 204, 206–8,
264; see also immigrants, illegal
military, Russian, 6, 13, 45, 245–7; budget,
245–6; see also army; navy; special forces;
weapons
military incursions, 189–91
Milošević, Slobodan, 172, 257–8, 263
Milov, Vladimir, 236
mineral water, 156, 185, 311
Miosz, Czesaw, 50
Mir space station, 243
MIRO, 316
missile defence system, American, 226,
250–3, 255–8, 266
missiles, 83, 190, 245–8, 256, 264;
American, 315
Mogilevich, Semion, 220
MOL, 233–4
Moldova, 145, 187, 258, 276, 310; and
Transdniestria, 110, 179–82, 192, 194–6;
Russian withdrawal from, 254–5
Molodaya Gvardiya, 153
Molotov–Ribbentrop pact, 146, 169, 179–
80, 218
Molyakov, Igor, 75
money-laundering, 109–10, 273
Montenegro, 291
Mordovia, 69
Moscow, 41, 49, 93, 184; Victory Day
parade, 4; apartment bombings, 9–10,
30, 35, 77, 106; and Ryazan bomb
incident, 34–5; 'White House', 39;
airports, 55, 88, 127; and nationalism,
56; prisons, 60, 64; Berezovsky's club,
62; demonstrations, 78; Nordost theatre
incident, 87; gay rights campaigners
attacked, 96; British Council office
raided, 99; cab drivers, 103–4, 299; anti-
Americanism, 104; racism, 105;

Litvinenko press conference, 106; and
Litvinenko affair, 108; William
Browder and, 127–8; museums, 136,
145; Red Square protests, 144, 304–5;
think tanks, 155, 236; as 'Third Rome',
158; Georgians deported, 186–7;
Estonian embassy attacked, 199–200;
Cold War visits, 248; proposed peace
conference, 264
Moscow, River, 133
Moscow bar association, 94
Moscow Carnegie Centre, 104, 154, 163,
262
Moscow Helsinki Group, 77, 97, 178, 304
Moskalenko, Karina, 94, 97
motorcades, 91
Munich, 154
Munich agreement, 147, 169
Murmansk, 76, 91
music piracy, 116
Muslim world, 262–3
Muslims, 97, 184, 203
Mussolini, Benito, 11

Nabucco gas pipeline, 215, 227–32, 234,
272
Naftohaz Ukrainy, 220
Nagorno-Karabakh, 146, 309
nanotechnology, 301
Nara, 192
narcotics, 266; see also drug abuse
Naryshkin, Sergei, 50, 291–2
Nashi, 102–3, 105; and Estonian war
memorial, 148, 199–200
nationalism, 18, 56, 69, 102, 134, 136, 156,
265
NATO, 147, 204; expansion, 5, 171–3,
205, 253, 259–60; and nuclear threat, 6,
315; and airspace violations, 13, 189–90;
and Baltic states, 16; and Cold War, 19,
147, 170, 247, 273; cooperation with
Russia, 58, 262, 277; and Ukraine, 101;
Russian views of, 155; and Georgia,
172, 185; alternatives to, 178, 266; and
Crimea, 193; and Estonia, 201, 255; and

Germany, 223; and Turkey, 228; and
Bulgaria, 230; and Russian threat, 247,
250, 255–7
navy, Russian, 13, 243, 246–7
Nazarbayev, Nursultan, 173–4
Netherlands, 19, 117; and history, 141,
149; and gas supplies, 213–14, 221, 226,
234–5
New Testament, 7
New Times, 81–2, 296
New York, 83, 123, 273
New York Stock Exchange, 129
newspapers, 4, 78, 82, 87; Mari, 98;
English-language, 194–5; Israeli, 264
NGOs, 13, 96–7, 100, 193–4; see also
voluntary organisations
Nicaragua, 147, 305
Nicholas I, Tsar, 157
Nicholas II, Tsar, 135–6
Nicolini, Mário, 308
Nigeria, 122
Nissan, 115
Nixon, Richard, 20
Niyazov, Saparmurat, 174–5
Nizhny Novgorod, 79, 295, 303
NKVD, 27
Nord Stream gas pipeline, 130, 209, 215–
18, 220–1, 226–7, 272
Norsk Hydro, 241
North America, 14, 17
North Atlantic, 246, 250
North Caucasus, 262
North Korea, 5, 251, 277
North Ossetia, 68
North Pole, 242–3
North Sea, 212, 221, 226–7, 246
Northern Fleet, 243, 247
Norway, 99, 208, 221, 235, 239, 242
Novatek, 238
Novaya Gazeta, 81, 87, 288–9, 296
Novosibirsk, 64
Novye Izvestiya, 34
NTV, 59–61, 82, 84, 214
nuclear power, 221, 231, 277
nuclear proliferation, 5, 71, 229, 249, 277

nuclear waste, 99, 135
nuclear weapons, 6, 13, 69, 81, 163, 166,
    245–7, 250–1; Iran and proliferation, 5,
    229, 248–50, 263–4; American and
    NATO, 20, 222, 251, 315; Hiroshima
    bomb, 144; Chinese, 266

October Revolution, 90, 137, 182
Office for Democratic Institutions and
    Human Rights (OHDIR), 178
OGPU, 27
oil, 12, 15, 69, 109–10, 129, 212, 242;
    pipelines, 21, 23, 63, 187–8, 213, 234;
    prices, 42, 67, 109, 113, 120, 188; and
    oligarchs' companies, 62–7; revenues,
    113–14, 117; state ownership, 118;
    foreign investment in, 126–7, 214;
    international market, 235; flaring of,
    239
Okhrana, 27
oligarchs, 8, 17, 22, 44, 47, 53, 317; Putin
    and, 59–67, 87
Olmert, Ehud, 287
Omsk, 63
ÖMV, 232–3, 316
opposition parties, 74, 85–90, 103
Oprichniki, 27
Organisation for Economic Cooperation
    and Development (OECD), 93, 293,
    318
Organisation for Security and Co-
    operation in Europe (OSCE), 14, 160,
    178, 181, 276
organised crime, 106, 111, 184, 205, 257
ORT, 61
Orthodoxy, see Russian Orthodox
    Church
Orwell, George, 103, 138
Ossetians, 182, 184–5
Ostauschuss der deutschen Wirtschaft, 224
Our Home is Russia party, 134
Oxford, 7, 63

Pacific Fleet, 247
Pacific Ocean, 246

Pakistan, 251, 261
Paksas, Rolandas, 172
Palestinian territories, 263
Pamfilova, Ella, 91
Paris, 100, 194
parliament, Russian, 8–9, 63, 152;
    elections, 12, 85, 92–3, 108; and
    centralisation, 164; committee on ex-
    Soviet region, 243; see also Duma;
    Federation Council
patriotism, 14, 26, 44, 101, 136, 146, 153,
    158, 199
Patrushev, Andrei, 292
Patrushev, Nikolai, 33–4, 194
Pemex, 238
PEN, 97
pensions, 134
perestroika, 7, 91
Perm, 145
Peter the Great, Tsar and Emperor, 142,
    150
pharmaceuticals, 116
Piebalgs, Andris, 218, 234, 236
Pinyaev, Alexei, 288–9
Piontkovsky, Andrei, 81–2, 267
PKN Orlen, 285
Plato, 7
Playboy, 246
Poederlee, 227
Poland, 7, 53, 58, 175, 290; foreign
    investment, 120; and history, 137, 140–
    1, 145, 151–2; imposition of martial law,
    144, 318; relations with Lithuania, 151–
    2; NATO membership, 171–2; support
    for Estonia, 199; exports, 204, 209;
    abrasive diplomacy, 205–6; and gay
    rights, 206; and competition law, 208;
    and 'two-speed' Europe, 209; and gas
    supplies, 213, 216–18, 221, 237;
    Germany and, 225; and missile defence,
    226, 250, 252; and 'rendition', 253;
    border, 266
police, 52, 96, 103, 105, 164, 170, 200; see
    also secret police; tax police
Polikanov, Dmitri, 56

political freedoms, 12, 28, 40, 43, 56, 71, 74, 79, 277, 279
political prisoners, 77–8, 199
Politkovskaya, Anna, murder of, 1–2, 68, 81, 83–4, 94, 281–2, 297
pollution, 95, 122
polonium, 2, 107, 283
Portugal, 19, 210
Pravda, 4
Presidential Council on Promoting the Development of Institutions of Civil Society and Human Rights, 91
PricewaterhouseCoopers, 115; and Yukos affair, 123–6
Prichodko, Sergei, 292
Primakov, Yevgeny, 32, 38, 285
Priština, 257
privatisation, 44, 153
Prodi, Romano, 210
professions, 51
Prokhanov, Aleksandr, 263
Promneftestroi, 65
propaganda, 3, 55, 61, 178, 277; Soviet, 51, 59, 102, 144, 170
property, private, 21, 45, 54, 109, 120
prostitutes, 49, 53, 102
protectionism, 109–10, 117
protests and demonstrations, 13, 74, 78–9, 82, 91, 95; Soviet era, 144, 304–5; against welfare reforms, 162, 237
Pskov, 189, 201
psychiatry, punitive, 23, 74–7, 91, 144, 305
Public Chamber, 91
public opinion, 38, 45, 85, 89–90; and Soviet Union, 70; and Duma, 92–3; and justice system, 93; and anti-Westernism, 154–5; and Orthodox Church, 156
public services, 57, 121, 279; in Eastern Europe, 206–7
purges, 137, 142–4
Pushkov, Aleksei, 261
Putin, Vladimir: and murder of Anna Politkovskaya, 1–2, 281–2; and America, 3–4, 154; personal popularity, 5, 10–11, 29, 38, 46, 57, 73, 89; rise to

power, 9–10, 22, 25–9, 38, 44–6, 61; and economy, 12, 20, 41–2, 47–8, 54; denounces NGOs, 13, 100; and collapse of Soviet Union, 15, 68–70, 140–1; as heir to Andropov, 20–1, 28; KGB career, 25–6, 219, 318; heads FSB, 25, 28, 319; and terrorist attacks, 29–30, 33, 36–8, 87; manner of speech, 30, 47, 287–8; and Yeltsin era, 40, 45, 47; and media, 60, 67; and centralisation, 67–70; and Beslan school siege, 68; relations with the West, 68–71, 154, 260–1; personality cult, 73, 102; blames others, 84; and presidential election (2004), 86; business interests, 87; and *Nashi*, 102–3; bans foreigners from markets, 104; denounced by Litvinenko, 106; and history, 141, 143–4, 150, 153; and religion, 156; ideology, 158–9, 161–3; and Belarus, 176; and Georgia, 184–5; support for Russian-speakers, 192; promotes intelligence services, 201; and Samara summit, 209–10; and energy policy, 211–13, 215, 231–2, 235; friendship with Schröder, 218–19, 223, 225–6; and Merkel, 224–5; military policies, 246, 248, 254–6; meets Bush, 248, 294, 307; engages Islamic world, 262; and China, 264; and CSTO, 266; and Roman Abramovich, 297

Qatar, 107, 235, 300
Quebec, 67

racism, 103–5, 139
Radio Liberty, 296
Radio Moscow, 6
radio stations, 55–6, 80–2
Raiffeisen Bank, 220
railways, 50
Rakhmonov, Emomali, 174
Rakimkulov, Megdet, 233
raw materials, 12, 53, 110, 114, 211, 214, 242, 259, 267

Reagan, Ronald, 20, 123, 223
rearmament, 13
Red Army, 7, 140, 143, 146, 148–50
Red Terror, 137
Reformation, 90
reformers, 8, 47
Reiman, Leonid, 297, 301
religion, 76, 90, 156–8, 307
Renaissance, 90
renationalisation, 118
REN-TV, 61, 81–2
research and development, 116
retail markets, 104
Revue Baltique, 149
Rhine, River, 4
Rice, Condoleezza, 108, 135
road safety, 91, 95
Rodionov, Igor, 171
Roma, 206
Roman Catholic Church, 158
Romania, 151, 172, 206, 291; and
   Moldova, 179–81; and gas supplies, 213,
   230–1; and 'rendition', 253; American
   bases in, 255
Romanova, Olga, 296
Romanov family, 135–6
Rome, ancient, 158
Rompetrol, 231
Roosevelt, Franklin D., 144
Rosneft, 49–50, 129, 214, 233, 264, 273,
   316, 318; acquisitions, 65–6, 118
Rosoboronexport, 247–8
Rossiiskaya Gazeta, 145
RosUkrEnergo, 220, 318
rouble, 9, 40–1, 67, 117, 175, 291
Rushailo, Vladimir, 33
Russian Academy of Sciences, 27
Russian Orthodox Church (ROC), 135,
   156–8, 307
Russian Research Centre on Human
   Rights, 97
Russian-Chechen Friendship Society, 97
Russneft, 65
Russophobia, 278
Ryazan bomb incident, 32–8, 60, 288–9

Rybkin, Ivan, 87
Ryzhkov, Vladimir, 92

Saakashvili, Mikheil, 183–7
Sachs, Jeffrey, 43
Safronov, Ivan, 83
St Petersburg, 10, 28, 115, 219; Putin and,
   25, 47, 49–50; nationalism, 56;
   demonstrations, 78; elections, 85;
   British Council office closed, 99; racism,
   105; investment summit, 123, 261
Sakhalin-2 gas project, 126, 225
Sakharov, Andrei, 136, 144, 295, 303
Salzburg, 232
Samara summit, 79, 209–10
sanctions, 271
Saratov, 83
Sarkozy, Nicolas, 210, 229
Saudargas, Algirdas, 284
Saudi Arabia, 17, 114, 118, 122
Savitskaya, Svetlana, 75
Sberbank, 64, 127
Schmidt, Helmut, 315
Schmidt, Yuri, 295
Schröder, Gerhard, 130, 143, 210, 215–16,
   218–19, 223–7
Sechin, Igor, 49, 129, 281
Second World War, 143, 146, 206
secret police, 20, 269
Serbia, 101, 172, 209, 257–9, 291
Serdukov, Anatoly, 292
serfdom, 167
Service, Robert, 303
Sevastopol, 193, 203
sexual abuse, 76; promiscuity, 122
Shakirov, Raf, 82
Shanghai Cooperation Organisation
   (SCO), 15, 177, 265–7
Shchekochikhin, Yuri, 36, 83, 289
Shell, 17, 109, 126, 316
Shenderovich, Viktor, 81–2
Shevardnadze, Eduard, 183
Shevtsova, Lilia, 154–5, 161
Shkval torpedo, 245
Shtokman gas field, 225, 239–41

Shuvalov, Igor, 292
Siberia, 64, 83, 98, 105, 126; deportations
    to, 150, 167, 180; gas fields, 239–40
Sibneft, 61, 63
Sikorski, Radek, 218
Silesia, 140
siloviki, 27, 47, 157
Singing Together, 73
skiing, 73
Skuratov, Yuri, 31
Slavic languages, 70
Slavophiles, 136
Slovakia, 19, 101, 172, 291; and gas
    supplies, 213, 217, 233
Slovenia, 213, 230
Slovnaft, 233
Smolensky, Aleksander, 52
Snohvit gas field, 240
Sobell, Vlad, 165
software, 115–16
soldiers, suicide among, 6
Solidarity trade union, 7, 147
Sonatrach, 236
Soros, George, 75, 129
South America, 236; *see also* Latin America
South China Sea, 266
South Korea, 240
South Ossetia, 110, 184, 311
South Stream gas pipeline, 230
Soviet Union, 3, 5; life in, 4–5, 21, 40–3,
    54–5; economy, 5, 21, 28, 39–43, 115,
    136, 143; collapse of, 7, 15, 68–70, 98,
    133, 140–1, 143, 152–3, 158, 180, 290;
    Putin and, 10, 15, 25–8, 68–70, 140–1;
    during Cold War, 19–21, 269–70, 278;
    Yeltsin and, 38–40; nomenklatura, 48–
    9; and ideology, 50, 131, 133; bases
    closed, 58, 259; Russian pride in, 70,
    135; penal system, 74, 76–7, 94, 97; civil
    society under, 96; youth movements,
    102; propaganda, 102, 144, 170;
    scientific legacy, 116, 121, 136, 143;
    industries, 118, 121–2; foreign views of,
    123; and history, 136–8, 140–50;
    national anthem, 136–7, 303; invasion
of Afghanistan, 138, 144–5, 262–3;
    annexation of Estonia, 145, 149–50;
    annexation of Baltic states, 152, 284,
    289–90, 309–10, 312; and Orthodox
    Church, 156; and gas infrastructure,
    212, 237–8; ties with Germany, 222;
    ban on pornography, 246; military
    legacy, 246, 249; anti-Semitism, 263;
    UN vetoes, 276; constituent republics,
    289–90
space race, 278
Spain, 206
special economic zones, 117
special forces, 245
speech, freedom of, *see* political freedoms
Stalin, Josef, 3, 21, 42, 75, 115, 133, 283;
    history and, 136–7, 141–4, 146–7, 149,
    151–2; reign of terror in Baltic, 182;
    deportation of Chechens, 286
Stasi, 26, 219
Statoil, 239, 241
Steele, Jonathan, 284
Steinmeier, Frank-Walter, 225
Stepashin, Sergei, 286
stock market, Russian, 66
Stockholm, 303
Stomakhin, Boris, 97
Strabag, 224
Strasbourg, 94, 97
Strategic Arms Reduction treaties, 250
Strategic Rocket Forces, 83
Strods, Heinrihs, 152
submarines, 246–8; *see also Kursk*
    submarine
Sudan, 248
Sudetenland, 169
Suez crisis, 144
Sukhumi, 183
Surkov, Vladislav, 158, 164–6, 281
Suslov, Mikhail, 133, 165
Sutyagin, Igor, 77–8, 94
Sverdlovsk, 39
SVR, 107, 201
Sweden, 150, 191; Defence Research
    Institute, 188; and gas supplies, 216, 221

Switzerland, 109, 208, 213, 218, 220, 260
Syria, 15, 83, 229, 248–9, 263–4

Tajikistan, 15, 174, 177, 266
Taliban, 259, 263
Tallinn, 15, 198–201, 227, 312
Tatars, 69, 136–7, 146, 203
Tatarstan, 67, 69–70, 97, 192, 262
tax police, 67, 286
taxation, 44, 48, 92, 117–18; and oligarchs,
    63–4, 66–7; and NGOs, 97; and
    renationalisation, 118–19; as proportion
    of GDP, 122; and Yukos affair, 124–5;
    and Orthodox Church, 156; flat taxes,
    291
Tbilisi, 190
telecommunications, 50, 119
television, 9, 12, 50, 59–61, 82, 84; in
    Mari, 98; Israeli, 264
Terentyev, Savva, 293
terrorism, 17, 29–32, 58; Moscow
    apartment bombings, 9–10, 30, 35, 77,
    106; Ryazan bomb incident, 32–8; and
    internet, 202; counter-terrorism, 266;
    see also 'war on terror'
Teutonic Knights, 150
thallium, 289
Thatcher, Margaret, 123
theocracy, 134
Third World, 318
Tiraspol Times, 194–5
Tkachenko, Yuri, 32, 36
Tlisova, Fatima, 84
TNK, 126
tobacco, 42, 121–2, 156
Togonidze, Tengiz, 187
Tokyo, 123
Tomsk, 297
Total, 241
tourism, 54
Toyota, 115
trade unions, 16, 122–3, 140, 302
Transdniestria, 110, 180–2, 192, 194–5,
    254
Transparency International, 18, 93

transport, 120, 162
travel, 4–5, 26, 51, 54–5, 102, 163
Trebugova, Elena, 82
Trenin, Dmitri, 258
Trepashkin, Mikhail, 36, 77, 106
Trotskyism, 302
Truman, Harry S., 144
Trutko, Marina, 75
Tsarist era, 90, 135–6, 150, 157–8, 167, 222
Turchynov, Oleksandr, 220
Turkestan, Chinese, 265
Turkey, 19, 54, 69, 106, 178; and gas
    supplies, 228–9, 234; anti-Americanism,
    261; and Armenia, 309
Turkic peoples, 69–70
Turkmenistan, 174–5, 177; and gas
    supplies, 219, 228–30, 234, 267
Turku, 297
TV-6, 61
TV-S, 61

UABC, 49
Ukraine, 140, 180–1, 275; Orange
    Revolution, 101–2, 162, 173–4, 191,
    194, 217, 259, 306; foreign investment,
    120; famine, 137; and Crimea, 146,
    192–3; withdrawal from CIS, 177;
    period of independence, 179; Russian
    influence, 194; and gas supplies, 217–20,
    240; and Bosnia crisis, 257; introduces
    flat tax, 291; language, 312; instability in
    east, 313
underwear, 102
unemployment, 43, 56, 143
Union of Right Forces party, 297
union state, 175–6
United Civic Front, 76
United Nations Declaration of Human
    Rights, 157
United Nations Development
    Programme, 14, 179
United Nations Human Development
    Index, 121
United Nations Law of the Sea
    Convention, 242

United Nations Security Council, 258, 276

United Russia party, 84–5, 88–9, 153

United States of America, 5, 20, 79, 93, 178, 240, 262; and 9/11 attacks, 3, 38; Putin and, 3–4, 154; relations with Russia, 4, 14, 58, 63; and former Soviet states, 58, 169, 173, 175, 181, 193, 198; and Yukos, 63–4; think tanks, 81, 101, 172; Russian refugees in, 84; support for Educated Media Foundation, 100; and Ukrainian Orange Revolution, 101–2; anti-Americanism, 104, 117, 154–5, 166, 222, 226, 253, 261; and Litvinenko affair, 108; economy, 116, 119; demographics, 121; and history, 139, 144, 146–7, 149; and global hegemony, 163, 165–6, 210, 261; and Germany, 222–3; and Turkey, 228–9, 234; and Bulgaria, 230; and former Yugoslavia, 231; energy independence, 235–6; military policies, 246–54; alliance with Europe, 252–4, 256, 261, 271; and Kosovo, 257–8; and Central Asia, 266–7; foreign investments, 272; federalism, 308

Unity party, 302

universities, 55, 116, 122

UNOMIG, 190

Urals, 39, 67, 265

uranium, 105, 250

Urumqi, 265

US State Department, 93

Uspaskich, Viktor, 173

Uvarov, Count Sergei, 157

Uzbekistan, 173, 177, 266–7

van der Veer, Jeroen, 126

Venediktov, Aleksei, 80–1

Venezuela, 15, 117, 235, 248

Ventspils oil terminal, 187, 285

Versailles peace treaty, 152

VGTRK, 81

Vienna, 232, 255, 316

Vienna Convention, 200

Vietnam, Russian bases in, 58, 317

Vietnam War, 139, 144–5

Vilnius, 7, 151–2, 284

vlastnaya vertikal, 159–60

vodka, 51, 135, 212, 294

Volga, River, 74, 95; basin, 222

Volgodonsk, 30

Volkswagen, 115

Volozh, Arkady, 116

voluntary organisations, 95–6, 99–100

Vory v zakone, 292

'war on terror', 3, 173, 253, 279

Warnig, Matthias, 219

Warsaw Pact, 4–5, 147, 172, 181, 204, 250, 259, 266, 315

Warsaw uprising, 151

Washington, DC, 82, 89, 109, 116, 144, 183, 195, 261–2

weapons, 6, 13, 83, 190, 245, 259, 263; industry, 121, 249; in Transdniestria, 181; *see also* aircraft carriers; arms sales; missiles; submarines; nuclear weapons

welfare reforms, 162, 237

Western Europe, 16–17, 19–20, 222; and history, 139, 145, 151; energy supplies, 188, 217; and Eastern Europe, 194, 204–6; and missile defence, 252

Westerwelle, Guido, 215–16

Winchester School, 53

Wingas, 226

Winiecki, Jan, 41

Wintershall, 216, 226

workers, 56–7, 123, 133; agricultural, 121

World Bank, 109

World Council of Russian People, 157

World Trade Organization (WTO), 18, 109, 217

'WWW', 265

xenophobia, 8, 23, 46, 102–5, 134, 138, 154, 157–8, 167, 187, 279

Yabloko party, 38, 81, 85–6, 89

Yakunin, Vladimir, 50

Yamal gas field, 239

Yandarbiyev, Zelimkhan, 107

Yandex, 116

Yanukovych, Viktor, 193, 312

Yavlinsky, Grigory, 38

Yekaterinburg, 39, 99

'Yelena', 75–6

Yeltsin, Boris, 8–12, 25, 29, 135; reconciliation policy, 15, 145, 152; and corruption, 31–2, 44; popularity, 38–9; and economy, 40–4; Putin and, 40, 45, 47; era of, 48, 51–2, 57–61, 70, 83, 89–90, 109, 120, 141, 145, 152–3, 156, 159, 264, 270, 317; and media, 59–60; and federalism, 67, 69; and rewriting of history, 152; and religion, 156; and Belarus, 175; and Germany, 223; and former Yugoslavia, 257–9; memoirs, 290–1; and Roman Abramovich, 297

Yevroremont, 51

youth movements, 55, 100–5, 300

Yuganskneftegaz, 64, 118

Yugoslavia, former, 5, 197, 231, 233, 259; see also Bosnia; Croatia; Kosovo; Serbia

Yukhanova, Nadezhda, 34, 36

Yukos, 62–6, 78, 109, 118, 123–5, 238, 271, 273, 306; Western interests and, 219, 236

Yuryev, Michael, 163

Yushchenko, Viktor, 101, 299

Yushenkov, Sergei, 36, 289

Yuzhno-Russkoye gas field, 226

Zagreb, 231

Zaitsev, Gennady, 35

Zakayev, Ahmed, 106–7

Zakharenko, Yury, 309

Zavadsky, Dmitry, 309

Zavtra, 263

Zdanovich, Aleksander, 33

Zeebrugge, 227

Zhdanov, Andrei, 200

Zhirinovsky, Vladimir, 134–5

Zimin, Ilya, 84

Zorkin, Valery, 93

Zubkov, Viktor, 120

Zug, 218, 220

Zyuganov, Gennady, 38, 45, 59